EVENING STREET REVIEW

NUMBER 34, SUMMER 2022

. . .all men and women are created equal in rights to life, liberty, and the pursuit of happiness.

—Elizabeth Cady Stanton, revision of the
American Declaration of Independence, 1848

PUBLISHED TWICE (OR MORE) A YEAR
BY
EVENING STREET PRESS

Editor & Managing Editor: Barbara Bergmann
Associate Editors: Donna Spector, Kailen Nourse-Driscoll, Patti Sullivan, Anthony Mohr, L D Zane, Stacia Levy, Jeffrey Davis, Clela Reed, Matthew Mendoza, Matthew Spireng, Ace Boggess, Kristin Laurel, Jan Bowman, Aaron Fischer

Founding Editor: Gordon Grigsby

Evening Street Review is published in the spring and fall of every year (with additional issues as needed) by Evening Street Press. United States subscription rates are $28 for two issues and $48 for four issues (individuals), and $34 for two issues and $54 for four issues (institutions).

Cover photos by Edward Lee

Library of Congress Control Number: 2022933301
ISBN: 978-1-937347-73-4

Evening Street Review is centered on the belief that all men and women are created equal, that they have a natural claim to certain inalienable rights, and that among these are the rights to life, liberty, and the pursuit of happiness. With this center, and an emphasis on writing that has both clarity and depth, it practices the widest eclecticism. Evening Street Review reads submissions of poetry (free verse, formal verse, and prose poetry) and prose (short stories and creative nonfiction) year-round. Submit 3-6 poems or 1-2 prose pieces at a time. Payment is one contributor's copy. Copyright reverts to author upon publication. Response time is 3-6 months. Please address submissions to Editors, 2881 Wright St, Sacramento, CA 95821-4819. Email submissions are also acceptable; send to the following address as Microsoft Word or rich text files (.rtf): **editor@eveningstreetpress.com**.

For submission guidelines, subscription information, published works, and author profiles, please visit our website:

www.eveningstreetpress.com.

Rosemarie Moore Morell
The Passing of Archbishop Tutu

One day past Christmas, twenty-twenty-one
Archbishop Desmond Tutu closed his eyes.
South African, he'd "fought" for peace and won,
In 1984, the Nobel Prize.
Appointment as Archbishop was a win:
Anglicans had faced discrimination.
Before Tutu, no Black had ever been
Archbishop in that denomination.
The archbishop helped get Mandela freed,
Then worked with him while he was president.
Their conquests we can see, or hear, or read:
Their legacy's in film, and song, and print.
His life devoted to equality,
He passed on Kwanzaa's first day: UNITY

Desmond Mpilo Tutu (October 7, 1931-December 26, 2021)
was a South African Anglican bishop and theologian, known for
his work as an anti-apartheid and human rights activist.
https://en.wikipedia.org/wiki/Desmond_Tutu

EVENING STREET REVIEW
PUBLISHED BY EVENING STREET PRESS

NUMBER 34, SUMMER 2022

CONTENTS

POETRY (CONT)

POETRY (CONT)

NONFICTION

FICTION

OCCASIONAL NOTES

JACQUELINE JULES
RBG'S LACE COLLAR

A judicial black robe
leaves room at the neckline
for a shirt and tie,
standard male apparel.

Was it designed for a man?

Not a woman like Ruth,
who adorned her neck with lace,
proud to display her difference,
to declare that nine women on the court
would be fair when the norm
for too long was nine men.

Her delicate collar of white crochet
made it defiantly clear
she dismissed
those who saw her gender
as a handicap to hide
rather than an asset
to be seen.

Jules

Ruth Bader Ginsburg (1933-2020) was the second woman appointed to the Supreme Court of the United States. A fierce advocate for gender equality and human rights, she gave passionate dissents of rulings she disagreed with, earning her the moniker, "The Notorious R.B.G."

THOMAS ELSON
MONTAGE OF MEMORIES

He, at six foot-three inches, remembered she was slightly taller. And, on that first evening, in high heels, she was towering.

He could not remember being asked to be her escort for her birthday dinner at the country club. Clouded in his memory was the birthday gift he must have given her. Nor could he remember picking her up or even driving her back to her parents' six-acre country estate.

But he did remember being introduced to her parents at the country club, and the *maître de* greeting her by name.

He remembered her basement with the two-lane bowling alley he never used, the soft drink fountain with every Pepsi product at the ready, the stereo system with soft music, and the easy feel of the leather divan on his skin.

He also remembered the way she inched closer, brought her long legs under her hips, smiled, partially unbuttoned her blouse, then leaned back, removed her shoes, and extended her legs toward him.

He remembered two more things: her legs were bare, and her feet were bigger than his.

Three Things

This morning, after the Sheriff and two state investigators left his office carrying boxes, the man did not return home—instead, he drove to a neighboring town and bought three things:

Dancing shoes.

A hamburger.

A shotgun.

The dancing shoes he delivered to his daughter whom he would never see again.

The hamburger he ate so he could think straight while he made his decision.

And the shotgun he will use in nine and a half hours—when he sits alone in an abandoned shack behind a line of trees in another state—and places it in his mouth.

HOLLY DAY
MOTES OF SPARKLING GLASS

You can teach brine shrimp to dance
by shining a flashlight into their tank
and moving it back and forth. They will follow the light
like a scarf of sparkling dust mites
like a swarm of swallows alighting for the night
like a cloud of gnats discovering a piece of rotted fruit
like a pulse of transparent blood vessels traveling along a vein.

What they don't tell you
in the manual that comes with the tank
that says shining a light into the tank will teach them to dance
is that you're really just tricking the tiny shrimp into thinking
that their hiding place been suddenly exposed to sunlight
and sometimes it kills them
and sometimes it forces them to change gender
and sometimes it makes them spontaneously reproduce
and sometimes it does nothing at all, because this whole time
the tiny specks of dust you shook into the water of your sea monkey tank

weren't actually brine shrimp eggs at all
but just bits of sand gathered from the shore of some faraway beach,
some beautiful, warm, tropical place
that you will never get to see for yourself.

Day

KNEE-HIGH IN THE WEED

The doctor laughs when I tell her my plan
was to give birth in the back yard, like my cat did her kittens
that it just felt like the safest place to me right now.
She says she doesn't do house calls, so I'll have to see her here.

I regret the touch of cold metal against my skin, all of the poking and prodding
the ultrasound that shows only the skeleton of the human child inside me.
I wanted so much for there to be a litter of kittens, and I tell the doctor this
and she laughs again and tells me only cats have kittens, my baby looks fine.

(cont)

At home, I am angry that so many things I say these days
are making people laugh, because I don't mean them to be funny, I don't.
I tell the baby inside me that most people don't take me seriously
and to not be surprised at the stories people will tell.

Day

TIM COE

Coca Cola bubbly light
caffeine laden base delight,
what perverse and jaundiced eye
wrought thy tasty chemistry?

From what vat or Petri dish
came forth thy form opaquely brownish?
What compounds did he require
to make our throats all burn like fire?

And what the blender, and what the art
could give this cola our collective heart?
For when our wallets began to speak,
they all declared, "C'est magnifique!"

What the hammer? What the chain?
causes that effervescence to remain
despite four hours between each grasp
it's foam still makes us sneeze and gasp.

When the stars threw down their spears
and watered heaven with their tears
did he smile, his work to see
did he who whipped up Tab make thee?

Coca Cola, bubbly light
caffeine laden base delight,
what perverse and jaundice eye
wrought thy tasty chemistry?

Coe

MIRIAM EDELSON
HOW THE MAPLE LEAFS AND DONALD TRUMP
CHANGED MY LIFE

The train whistle beckons. Its tone signals the incomparable sound of heavy railcars moving. "Take me away," sings the whistle, beating its path behind my bedroom door. Out to the back I run, only to glimpse the tail lights of the night train as it transports goods to distant shores. My adventure has me blast out the gate, but no further than our tame suburban back yard. Now that the train is gone, I can hear the leaves rustling above my head. I am disconsolate.

Today in the fourth grade we hide beneath tables in the hallway. "Shht!" the teacher says, telling us to grab our winter coats from their hooks. We crouch down, trying desperately to be quiet, for about five minutes. We learn later this is an "air raid drill" and that we're not to feel afraid. Just stay silent and covered.

It's an odd exercise, I think to myself. As if my little brown woolen coat with black toggle fasteners would protect me from bombs dropped by the enemy. In the fourth grade there isn't any discussion of who that enemy is and why they might pelt us with bombs. This also strikes me as odd, curious as I am.

At home, I get the drift from my parents that the air raid drills are more of a made-up danger and not to worry about them. Just listen to the teachers, they say. They call it the Cold War, not something I understand. This is the beginning of an inkling that my parents are different. They do read me children's folktales from a book that comes from the Soviet Union. The stories are not very different from those in the other books we read together, but I gather the book is somehow cherished.

A few years go by. There never is a bomb. At least not here at home. In Vietnam, where I now understand there is a hot war, lots of bombs explode on people's houses, wrecking their communities. In this house, we are against the war. My eldest brother burns his draft card. My parents are concerned. Then it turns out my brother has a serious back problem and is rejected anyway. Crisis averted.

*

It is 1968. My father campaigns for Senator Eugene McCarthy of Minnesota to become the Democratic nominee for president. He is a Senator, an economics professor and a poet, who runs on an anti-Vietnam war platform. In the end, his campaign unravels on a technicality. It is my father's turn to feel disconsolate.

At that time, a cartoon from the New Yorker magazine is tacked to the kitchen cupboard closest to the telephone. A man is sitting on a window ledge, way up high on a building. "We'll move to Canada so you don't have to choose between Humphrey and Nixon," it says.

The war in Vietnam is ramping up and protests capture the national news each night. We do, indeed, move to Canada that summer. My father sells his arts and crafts supply business and we have meetings at the Canadian Consulate to apply for landed immigrant status. At the latter, we children are shushed and told not to say anything. Later, we say goodbye to lifelong friends on our street. I feel sad, but it's also an adventure.

Before crossing the border, we camp a couple of nights in upstate New York and visit with my parents' friends in Corning, where the famous white casserole dishes with light blue flower patterns are made. We enter Canada on July 15th, 1968 at the Peace Bridge that spans the Niagara River from Buffalo, NY, to Fort Erie, Ontario. It's a very busy commercial route and big trucks are everywhere.

For my mother, returning to Toronto after twenty years in the United States, it is a hopeful move. Many years before she had joined a group of progressive graduate students in social work in Pittsburgh to study group work—as opposed to individual case work. This distinction reflected a systemic analysis to overcoming problems of poverty, immigration and family disputes. She has a job lined up in Toronto working as a geriatric social worker.

Her mother, Polly, is still alive in 1968 and lives in an apartment in uptown Toronto. She is glad to have my mother closer and welcomes us warmly. So do my mother's brother and his wife who live nearby. We settle at the northern city limits of Toronto, a place public buses don't even reach on the weekend.

There were lots of benefits to Toronto for young teenagers. We are allowed to travel alone on the bus and subway to downtown, something unheard of in New York for youngsters our age.

We enroll in new "open-plan" schools. Characterized by large open spaces, carpeted for easy gathering on the floor with classmates, the school specializes in a non-structured approach to learning critical thought. I soon earn the honour of playing the national anthem, "O Canada," in the mornings at assembly. I begin to feel that I have a stake in this new country.

Coming from the United States, language is not a barrier. But my accent is. We call our dog "Sugah" for Sugar. And say "cawfee," for coffee. Desperate to fit in at twelve years old, I lose my accent quite naturally over the course of our first year.

*

Living in Canada is not so different thus far. I still feel the pull of the United States and am not quite at home here. I remember saying the "Pledge of Allegiance" every morning at school and learning about American history. I know who won the war of 1812. I remain in touch with a couple of friends in New York; one comes to visit during the holidays.

One Saturday night the family is watching Hockey Night in Canada on television. It is about six months after our move. The New York Rangers are playing the Toronto Maple Leafs and there is a great deal of excitement in our house. Henderson, Keon and Bower are on the ice for the Leafs. We were not hockey fans before, but now this is something we do. Halfway into the game, I realize that I am starting to root for the Toronto team. A milestone is passed. It doesn't matter that they lose the game.

This burgeoning Canadian identity does not follow a linear development. In 1970, during the October Crisis, Prime Minister Pierre Elliot Trudeau declares the War Measures Act to deal with the political situation in the province of Quebec. My father is against it. He says it is an unnecessary limit on civil liberties. He questions living in a country where the leader has the unfettered ability to enact such powerful law. When I ask him if he will seek Canadian citizenship, he says no. This makes an impression on me.

For myself, the question comes up some years later when I am in university. I am active in the student movement, vocal in the media around issues of tuition, student assistance and international education. My parents urge me to apply for Canadian citizenship since I am so involved and publicly outspoken. I take the necessary steps to do so and for many years carry dual citizenship.

Time passes and I feel a part of this country. I help in a few election campaigns; I vote each time I have the chance. I give up my American citizenship not long after Trump is elected. There is no New Yorker cartoon tacked on the cupboard, but I know Canada is my only country, my only home.

First appeared online in *Adana Literary Journal*

JAMES FOWLER
ANXIETY NATION

Not your typical suburban cocktail
party, tongues loosened by drink.
Listen carefully, you'll hear
what keeps each one up at night.

The natty-looking man confesses
he's plateaued at work, struggles
to compete with savvy young turks.

A sympathetic stranger shares her fear
she'll have to take extended leave
to care for dilapidated parents.

Mingle further and pick up talk about
calming meds, their side effects,
what they do and don't mix with.

The guests tend to gather by kind:
socially nervous in cozy nooks,
catastrophists around the snack table.

It's more than talk therapy, a chance
to air darling, addictive torments.

Muffled yelps escape a back bedroom,
where the more intrepid strip
and worry one another with fret sticks.

Those fearful of dying alone are to fish
in a cardboard box for a shelter puppy.
Demur, and they must go home with
a fellow lonelyheart, gender a crapshoot.

The night climaxes with the swap,
troubles in a bowl blindly exchanged,
gambling debt for cosigned mortgage,
fixed phobia for free-floating neurosis.

(cont)

Predictably, swappers trade back
in private, claiming a bad fit,
able to sleep a little better
once their nagging bedmates return.

Fowler

RACHEL SQUIRES BLOOM
DO UNTO OTHERS

You lose 90 percent of your body heat
through your head, so wear a hat
our CCD teacher admonished, Sunday School
held on Wednesday, as Sundays
were too valuable to parents sleeping
it off or herding kids to sports.
These teachers were aged-out mothers
and one father whose own children fled
to community colleges, held standards of sitting
still and raising hands like eager flagpoles,
habits nearly extinct in weekend-inspired
kids-these-days. The '60s backwash emphasis
was on New Testament Jesus as man
among men, humble and sad, eager to offer
that cheek as he skimmed across water
and performed domestic miracles
that would surely endear him to a generation
raised on Pop Rock and Partridge Family.
I once overheard our teacher in a group
of like-minded upstanding citizens now
known as bigots use the word *n-word*.
The context was South Boston busing,
the viciously ignorant faces framed
on our grey TV screen were white ones,
hate and grimace on the same faces
in the daily *Globe* and *Herald,* front page
of the newspapers he delivered by boxy truck,
his real job, before even birds were awake.

(cont)

I pictured heat radiating from a head,
Heat Miser-like, trapped by stiff wool.
That 90 percent was suspect; why not
the precision of 87.6 or even odd 93, having
learned by seventh grade to attach numbers
to the world. Questioning his figure tumbled
me into a burrow of doubt. When,
adoration in his eyes, our teacher spoke
of Jesus' love of us I knew he meant pale us,
not the wider *us*, tougher to love at our
neighborhood's perimeter. Listen I did,
and watched and learned.

Bloom

FREDDIE

You were seven, I eight
when TV news informed us
that Freddie Prinze had killed
himself. Knee to worn
pajama knee we sat in post-dinner
twilight in the cluttered den
with its fatigued sofa and sad
chocolate paneling discussing
How would this happen?
How could a body end itself?
Never mind why.

We practiced being the only dead
that we knew, lying statue-like,
hands crossed over chest
like waxen Grandad had lain.
Then we splayed like Jesus
pointing in all directions,
who we saw weekly in pale wood
carved like loved marble, hanging
anorexic and sorrowful, Caucasian
eyes watching miraculously
from beneath closed lids.

(cont)

We knew nothing of Quaaludes,
depression, comedic ambitions,
the racism that *Chico* parodied
and rode like a pony. Innately
we knew to side with Chico,
that Underdog Dad always said to root for.
We knew that knives killed, concluded
Freddie must have stabbed himself
in the head, that seat of thoughts
like those taxing our minds trying
to assimilate this new news into
what we knew. Again and again
we acted this out, squealing with fear,
with how funny we looked
parodying dying, death, laughed
at this tragedy, inexplicable,
and so far away in some
two-dimensional kingdom.

Bloom

KATE LaDEW
GLISSANDO

The little girl works at the factory from 5 in the morning 'til 9 at night, rising when the moon is still caught up in a dark bulleted with stars. She always hears her mother ask the colliers for the time and they always answer the same way and the little girl always waits for her to crawl into their bed and wrap her arms around her ribs so they can watch, ear to ear, the sea of men wade through the fog to the dock and the ships. Coal weighted coughs rise and fall like fingers in a fast slide over piano keys and when the music fades and the colliers are out of sight, she and her mother clasp hands and tiptoe, so as not to wake the day, into the dirt floor kitchen, slicing two thin strips from the loaf of bread already pockmarked blue at the corners, like a constellation in negative.

The little girl's mother scrubs under her arms, the back of her neck, water cold in the bucket with no bubbles, just a thin slime of soap on the surface that smells like damp and rot. The little girl dresses herself, shimmying the scratchy fabric over her hips, rolling up dark tights that sag at the ankle and knees, tying the broken laces crosshatched over each boot into a knot and folds herself over in one of two kitchen chairs as her mother braids her hair, pinning the plaits in the back so they don't catch in the spindles. Then the little girl and the little girl's mother walk the five miles to the mill and wait.

When the gates open, the little girl and her mother pass by the picker-houses, tiny fluffs of cotton settling on their hair and shoulders, floating in the air like flurries of snow. The brown faces through the sweating windows always look once before looking away, and the little girl always feels her mother's feet quicken, her hand pull. She never sees the brown faces anywhere else and wonders where they go when they're not here.

Spinning machines stretch out like long legs of a hairy spider, each frame racketed with spindles, each spindle with their own bobbin to fill. The little girl's mother guides the fiber through the machines that clean and smooth the cotton into rolls, folded together by the finishers. Women take the folded rolls into the main building and the little girl doesn't know what happens to them before they become shirts and dresses and underthings.

Last week, the man who watches them all from the balcony came to her mother and told her soon she was going to tend the looms in another part of the mill where they're woven into cloth. The little girl would brush the lint from the looms and watch for snags. This excited her mother, because her pay would be increased and allow for short breaks in between their piecing of bobbins and when the doffers came in to change the spools. This excited the little girl because she would finally find out how it all happened.

Today, the little girl's mother continues to guide the fiber through the machines, the little girl sweeping up the dust that always collects under their feet. She receives no pay for her job, but it keeps her close and watchable and in a few years' time she can begin to learn the more complicated workings of the mill and start to help with the daily expenses.

The little girl's mother coughs, dry and rattling, and the little girl squeezes the tips of her mother's fingers, the same level of fright she always feels rising as she watches the tendons in her mother's neck tighten, the little blue vein in her forehead throb, the tears collect in the hollows under her cheeks. The cough always lessens after they get home before almost fading away, so the little girl closes her eyes until she feels her mother squeeze back and it's okay again.

The little girl and the little girl's mother always walk home together. The men who wait in the dark for the factory's closing whistle are less likely to grab at them that way (though the little girl remembers once running three miles home without stopping as her mother screamed behind her *Hurry, Hurry* before a dirty hand clamped over her mother's mouth and she was enveloped by shadows. Hours, days, weeks, months later, her mother very slowly opened the front door, a smear of blood under her nose, at the corners of her mouth, and would not let the little girl touch her until she heated water and scrubbed herself, standing naked in the kitchen. When they climbed into bed, the little girl's mother apologized into the little girl's ear for using so much soap, promising she would replace it before their Saturday night bath and the little girl did not know why her mother began to cry when she told her it was no trouble, she didn't mind less soap if her mother needed it). But at noon, when they're allowed forty minutes of free time, they don't eat together, the little girl's mother allowing her to walk the mill grounds, while she has lunch with the other women, sitting on the coiling roots of the Quaking Aspen in the corner of the lot. The little girl always stops at the end of the main brick building and turns to wave at her watching mother, before carefully maneuvering out of sight and toward the thin break in the fence, tumbling into a run as she reaches the town and all its unfamiliar adventure.

The little girl never has long on the macadam roads, crushed stone hot and hard under her feet. Lately she's spent it rushing from tree to tree, throwing her back against the bark if spotted, until she makes it to the wealthier section, the houses crisp and white as cut apple, porches long and wrap-around. One house intrigues her the most because another little girl lives there, and she can watch her through the open window as she plays the piano with an old man sitting beside her, lightly tapping her fingers with a ruler when a wrong chord is struck. She imagines herself in the corner, waiting her turn, or maybe beside the other little girl. They can be sisters, twins even, and learn everything at the same time. She will wear blue and the other little girl will wear pink, the only way to tell them apart, and they will be each other's shadows and eat cookies and sweets in a dining room with a long table and a lace tablecloth and everyone in all the big houses will visit them every day and sometimes the little twin girls will turn these people way, only needing each other and the little girl's mother, who will be their mother and wear her hair half up and half down in cascading curls and a diamond headband and she will never have to do anything except be their mother and take long hot baths in the afternoon and every room will smell of baking bread and honey and feel clean and cool and just right.

The little girl clutches her knees to her chest, sitting at the very edge of the other little girl's yard, unnoticed in the shade and thick branches of the unkempt empty lot beside the columned house. When the little girl is not dreaming of living in the house, she likes to make up rhymes to the tune of the piano, digging the letters she knows into the dirt. She's been repeating one over and over, made up some morning as she and her mother watched the colliers on their march: *the men rise and fall, in the dark of the sea, like fingers tumbling over piano keys*—(one night not very long ago, the little girl's mother brought the bottom of a wooden box into their bedroom and poured a thin layer of fine, soft sand into it. She began tracing shapes into the brown and yellow tinted granules, forming a chain, then brushing it smooth. The little girl did not ask where she acquired these treasures, she doesn't know and doesn't much care how they get anything, because her mother is good and true and nothing could be the matter. That night the little girl slid off the bed, crossing her legs and looking down as her mother continued to create magic. *This is where glass comes from,* her mother said. *You heat this until it melts and pour it into molds and wait till it's cool.* The little girl looks up at their one-bedroom window and back to her mother's big wide smile. *Yes*, she nods. *This,* she picks up a handful of sand and lets it drift though her fingers, *is what that,* she tilts her head towards the foggy pane, *used to be. Now,* she takes the girl's hand, folds her middle, ring and pinky finger down, grasping the little girl's pointer finger and using it to trace a shape like a ladle, *this is how you write your name.* The little girl does not look down at the shapes her finger makes in the sand, and her mother has to start from the beginning, urging, *Pay attention, this is important.* The little girl is feeling the pulse of her own wrist under her mother's hand, the warmth of their bodies as they lean their heads together, the slowing of time as nothing exists except the two of them and there is nothing to do but this and nowhere to be but here. She's watching the light that lives inside her mother bloom and expand until it bursts the whole world into phosphorescence. The little girl doesn't mind if it takes all night) *the men rise and fall, in the dark of the sea, like fingers tumbling*—The little girl looks up as a flat chord sounds and then again, and again. The other little girl is slamming her fists against the keys and the old man is standing up and moving away, crossing his arms and shaking his head. The other little girl stands up too, the piano bench scraping back and she holds her arms, hands still in fists, straight at her sides, long blonde hair kicking up like horse's legs and stomps out of view, the pink satiny light of her dress flashing.

The little girl holds her breath, watching the old man. His head drops, rests there a moment, and then he is opening a little satchel and stuffing sheets of paper into it, clasping it shut with force and does not stomp but strides through the doorway. The little girl crawls along the edge of the yard and sees the front door open, calmly but firmly shut, and the old man descends the stairs and walks down the front path, satchel under his arm. The little girl edges back into the shadows, hovering a moment before creeping out to the end of the lot, the old man's back receding.

Suddenly, there's a vehicle in the road, the dust seeming to fall up from the ground, clouding around the silver sparking buggy. An electric car. She's seen the man who watches them all from the balcony leave the mill in something just like this. Behind the electric car comes another vehicle that looks like a milk wagon with no milk, a long sheet over whatever it's carrying.

A man jumps out of the electric car, removing gloves and stuffing them in a trouser pocket. He leans over the door and retrieves a straw hat with a wide black ribbon, combing his hair with one hand and pressing the hat over it with the other. He looks all around, as men position a ramp behind the wagon and push something down it.

The little girl takes as many steps as she dares into the road, holding one hand over her eyes to catch a glimpse of this mysterious cargo. She leans forward, feeling a twinge in her back when a sound reaches her ears and she stands up hurriedly.

Yes, you there. And the man is taking off his hat and waving it at her. *You, girl. Come here.*

Her first instinct is to flee. She might be late already. She has no idea how long this has lasted. But the man is walking towards her and his suit is very new and his shoes are very shiny and his face is clean-shaven and beaming and the little girl smooths her dress and clasps her hands behind her hurting back and walks forward.

I want to show you something, the man says. The little girl says nothing. His voice is as new as his suit, as shiny as his shoes. *As long as you're here,* and there is amusement in his voice. He holds out his hand. *You might as well see what I've bought.*

She follows a step behind him, stopping when he looks back, starting again when he looks away. There are sweaty men in white uniforms by the wagon, dust caked at the bottom of their overalls, wiping their brows with the backs of their arms. The man in the suit seems unaffected by the heat, his face dry and serene and he nods at the men. *Just a minute,* he says. *We have a traveler who wishes to see the spoils of our journey.* Between the workers is a rectangular bulk, draped by a sheet the same color as their uniforms. The man in the suit clicks his heels together, pulls on the edges of his vest, holds a finger up, then lowers it. Bending at the waist he snaps the sheet away in one motion to reveal a piano the color of nighttime, gleaming and glinting in the unrelenting sun overhead. The little girl gasps, involuntarily clapping her hands against her cheeks, mouth agape. The man shows his big white teeth. *Methinks we have a success, gentleman,* he says to the workers who only wipe their brows again. *The lady appears overjoyed at the purchase.*

The little girl giggles, eyes sweeping back and forth. She's never been close enough to touch anything so grand, so fresh and new.

Do you like it? the man asks.

The little girl nods vigorously, heart beating fast. This is the most beautiful thing that has ever existed. *But you already have a piano,* she says. There's a long moment before she puts a hand over her mouth. Her heart beats faster. The instinct to flee comes racing back into her limbs.

What's that now? The man says, but he is looking up at a second-floor window of the columned house, at the little girl looking past the glass and down at him. He holds up his hand and the pink ruffles of the other little girl's sleeve raises. The man holds this stance before angling his straw hat and catching sight of the little girl below him, her presence seeming to surprise him. He laughs a short laugh. *You mean the harpsichord?* he says and the little girl is frightened—he will know she watches, he will make her leave and never come back—but the man only laughs again. *The neighbors do complain and now,* he tilts his head at the shiny black piano—the little girl squints her eyes, conjuring the instrument she's been listening to for weeks and wonders what the difference is— *they'll have even more to complain about.*

The little girl is counting the keys in her head, imagining the sound they make, when she hears the man clear his throat. *It's very lovely,* the little girl says quickly, hoping this is right. *I do so love pianos.*

Do you now? the man says, arching a brow. *Have you ever seen a piano?*

And the little girl points at the laminated hardwood box between them and the man says *Ha!Ha!* a real rumbling laugh and the little girl is confused and delighted as he gently grasps her shoulder and pulls her to the keyboard. *Go ahead,* he says. *We'll see if it's as good as the salesman claimed.*

The little girl bites her lip, feeling the tremble in her teeth. She lifts her hands, holding them out as if warming them over a fire. Flexing the tendons, she winces, the weeks old tenderness in her thumbs flaring, a feeling like bone scraping against bone, the same feeling in the small of her back that wakes her up at night. The little girl swallows, sensing the man's waiting like a physical thing, and carefully, carefully, fits her fingers over eight keys, depressing them all at once and stumbling back, the noise loud and bright. The man laughs that same laugh, throwing his head back and the little girl wants to make it last forever, so she glides the edge of her palm clumsily over the keys, one after the other, the sound like falling down stairs. The man presses close to her and makes the same movement. *That's called a glissando,* the man says, fingers sliding as the keys erupt. *Or gliss, as the musicians say.*

Glissando, she whispers, the word perfect and new in her mouth, like an opening to a whole world full of notes and sound and beauty and unexpected things. She smiles up at the man and he smiles back, stoking a little ember of bravery that always lay hidden in her heart. The little girl says, carefully, carefully, leaning in like a secret, *The men rise and fall, in the dark of the sea, like a glissando tumbling over the keys.* Her eyes look into the man's, back and forth, back and forth, waiting for a nod, a look, a sweep of the hand, *Oh, it's you, finally. We've been waiting for you, right here, where you've always belonged.*

The man blinks, gaze startled, eyebrows coming together as if looking at something too bright. *Well,* he says, straightening. *I'm sure a little girl like you has somewhere to be.* He pulls out his pocket watch, opens it, shakes his head, closes the watch, slips it back into his vest pocket, and waves his hand at the little girl as if shooing a fly from food. *Go on home now. Maybe your daddy can buy you one too, someday,* he says. The workers, who were using the man's distraction to catch their breath, leaning against either side of the piano, spin back into motion as he says, *Hurry, Hurry,* clapping his hands and snapping at them like two troublesome dogs.

The little girl waits, looking at the man as he looks up at the now empty window. And then he is walking away and the piano is gone and the road is clear and the little girl watches her words vanish in the air, dissolved like a faraway tune after the slam of a door. The world as she knows it is restored, dust and dirt and a long walk for a mill child on her way back to the looms, and not one thing more. She never goes back to the house.

A year later, men in suits and shoes just like the man with the piano, tug at her pinned-plaits, usher her into an unfamiliar room, while she looks back at her mother who drums one hand nervously over her heart before a cough doubles her, and the little girl is in the room and the door shuts and she feels herself lifted into a leather chair with wrap-around arms, sinks into it, boots an inch off the floor, arms draping loosely, her body still vibrating from the chugging of the mill. The little girl watches the men's lips move under their mustaches, missing every other word as she rolls her head to the side, rubbing the bad-sleep bruises under her eyes, and watches a younger man depress keys on a machine that looks like a cash register cut in half. A circle of paper slowly diminishes and curls on the floor, it's dull white filled with ink dots and dashes, the click-click-click soft and off rhythm. The little girl's eyes close and she's back in her reoccurring dream so lovely it makes waking up worth the memory. She's twirling in a pink foam that is the cascade of her dress, weightless and clean, as pillowed clouds surround the incandescent columns rising her mansion into the baby blue of the sky. Her mother's hand is soft and smooth combing through the curling rolls of her hair, flashing a million colors at once like a pearl layering in beauty and they tumble into a sleep that lasts days and might go on forever, because there is not one thing to do here except breathe in the endless smells of flowers and baking bread and warm honey and the calm, rosy cool of the air enveloping every slope of skin, the feel of her mother's arms around her full belly, muscles slack and sleepy, a quiescence so deep it takes up everywhere, and there is the sound of a piano dropping into a melody perfectly timed to the beat of her safe, happy heart—

A sound like breaking lifts the little girl's chin. She bolts awake to a man's middle finger striking the palm of his hand once, twice, a barrage of questions battering her ears, and his face is so stern, his body so close, she answers without inflection or pause:

- 5 to 9 -
- her 6th birthday -
- 2 years -
- dead -
- arm caught in a turbine -
- 30 minutes at noon -
- a slice of bread and cheese -
- no breakfast, no dinner -
- stop the frames, take the flyers off, take the bobbins off, carry them to the roller, replace with empty ones, set the frame going again -
- the strap -
- 5 lashes for every minute late -

- 5 miles -
- 3 am -
- deformed? -

(the little girl pauses, blinking rapidly as a hand strikes the desk)

- yes, my back, my fingers -

And she holds them out, as they curl involuntarily, knuckles swollen, stands up, shoulders arching forward, waiting while the men speak in whispers, their own straight backs turned away.

The little girl, finding herself forgotten, slides back down into the chair, mouth exhausted, she's never spoken so many words at once to strangers. Lolling her head, the young man sits, hands in lap, the strange machine now silent. She traces the dots and dashes with her eyes, seeing sand in a wooden box, fluttering her lashes as the young man's voice drifts towards her.

It's a phonetic code, he says, picking up the curl of paper and holding a section out, tugged flat like a banner. *They stand for words. These are all the words we've said.* He lets the paper drop as she leans forward, the pain in her back pulsing. Floating his fingers over the keys of the machine, he ghosts them back and forth. *I listen to your words and make them into sound, and then ink, and save them all so we can transcribe them back into words and, when the time is right,* he ghosts his fingers again in one sweep, *speak them out loud so everyone can hear.*

Glissando, she says, and the young man tilts his head.

What's that now?

The little girl smiles and it's sad.

Snap-one-two breaks the quiet and the men in suits all cross their arms. The stern man asks, from under his mustache, a question.

Later that night, when the young man is alone, angling his desk lamp to turn the inked dots and dashes into sound, into words, and back to ink again, he pauses as the bell of his typewriter dings, presses the carriage return lever, turning the paper up and, moving the carriage back to the start of the next line, mouths the last question and answer of that day. The words drift into his brain and back out again as the slugs of metal imprint them on the paper, glowing yellow like a beacon in the dark of the room:

Commissioner: State what you think as to the circumstances in which you have been placed during all this time of labor, and what you have considered about it as to the hardship and cruelty of it.

Female Millhand: …(the witness was too much affected to answer the question).

ANN SILVERTHORN
IN THE PLANETARIUM

I hold you on my lap, your legs
dangle, you're getting so big.
We both look up at the many
paneled dome, into the night sky.
Small white circles arranged into
characters, stories and dreams.
We feel small, overwhelmed by it all.
The hair on your head tickles my chin,
my arms encircle your waist.
So what will you be? Who will come
after you? We are here for less time than it takes
light of the stars to reach us. From those stars,
we are already gone.

Silverthorn

DS MAOLALAI
THE SNOWFLAKES

of course
our life together
might be whittled down
to a slight collection
of chances,

though then
of course, so too
might any other life.
we've both been lucky,
both think ourselves
remarkable,
but also then,
so too does everyone;
we're not quite
remarkable there.

(cont)

a phrase
(somewhat killed
I admit in modern use,
though suitable anyway
given our politics)
says snowflakes
aren't identical,
but tell someone that
who's walking
in a blizzard.

Maolalai

STEPHEN J KUDLESS
A WOMAN WITH BROWN HAIR

After the coffee that completes my midday meal, I find the time in the square a most felicitous means to launch into the afternoons. I have been taking this hour respite for more than a year now, and it has become rare for me to depart from this daily, weekday schedule. It was about two months ago during one of these post-prandial relaxations that I first saw her. My eyes were not drawn to the long legs plunged into stylish pumps or the trim fit of her mauve overcoat. Oh, no. While legs and shapeliness are surely fascinations to savor, on that day, my unsuspecting glance was stopped by her hair.

Her hair was brown, not a color that generally inspires excitement. I was struck by its soft falling towards her shoulders in what seemed to be undulations as she strode by. The strands flowed to her clavicle and splashed up again, threatening to spill over. I could not recall ever seeing air with such liquidity. When she sat on the bench across from me and a bit farther along the walkway, the soft movement, like lava running down a mountainside, stopped and collected in pools near the base of her neck. I imagined that this was a temporary delay and was proven correct for with each motion of her head, the torrent of hair was released to continue on its sensual course.

Thus, began what I like to call my "affair" with this woman with brown hair. Every day, or more correctly nearly every day, we shared the square across from the university buildings. Scores, perhaps hundreds, of people passed through this urban green—mostly rushing to meetings, dashing to the bus or underground, with a few, couples mainly, ambling at leisure while spending what looked like pleasant moments. I did notice several *other* returning faces in addition to hers—the fellow who carried a briefcase held secure with large elastic bands, the gentleman and his wife who lingered near the statue of Gandhi from time to time to chat. (Of course, it is my surmise that they are husband and wife, but there was something of the married sort about them and a scent of the furtive.) Naturally I noticed Charley, the chap who runs the coffee bar in the university hall basement across the way and his old dog on their daily romps. I came to know his name because a number of other park visitors called him by name as they passed. He and his dog, I concluded, are local celebrities. All of these people had their peculiar attractiveness, but it was the woman with the brown hair who changed my p.m. visits and caused my mornings to devolve into mere preparations for the hour to come in the square.

Last Friday, a cool day with sparse sunlight, she sat in her customary seat and removed a small sandwich from her purse. This is remarkable because she had neither eaten nor drunk on earlier afternoons and so I was quite surprised. She was wearing a blue jacket from which she repeatedly swabbed away imaginary crumbs after each nibble. I call them "imaginary" because I could not see that any had actually fallen from her lips as she ate. Shi is so proper, you see. She handled her morsel with a delicate grasp, and as often as she dabbed at her jacket, she dabbed at her lips with a small napkin. She chewed daintily, lips closed and only the front of her mouth moving. Although her chewing was gentle, to my delight the little movements produced the effect I so admired about her hair. I have never enjoyed watching a person eat so much.

Such a lovely flower as she, quite naturally, must have a name. But, of course, I cannot speak to her, and so learning her name by the usual means of conversation is impossible. I would so love to know it because such knowledge would increase my sense of intimacy with her. I assume, as I must, that she has not taken any notice of me at all. How could she? In these brief moments in the square, she is always occupied with the stuff of her undoubtedly busy life, with her desires, her needs, her thoughts. One day she reads, another she speaks on her mobile phone, and on other days she casts her eyes about simply ingesting the loveliness of the trees and flowers of the park Still, I wonder, indeed *wonder*, of her name. I have considered naming her myself and have made a mental catalogue of possibilities. I would, on one day, call her "Angela," perhaps. She is, after all, seraphic. On another day I think she is a "Nadia," a name in which the feminine vowels are only briefly interrupted by interloper consonants. Perhaps she is a "Gabrielle" or a "Solange." Perhaps not, though. She is not Gallic, I decided. This name business is maddening, exhausting, and —in a peculiar way distracting, for the silent moments imagining appellations take away from my time of pleasurable observation. I will abandon this pastime.

Yesterday was a momentous one in our relationship. Both of us were in our respective places, sitting quietly. My hands, as they are usually, were folded neatly in my lap and her hands were busy running through the pages of a small book. It appeared to be a notebook or address book, not a novel or other entertainment. At one point, she paused from her page turning and stared—I think she stared—at the leaf before her. Quite to my surprise, then, she raised her head from the page and turned. Her movement was so rapid that I had not any time to avert my glance. And so, our eyes crossed. More than crossed; our eyes locked for the briefest second and, in that instant of thrall, I saw the glistening pearl of a tear in the corner of her left eye, near her nose line. I felt an urge so strong, so coercive, that I sense it still, a day later. I wanted, more than anything, to speak to her, this brown-haired beauty who lights my days. But, of course, I could not.

That moment, however, became a window open wide through which I saw myself standing, approaching, and talking to my nameless woman. In this apparition I imagined her voice, whispery yet firm, recounting the cause of her upset, the reason for her tears. I, quite naturally, listened all the while absorbed by her beauty. I offered consolation, and in an act of atypical boldness, I extended my hand. In my larger, coarser paw her fingers felt like little wet petals, and she let me hold them as I supplied a verbal unction to her wounds. 1 saw myself sit beside her, close enough so that I maintained her hand in mine. As quickly, though, as this window dream opened, it closed.

Our eyes disengaged. She looked away, towards the statue of Gandhi with its ring of flowering plants as I dropped my head and gazed at the walkway at my feet A small flurry of motion captured my attention, though, and I raised my nodding head an inch or two to find her, my nameless lily, walking towards me on the pathway. I felt my pulse shudder and thoughts raced through my head with the speed of light, thoughts that I had not allowed myself to entertain. Would she notice me? Would she speak? In a few short steps she was directly in front of me, and my eyes, still slow in rising, were now ascending, past her legs, her mid-section, her shoulders, and—finally—her face with its billowing cloud of soft brown hair. She was almost beyond me, then, with her perfume still riding on the breeze.

I felt a hand tap very gently upon my left shoulder and, with an uncharacteristically speedy shift of my neck, I turned and faced in the direction of her steps. At the same time, a feminine voice broke my reverie.

"Professor James," the voice said just wove a whisper, " Professor James, it's time to go."

I nodded slightly. The nurse bent and daubed my lips and chin, removing a small trickle of saliva that had reached my lower jaw.

"Are you warm enough, Professor James?" she asked

I again nodded slightly, but she was already straightening the blanket across my legs and lap, tucking it into the corners of the wheelchair against my hips.

I felt her release the brake and begin pushing, very slowly at first We bounced along, past Gandhi and his flowering plants towards my apartment in the university housing.

"Well," she said, "we had another nice visit today, Professor James, didn't we? We'll be back tomorrow. You love it, don't you?"

I think I nodded, but I am not certain. I should have, because I was already anticipating it—the slow morning, the delay, the dressing, the preparation, the bumpy ride to the square. Tomorrow would come and with it, another hour to spend with my woman with the brown hair.

VINCENT J TOMEO
CHARGING A CELLPHONE

My son visited me in the hospital.
The whole time he was on his cellphone.
I was on life support, struggling to breathe, survive!

His phone was losing its charge.
So, he pulled the plug to charge his cellphone.

Tomorrow,
There will be a virtual funeral.

Tomeo

PERCEPTION

Went skiing.
The ski lodge attendant attached a tag to my ski jacket.

Forgot to remove the tag.
The next day, in New York City,
A lady approached me in a reprimanding manner,
I've seen everything, she said.
Young man!
Why are you wearing a condom on your jacket?

Madam!
This is proof of payment.

Tomeo

VINCENT VECCHIO
(INSERT NAME HERE)

(insert name here) was her name.
The oxygen & the hearth
       to my zodiac flame.
Mon one-in-a-million Cajun Dame
W/ a spicy mirth and smile
T'thaw even the most icy-clawed crocodile,
Blushing in a rush t'crush down his obelisk
Of bro-man-dude-thing masculinity, his fingers crossed she'd linger
Just a smidgen longer, lost in the religion
Of her Ziggy Stardust pizzazz; the brisk,
Scat-singin' jazz of her laughter
       cleansing the jejune lesions of the soul.
The soft solace of her gaze
       oft the only lighthouse among Life's haze.

(cont)

Not a day passed
      We weren't having fun:
Holly jolly love llamas
      lollygaggin' in the Mississippi sun.
Hakuna Matata. No drama t'preach,
Sippin' on our cheap two-dollar gas station
                pina colattas
      on Biloxi beach. Outlandish as Easter Island statuettes
Standing in awe on the edge of the world
W/ all its catastrophe behind us; our peacock feathers unfurled
& our skin…O our skin electric off Freedom's mojo in the air,
Feeding loquacious seagulls our crumbs
      as they'd strut their bums
      along the teasing tide
Clawing out t'where the mermaids would surface
W/ their inquisitive eyes:
"What kind of ooey-gooey enigma is this?"
They'd wonder. "Their intimacy tells no lies…."

Guitars, radios,
Cigs and beers,
Lights along the bridge,
Kisses on the piers.

Those would be "the days:"
Our cosmic kitties all a purring.
W/ tails alluring in a sway…&
Our cameo in the interstellar flic
We call Love picture-perfect as the Titanic,
Where I was Jack, and she was my Rose,
And despite all the dangers we'd be exposed,
I'd never let her go…
We could spend an eternity
      gallivanting from all evil….
And when we'd grow bored of the land,
We'd waddle into the sea hand-in-hand,
Diving down to the depths of its floor
Where entranced we'd slow-dance forevermore.

(cont)

Memories I'll never forget.
Romance I'll never regret.
I miss you…. Whoever you are.

Vecchio

MARTIN WILLITTS JR
LEFT BEHIND

This morning a town rolled by
for no particular reason, on roller skates,
to somewhere else in a hurry, and I couldn't,
for the life of me, ask where it was going
or why it was in such a big hurry.

The town had streetlights where young love
could freely express desire, lit from love
being displayed. There were small-minded stores,
where mannequins, fashionably dressed,
waved without arms or hands.
A school recited the alphabet
in cursive. A woman aired out a house
as it wandered by, the house lost in deep thought.

It's not every day you see a town walking by
like a parade, in a hurry to escape
whatever it left behind. In the rear,
a man tipped his hat, pleased to be seen
and not considered an illusion.

Then, another town moseyed along,
complete with pee-wee baseball.
Another town with empty boxcars and parakeets,
and another town with a post office trying to change
all the new addresses.

(cont)

I was beginning to feel left out.
I wondered about all the excitement.
Where was everybody going? My shoes followed,
leaving me behind, disjointed, confused by the towns.
Then, my buttoned shirt walked off, wearing a tie.

I stood on empty space, trying to decide what to do next.
Then, my decisions left me behind to fend for myself.

Willitts

CHARLES RAMMELKAMP
ALMOST AS INTIMATE AS KISSING

"Jerome!"

We reach in for the handshake, but then we realize the situation, both of us behind shopping carts at the early morning people-over-sixty grocery hour—like the early-bird dinner the retired Floridians eat, only in reverse—face masks obscuring our mugs, thin disposable gloves covering our hands, like a second layer of skin.

For a couple of weeks, before the six-foot social-distancing rule took effect, the elbow-bump had been trending, and I'd come to like it, as if it were a move on the basketball court, a fake, a fade, a wide-open J.

Jerome and I had had a regular Sunday morning game of one-on-one on the basketball court at the gym, first to score eleven, for close to a decade, until the day my ACL snapped like banjo strings, and I collapsed to the floor, unable to stand on my right leg, wobbly and unstable as a string of al dente spaghetti. Jerome had driven me over to the emergency room and called my wife.

Once I'd healed—I was deep in my fifties by then—we never played another game. But when I took up swimming laps in the pool, before long Jerome, too, joined the little band of early-morning before-work swimmers. We continued to talk basketball up in the locker room, sweating together in the sauna, shaving at the wash basins, showering in adjacent stalls, sitting on the bench in front of the lockers, getting dressed. Kobe, Lebron, the Lakers, the Celtics, Golden State.

Even after we both retired—me from Sales, Jerome from the

Law—we continued to show up at the gym before dawn, join the group of swimmers, swap stories in the locker room, then go our separate ways.

Now it had been a couple of months since the gym had closed; governor's orders.

"How's it going?"

I shrug. Such a simple question, but oh, what a complicated answer! So much had happened the past few months. On top of the pandemic, the George Floyd murder had recently happened. My wife and I had social-distance protested at a local rally, standing silent for eight minutes and forty-six seconds, the length of time the police officer had knelt on Floyd's neck. Jerome and I talked politics, too, but this chance meeting in the grocery was more personal than that. The question was more elemental. *How is it going?*

"I was just thinking: I'd be on my annual Chicago-Minneapolis swing about now, if I were still working, talking to clients." Somehow the response didn't seem adequate.

"Tell me about it. The courts are closed to the public. Only essential staff, only emergency matters. Glad I got out when I did."

We share a grim laugh. Gallows humor.

"How's the family?" Jerome's father, long dead now, was African-American, his mother, still alive in her mid-nineties, Italian-American. Jerome married a Scandinavian blonde named Elsa. They have a couple of daughters whom I've never seen; they have their own families out in Oregon or California or someplace. Jerome and I never actually socialized outside of the gym, though once, many years ago, we did have a beer together after a basketball game.

He shrugs. Another complicated simple question. "Yours?"

I shrug, too. My son's career Army, stationed overseas in Frankfurt. He tested positive for COVID like so many of his men, and self-quarantined away from his wife and children for a couple of weeks, but he was never seriously ill.

"Good to see you," I say, almost apologetic because it really is great to see Jerome, even if I can't express it. This is the *friendship* I've found so absent from my life these past months. This is what all that isolation makes you hungry for. My glasses have fogged up with the conversation, my breath clouding the lenses up from under the mask. We push away in opposite directions in the breakfast cereal aisle. "I understand the NBA's talking about having a short season and playoffs, under strict conditions. Too bad it had to happen this way, you know? I thought this might be Milwaukee's year."

"Yeah, or maybe the Lakers."

There's so much left unsaid, but we're blocking the aisles. I can see the same yearning that I feel for something *normal* in Jerome's eyes. But people are waiting for us to get out of the way, so we move on, resisting the impulse to fist-bump—or even shoulder-pat.

CRAIG COTTER
AYAZ MARHONI & MAHMOUD ASGARI

The Iranian government
held a public execution

to murder gay lovers Mahmoud Asgari, age 16
and Ayaz Marhoni, age 18.

They were arrested at 14 and 16, tortured 2 years
and forced to tape a confession that they were in love.

Handcuffed together
before their public execution

photographs show them crying
as a microphone is held in front of faces.

Instead of building gallows
that snap the neck instantly

they were hoisted slowly
nooses around their necks

and strangled to death over 20 minutes.
Mahmoud jerked so much

one of his sandals came off.

—Publicly executed in Edalat (Justice) Square in Mashhad,
   northeast Iran, on July 19, 2005. The facts are disputed.

Cotter

DONNA PUCCIANI
SQUIRREL WITHOUT A TAIL

A warm-bodied, acorn-digging
ball of gray has been ambushed
from behind by a predator

who bit off the whiff of fur
that used to be a tail. Or perhaps

she was caught by a runaway
lawnmower and lucky to get away.

How many happenings cannot un-
happen—a child's handprint in cement,
the dance of falling leaves or snowflakes,

the riddle of tides, the ache of old bones,
the map of the world drawn in wrinkled skin,

small creatures consumed by large,
a boy's growth marked in pencil on a wall,

or the final curtain call in a velvet theatre,
the last of the applause drifting like fog
among the intermezzos and empty seats,

and the house lights dimming,
mothlike, one by one.

Pucciani

JOHN GREY
OCTOBER ON BROAD STREET

Autumn in the inner city,
backyard trees,
even the rats that forage
in the lumps of leaves,
change color—
a stray dog figures he can chase those rodents
all the way back to Norway
but they laugh at him
by breeding more and more.

In a hollow under the house,
a groundhog digs himself in.
Boys, on knees,
seek him out with a flashlight.
Someone tosses a firecracker
in the direction of the den.
They're lucky the whole place doesn't burn.

Every oak and elm
drips like a leaky tap,
as the dead collect
between their roots,
or clog drains,
or take to the streets.

Insects die out.
Worms sleep.
The stray dog huddles in the doorway of a church.
"Make way, mutt," says a homeless man.
"That's my spot."
The dog's accommodating,
becomes a cold night's blanket.

Two kids see all this
from a second-floor tenement window.
This is the world
when nothing else is.

Grey

RICHARD COMPEAN
ON THE BEACH

On this Thursday morning the alarm did not go off because Nathan had not set it to go off and because he did not want it to go off—not today. He wished he had people to see or places to go, or even, like Gregor Samsa, at least a family to work for.

His torpor had started on Monday and repeated itself on Tuesday and Wednesday. Nathan had awakened, alone, and thought, *Who gives a fuck about me?* He mused that he could sleep for the rest of the morning, or the whole day for that matter, and no one would care.

Yes, he had a job that allowed him to work from home, and a condominium in a nice neighborhood, and food in both parts of his refrigerator. But last week he had worked extra hard to complete his part of the revised program that others at work would not be looking at for at least another week.

Since he had no deadlines to meet this week, he had actually gone back to sleep on Monday, not reawakening until after 1:00 p.m. On Tuesday he could not stay asleep past 11:00 a.m. And on Wednesday, he only made it to 9:30 a.m. Clearly, sleeping in was not the answer. Nor was watching movies or binge-watching TV shows on Netflix or Amazon. He had grown tired of everything he tried to watch.

Since Wednesday evening was the eve of his fiftieth birthday, he decided to take stock of his now miserable life, find the places (especially the more recent ones) where he had gone wrong, and maybe do something about them or change his ways.

The problem was that doing something would involve other people, and right now, especially in a time of required social isolation, there were no other people. The last time he had had a conversation with anyone about anything that really mattered was after his recovery from heart bypass surgery, nearly a year ago. It was a conversation with his sister about their lives without their parents. Nathan could not remember any details.

Since then, his only interactions had been with those he worked with, at lunch or at occasional Friday after-work happy hours. Now the restaurants and bars were all closed because of the pandemic, so he would go days without speaking to anyone or seeing anyone, except on his daily late afternoon walks. And usually who he saw were people wearing masks and walking or jogging in the opposite direction as him.

Nathan's father had abandoned both his mother and her children long ago, his sister had moved to Amsterdam with her husband, and he had lost touch with both of his ex-wives. He had no children by either. His first marriage had lasted almost seven years, the second only three. For the past ten years, there had been some occasional relationships, mostly what he would call flings or affairs. He even wondered now if he still remembered how to do it, if the beast was virtually dead.

Now there was no one who might care if he got up, or even whether he lived or died. He could go for his usual walk, but today was not a usual day.

It's my fucking fiftieth birthday today, so I have to do something different, he thought, or maybe said out loud, enough to reach his feet and ankles, to get his hands and arms to push aside the bedcovers and lead him into the shower, after which his fingers put shaving cream all over his face, grabbed the razor, and shaved off many days of stubble.

The figure in the mirror, even with a clean shave and combed hair, looked to him like someone who was seventy or eighty, not fifty. What to do?

As he walked toward the home office that had been his living room, he saw some charts he had prepared, sitting on the laminator he had brought home—way back before the pandemic—from his office. They were about fifteen inches square.

It would be easy to create new ones, so he decided—not knowing why—to make two laminated posters, with the same big, bold printed message on each side, one in red and one in violet. After all, why not make the color printer useful? The messages in red and violet were the same: "**I AM 50 TODAY**." By punching holes in the corners of each laminate and stringing them together with shoelaces, he created a sort of old-fashioned sandwich board that he could wear while out walking. He also decided to walk somewhere different today, along the beach.

As he looked for the shorts he had not worn since last year and sandals to wear instead of cross trainers, from the window of his neighbor's condo he heard The Rolling Stones starting to sing "You Can't Always Get What You Want." *Thanks a lot, Mick*, he thought. *That's just what I need to hear, alone on my fiftieth birthday.*

He drove toward the marina, parked his car, and found a stretch of about a mile and a half that would provide a good round-trip workout of afternoon sunshine and ocean air, if nothing else. From his car it was a block to the beach entrance, so he carried his sandwich board birthday sign there, then put it on and walked to the edge of the water, setting out north toward a rock formation that would be his turnaround point.

He got all the way there without anyone saying anything to him. Only a young boy and small girl, while looking at him, turned to say something not to him but to the older man at the beach with them. No one else seemed to notice either Nathan or his sign.

More than halfway back, just when he was muttering to himself about what a stupid idea this had been, he heard a child's voice ahead.

"Grandpa, here comes that man again," Nathan heard the boy say.

"Which one?"

"The one we saw with the sign on his stomach. And he had it on his back too."

"You mean the man that was crying?" piped in the little girl.

"Well, Pauli and Anna, please don't stare at him. I don't know if he's crying or not, but just keep a distance from him as you've been doing with others."

Anna said, "Fine," then asked her grandfather about the man's sign. "What does that mean, 'I am fifty today'?"

Her grandfather said that it probably means that today is his birthday and today he is fifty.

"Almost as old as you, Grandpa," quipped Paul.

As Nathan's trajectory around them brought him closer, little Anna looked at Pauli, then at her grandfather, put out her hands like the symphony conductor she had recently seen on TV, and began to sing, loud, clear, and joined by them:

"Happy birthday to you. Happy birthday to you."

Nathan heard them and had to stop and listen.

One of the things he always used to hate while dining in restaurants was groups of individuals at a nearby table, led by waitstaff with cupcake and lit candle, arriving to sing "Happy Birthday." Even more, he had hated hearing other diners join in. Whenever it had happened, he had considered it so tawdry that he refused to join in.

Today, too, Nathan did not join in with their singing, not even for himself, but others nearby did. And as they sang, he heard not "Happy Birthday," but instead, in his mind's ear, he heard the London Bach Choir joining Mick Jagger in bringing the song his neighbor had started to a close: "If you try sometimes, you just might find, you get what you need."

J TARWOOD
A TEACHER FROM THE MAINLAND

My Chinese teacher
never had a word like ours.

He spoke Mandarin all day.
We spoke street.

In school, teacher, student,
pretend, but he reads

books, he believes
what he says,

which strands him far away
among big sayings

nobody wise would mean.

In class, he so loudly
cared, we laughed,

getting him red,
shattering his face.

He didn't know anybody.
He could only imagine.

That made a contradiction:
him there, us here.

Tarwood

FRANK H COONS
WHAT I KNOW OF THE PARANORMAL

is obscured by myth and mysticism
plus, a dab of psychic research.
    I've never seen a ghost and I'm not
holding anyone's breath, but under
    the right ectoplasmic circumstances—

well, let's just say the impossible
    happens every day to the extent
we are constantly hammered by happenstance
    that challenges brains far bigger than mine.
And if on some nights, I see a being
    vaguely resembling my long-dead father

    working in the garden, dead-
heading chrysanthemums or spreading peat moss
    into the soil, I will choose to call this apparition
neither phantom nor poltergeist,
    but the purest kernel of memory
that animates a distant narrative.

    I can't quite join him
in the gloaming and till that midnight loam,
    but I can raise a glass of his best
bourbon and toast his semi-present image
    before he disappears again into his heaven
where I will or won't join him when I finish.

Coons

R CRAIG SAUTTER
NORTH OF NOWHERE

North of nowhere was where I was headed when I heard the wind
warn me I was traveling up that way for good, which I feared was probably
not so good.

I'd spent a couple of years south of nowhere at a branch college, came back, got stuck there wishing to god I could just leave, but never did, until now. I guess you can figure out that like lots of folk, I grew up nowhere and I was going nowhere fast.

It was way past midnight. I'd left a couple of hours earlier, after I saw Jade riding home up the long driveway with Carson Drake, her supervisor on the second shift at Anton Screw and Bolt, which seemed pretty appropriate. She figured I still would be at Sutton's Bar & Grill downtown on a Wednesday night drinking with friends and listening to a live local band, like I usually did. But I wasn't. I just jammed some shirts, pants, socks and underwear, and my Kindle with some books and my scribbling into an old army knapsack left over from my old man's Asian tour and headed out the back door before she even got done and moseyed in the front. It had been her mother's place before she died of cancer a year ago, so I had no stake there. And my Ma had gone earlier, same thing. They both worked at the bio-fuel refinery south of town.

I headed out through the rear woods, across to the county road, and didn't look back. The field was sort of muddy in places since it was late winter and recently rained a bit. I got up on the highway and stuck out my thumb not knowing where the hell I was going, except north. I knew it was finally time to take off. I'd put on a pair of gloves and a black knit cap since it was still pretty cool out. My backpack was fairly heavy. I was used to driving everywhere, had gotten a little too fat, not that fat, but low energy, weaker legs than when I ran track in high school. I figured Jade could keep my old red Chevy. At least I left her something to remember me by.

Jade was a good looking, fairly tall girl, brunette, smile like a headlight, real nice shape. And she was smart. That's what I really liked about her, witty and funny. She always had a good line. She even beat me in chess once in a while, and was always doing math puzzles. I guess she's why I overstayed my time nowhere. I met her just before I left for school. Then we took up again when I came back to work for Miss Sylvia in her old bookstore and tea room down off the town square on Maple in an old 1890s red brick building her father left her.

Miss Sylvia is about 80 now, but first ran her store as a newspaper and gift card shop, back when folks bought gift cards and newspapers. Then after she expanded a little, folks stopped by for coffee and a roll on their way down to the plants for first shift. When the Internet came in, she started selling books mostly by mail. That was my so-called job when I got back from school, to log in used book titles and drive them over to the post office when she sold one, which was pretty often. Then she started buying old hard-bound books and rare collections when folks died or moved out looking for work, catalogued and posted them online. She went to a lot of auctions all over the county and beyond if she got a good tip.

Her old dying store business really took off, at least enough for her to open the coffee, tea, and reading room with its oriental rugs and cedar bookshelves. She took care of the early morning business herself, worked on a pour-your-own honor system during the day, and hired high school girls to work after school when a lot of kids and folks with nothing to do or who were getting off shift drifted through, or they just wanted to grab a table to read. Some folks hid their pints and freshened up their tea. She didn't care none. She had old and interesting books, intellectual subjects that she collected from some college libraries when they threw them out, some picture art books, paperbacks and mysteries she didn't care about, stacked all over the place and didn't even sell those. You could take copies with you if you said you'd bring them back, which most folks did. She didn't really care.

Her real business was with the good hardback volumes and collections she kept upstairs. That's where she stored her father's old oak roll-up desk, her computer on a side table, her easy chair and rocker, and an old brass bed that had been her grandmother's way back. She ate almost every meal at the restaurant around the corner, Ruthie's, although she had a small refrigerator upstairs and some kitchen equipment on the main floor. She didn't need much, she told me. Old Sylvia liked me, I guess because she liked my Ma first because she used to buy gift cards for birthdays and so forth. Old Sylvia even hinted I could take over when she moved on to the big bookstore in the sky, where all the wisdom of this world and others is kept in big books on shelves as long as the eye can see. That's what she used to say and laugh her funny laugh. I don't think she was religious or anything, just kind of mystical, a lovely old woman who I'm sure I'll miss. Anyway, it was a place to hang out and read and waste time and talk or flirt with the high school girls. I didn't want to work in the plant or refinery like my Ma had done so long. I didn't want to do much of anything really. And like I said, that's where I first met Jade.

She was a high school senior when I first saw her and we took to each other pretty fast. Then I went away for a while, and when I got back, she wasn't working there anymore, but at the plant to help pay for her sick mother's medical bills. Then it got complicated fast, if you know what I mean. When her mother died, I moved in and I thought we were square. But Jade was too restless and attracted lots of looks, which she was glad to return, and I could see it was going nowhere with us, and then she started messing around, I guess. Anyway, I warned her I couldn't take that, I mean psychically, and she said none of it was serious like us. But you know how that goes after a while. She was younger.

Not a lot of traffic comes along on the county road after everyone's punched in on third shift, so I was just walking along until someone did. The clouds were fairly thick, covering a half-moon. I could hear a couple of owls, and maybe a polecat or two. I started singing to keep myself company, whistling a little too. I must have walked an hour with only one or two cars passing, not daring to slow down for some stranger out late on a dark road. Who can blame them? Then about 1:30 or so, I heard a pick-up with a blown muffler slowing down, pass me by, and hit its brakes. It had out-of-state plates. I ran up to catch a ride. I was cold. The driver flipped open his passenger door. As I got close, I spotted a couple of rifles on his rear window rack. That's nothing around here. I never saw the dude before. He was about 45 or something, had an uneven crew cut, was kind of heavy, sweating on his forehead, and wearing a shit-eating grin on his face.

"Hey buddy, need a lift?"

"Sure. Cold out here."

"Lonely too?" he added as I started to step up.

That stopped me fast. I could see he was lowering his hand down to his crotch. "Damn," I thought, "I don't need this crap."

"Well, I guess not really," I said. "Just walking home. I'm almost there. Got off the bus in town a while back" I lied. "Think I'll just walk. I need to slim down."

"Be a lot easier to ride for a while."

"Thanks anyway for stopping." I tried to be polite.

Next thing I know he's reaching for his rack and pointing one of his rifles my way. "I think you should get in. If you're not lonesome, I am."

"If you say so," I faked as I grabbed the side door, slammed it on his barrel, and dodged to the rear out of his line of sight, ducking down as I took off running. Almost simultaneously a shot blasted through the door which had smashed against the barrel. I shifted to the side and rear of his pick-up, slipped down a small gully across a stream, tumbling down, losing my old man's knapsack. He jammed it into reverse so he could try for a clearer shot. I got up fast and raced for the woods a couple of yards beyond, dove behind a tree. The next two shots blasted bark behind me. Split wood went flying. I heard him opening his door, getting out of the driver's side. I got up, broke into a full run, weaving through the old oak grove and thick hickories, headed south back the way we'd come from, and then cut into a field of broken winter corn stalks, swerving like a halfback, getting down low, then almost crawling. He fired wildly a couple of more times where he thought I was, where I'd been. I heard one shot whiz by and hit the mud about three yards ahead and rolled right several times, but he was firing blind.

"God damn punk," he yelled out, "Next time I won't miss, you son-of-a-bitch. And I'll be looking for your dumb ass, you dumb bastard, you can be goddamn sure of that. You think you got away. You ain't safe no more, punk. I'm coming back for ya."

I stopped moving. I heard him get back in his truck and squeal off, peeling rubber for 25 yards or so.

I lay out in the field panting at first trying to catch my breath, lay there on the cold ground for what must have been an hour, maybe more. A few cars and trucks sped by. One slowed down, twice, going each way, stopped for a while, its engine idling, its muffler burping loudly. I figured that had to be him. Then he went on, after he fired two more shots. I just kept looking up at the dark clouds rushing by, the moon shaded behind their long strung-out formations, wondering what to do next. Eventually, the clouds broke open a little and the half-moon dully lit up the silent field. I figured it was clear and made my way back through the field and woods looking for my old man's backpack, which I eventually found after about fifteen minutes. My phone was in there, and I saw it was already 4:15. Folks would start heading into toward town and work soon. I got back on the road and continued north.

I felt a chill when I heard another car coming up behind me. But I didn't hear the busted muffler. It wasn't the pick-up. It was an old blue Nissan. I recognized it, Lizzy Raymond's car. She was getting off work from the all-night diner down south of town. She's about 10 years older than me, pretty too, always friendly when she waited on me, like she was to everybody. I was surprised she recognized me, covered with mud, shivering, looking kind of freaked. She pulled over and rolled down her side window.

"What the hell happened to you? How'd you get so damn muddy?"

"Been a long night."

"I guess. Better come with me, honey, you need to warm up, and a shower."

I did, but that's another story that I rather not tell right now.

WILL HEMMER
NIGHT FLIGHT

In the dim cabin of a plane,
where the only light is my reading light,
a child curls under her blanket and looks at me.
Am I right in this? I wonder.
She smiles shyly and hugs her doll.
I want to touch her gently on the nose
to see if she will giggle,
but men alone
do not touch children
not their own,
and so I quiz her silently
on the right financial moves,
and does she know a cure
for falling hair,
and isn't loneliness
too harsh a price to pay
for withholding love?

She watches soberly,
then yawns and,
dropping her doll
on the seat between us,
closes her eyes….
and I see
in the glassy stare
of the sprawled doll
only myself
and through the portal beyond
the night sky.

Hemmer

SAM AMBLER
CEPHAS, THE ROCK

Islam! and Christendom!
Are you ready to rrrummmble?!
In the corner on my left,
we have Achmed Suleyman,
aka "The Mule," draped in pitch-black
like the sacred Kaaba,
carrying the weight
of over one billion Muslims;
and in the corner on my right,
we have Cephas Simon Peter,
aka "The Rock," swathed in red linen
like the Blood of the Lamb,
weighing in with more
than two billion Christians.

All right, contenders,
you know the rules,
no hitting below the belt,
no kicking between the thighs,
no demonizing.
Good, then shake hands
and go back to your corners.
When you hear the bell
show us some preordained choreography
like we've never seen before.

Ka-lang! I tell you folks,
I've never seen such spirit
exhibited here in this ring.
The Mule and the Rock
virtually leap into the canvas center
circling, stalking each other,
swatting their nasty hadith qudsi
and sly proverbs aside,
looking for the other to falter.

Oh my God, do you see that?
In one swift move,

the Rock twists the Mule
into a papal miter headlock;
then like a flash of lightning
the Mule achieves a full reversal
with a Meccan hajj stroll.

This is a battle made in heaven, folks,
the Rock might be a little older,
but he's got a lot going on.
And the Mule, well, that stubbornness of his
could pay off big-time.
There, you see it?
The Mule issues a fatwa
out of the side of his mouth
while maneuvering the Rock
into an Ayatollah Khameini clench.
The Rock vacillates through his grip
and reciprocates
with a Damascus Road feint
into an apostolic nuncio's twist.

The Mule doesn't stay still long.
He declares "jihad" and hurls himself
against the Rock's gravel pit.
The Rock reels, spits out "crusade,"
and rolls over the Mule
with an Inquisitional body tuck.
Oh, my Lord, folks, I'm not sure
they can dish out much more of this.

Ka-lang! There's the bell,
and just in time too.
We'll be back after these words
from our sponsors
for the surprise ending
that will leave the whole world aghast
wondering what to do next,
so please don't touch that remote.

Ambler

THEY WENT UP TO HEAVEN IN A CLOUD

O planet Oprah,
as you swing
through the cosmos
in your orbit on high,
be kind to your moon,
Gayle, who regulates
your tides and activates
your werewolves;
and do not ignore
your asteroid belt,
Stedman, who encircles
your girth and amplifies
your mirth.
O planet Oprah,
three is not a cloud,
…um…crowd.

Ambler

ANTHONY J MOHR
ON VALLEY VISTA

The three young women seem on the edge of adulthood. Each has blonde hair, straight and almost as long as the tan legs that carry them along Valley Vista Boulevard, an ideal place to walk. Valley Vista is also an edge, the last street before the San Fernando Valley gives way to the Santa Monica Mountains.

Dressed in matching T-shirts of yellow and blue——I'll bet their iPhones also look alike——they laugh their way past the houses and lawns.

I'm across the street, so I can't hear what these gazelles are saying, save for stray words like party, cute, and Porsche, but I can't help trying to listen.

They arrive at the corner of Stansbury Avenue, one of the choicest streets in the area. Jacaranda trees line it, purple branches blooming rich and full, forming a canopy over the pavement.

Before the trio turns the corner, a husky woman walks toward them. She has muscular legs, and her short black hair is slightly darker than her skin. They don't notice her approaching. They don't notice when she leaves the sidewalk and steps into the gutter, making way for them to pass while they continue to chirp at each other, like the birds nearby.

A police helicopter chop-chops overhead, flying low. They don't notice that, either, but she does.

EDWARD LEE
THIS HOUSE WE BUILD

This house we built
still has some
unfurnished rooms,
like secrets we know are there
but do not need to know,

and we keeping building
with every kiss
and tender touch,
every silent moment
of contentment
as we lie beside each other at night,
not needing to be anywhere else
but in this house
we have built
around ourselves,
rooms both unfurnished
and furnished, secrets both
silent and known.

Lee

AYMON E LANGLOIS
ODE TO A BOOKSHELF

Beneath the window,
next to my desk you sit and
hold multitudes—
worlds built of words—
between wooden boards.

>There's Stevenson's "strange,"
>   beloved *Case*;
>   Dickens' *Expectations*—a present
>   for exceeding my own…
>   there's the Eliot that haunts
>   me, going on April;
>   and two first edition Carvers, one signed
>   from a small bookstore in
>   upstate New York.

It'll be time for an upgrade
soon, you'll be off to Goodwill,
then another's bedroom or office
where, perhaps, you'll lament bearing the
burden of Darwin, Galileo, Newton, and Copernicus
or where, maybe, the worlds I compose will come to sit
besides those by whom they were inspired.

Langlois

TINA EGNOSKI
HEMINGWAY FEEDS THE DOLPHINS

Marine Studios,
St. Augustine, Florida
September 1947

Mullet are heaped in a pail by the holding tank. They hint of rot, to his nose at least. The girl, fistfuls in each hand, docsn't seem to notice. Or she's uscd to it, spending whole days unattended at the park.

Two dolphins, noses high, chitter. She tosses the fish. Direct hit, right in the maw. He wonders if she should be so indulgent. Don't they starve them until showtime?

"That's Dolly," she says, pointing to the dolphin on the right. "She's the highest jumper. Sometimes I give her extra."

"Is that allowed?"

She shrugs.

"What do you call the other one?" Hemingway asks.

"Splash," she says.

She's Baskin's daughter. No, niece. He's met her before. Susie? Sally? Maybe, seven. Her hair is the bristles of a scrub brush, the ends twigged from salt air and humidity. It's the color of sea oats. As a boy, Bumby's hair was that color. Later, it darkened. The way everything— eyes, skin, heart—does.

His chest is warm. From the sun, from the gin he left on the bar at the Moby Dick Lounge next door. A kitschy place that Baskin manages. Fishing nets and buoys hang from the ceiling. Norton Baskin, not a hearty drinker, but he holds his own. He's a listener, a skill that puts his guests at ease. He had hoped to see Baskin today. He needed a listener.

The problem is cats. Mary keeps bringing home more cats. Kittens really. Strays from Havana. And they keep losing them. To falcons, he supposes. Or they wander off the property. Once, he found a carcass down by the road and buried it before Mary could see. It has been over a year since she lost the baby, and still, every dead cat is a reminder.

For some reason, Baskin never showed. So, Hemingway paid the bill and came here. No Baskin, but he found the girl. The front of her white cotton dress is gummy with fish slime. He envies her youth, her innocence. She doesn't know who he is. Doesn't know he can't put pencil to onionskin, fingers to keys. She won't ask him when he'll write the big one or win the big prize. Critics ask. Readers ask. She won't and he won't have to say, *I did. I wrote the big one and they nailed me on the cross.*

He bets she doesn't even know that the actor who comes here to film the jungle movies is beloved all over the world. He imagines Weissmuller hoisting the girl onto his shoulders, parading her around for the cast. So easy, his strength, his charming smile. Hemingway has seen *Tarzan.* Didn't think much of it. Didn't much think of it.

"Hey, mister," says the girl. "You try." She toes the pail.

The dolphins nod, chitter again, encouraging him. He scoops and lobs, missing the target. They don't care—they dive and recover the mullet, come back for more. Splash has a scar just to the right of his blowhole. That's the only way to distinguish the pair.

With a handkerchief, he mops his forehead and his greasy hand. September and still the sun is full of spite. The way it beats down on him. Cruel as life. The life that beats down on him. The death that beats at him. Friends, rivals. Anderson is dead. Joyce is dead. Stein. Fitzgerald—dead so long. Now Max. And the cats. Two turn up dead and Mary brings home four more. Life goes, as it does.

The girl trails her fingers in the water. The ripples excite the dolphins and they flutter backward. No, *flutter* isn't right. What is the right word? Max would know. There isn't an editor alive who can match Max Perkins.

"You're that man," she says.

She knows.

"My uncle's friend," she says.

No, she doesn't.

"Yes, I'm that man,' he says, pleased to be known as Baskin's friend.

"You write stories," she says.

"Yes, I do, young lady." So she does know.

She laughs and it sounds like applause. "I'm not a lady. I'm just a kid. My aunt Marjorie's a lady. She writes stories too. A lady writer."

"I know," he says.

Fine writer, Marjorie Rawlings. Damn fine book, *The Yearling*. To him, not even her best. They should read *South Moon Under*. *They* meaning everyone. She won the big prize. She had her own film crew. The girl—she probably met Gregory Peck.

Is Baskin Marjorie's second husband or third? No matter, she's not like his Mary. She's independent. When he visits, Baskin tells him she's at their house in New York or home in Cross Creek. She's in Atlanta or St. Louis. They never seem to be in the same place.

He should leave. He has hours ahead on the road, then a boat across the Strait. But home—he doesn't want to be there. Mary can't stop crying, can't stop bringing the crying kittens. How many drinks did he have? Two. Four. He lost count. The gin here is never cold enough. He needs to let Baskin know.

He misses Baskin. Misses Max. He misses the baby that wasn't a baby, but cells lodged in one of Mary's fallopian tubes. Will she ever be the same? Will he?

The girl slides her hand in his. Sticky. Warm.

"You're my friend too," she says.

The wind lifts her hair, revealing pink-pale scalp, easily burned. He wants to touch it. If he does, though, he knows it will all vanish—all that he has. And he has much—even in death and sickness. He has Mary and she will get better. He has the boys, Bumby, Patrick, and Gigi.

And words. He has words to put on paper, books waiting for him to complete. Even without Max, without the prizes. And the cats, so many cats now, arriving almost daily. They'll hardly notice when one goes missing.

He has a new friend. She's fresh and young and open for all that life has to offer.

For all that life.

JUSTINE MCCABE
ODE TO INSOMNIA

Who knew
that late
life
insomnia
would birth
opening
lines
to poems
yet to be
written
in dreams?

McCabe

SUSANNE VON RENNENKAMPFF
CLOSE OF DAY, HARVEST

And still the heart wants more,
impatient, restless,
until, across the field,
a group of poplars are lit suddenly
by late sun freed from clouds.
The hawk who kept you company
through the long afternoon
settles on golden stubble
nearby, shakes dark wings,
gazes into a distance
you both seem to know.

von Rennenkampff

RELIEF

Early evening, and I am on my way home.
Another day coming to an end, my mother
ready for the night, not of her own choosing
but because it is time:
she is only one in the queue, others
are waiting/not waiting,
just like her. What else is there now
but this waiting, not waiting
for something she doesn't even know
will come, sooner or later, death
abstract, not linked to her
or anyone she knows, has known.

I tuck the blanket around her.
She is so small in this cocoon,
always cold—some things at least
don't change. She asks for her book, the glasses
the nurse already folded and left on the sink
for the morning shift, not expecting
this request. Is it a practiced pattern

(cont)

she clings to, a way
to ease herself into the long and lonely night?
If I ask her tomorrow, will she remember
the smallest fraction of what she read tonight?
And does it matter?

I step into the fragrant evening, the day
holding its breath, like me,
the air still, sated
with all this quietness.

Anticipation. The sky heavy
with the promise of rain,
in the distance
the small voice of thunder.
My body tense
after another day of watching helplessly,
explaining and listening patiently, coercing
to take another sip, another bite —
for what?

The air matches my tenseness, longing
for the discharge of pent-up energy,
but not yet, not yet.
Knowing it's imminent
I will the rain to wait, am caught
in this state of suspension, brush
bare arms deliberately
against the coolness of hedges
lining my path.
The scent of peonies mingles
with that of charcoal, finally
pushing aside the smell of urine
and hopelessness.
Can there be a cleansing, even
temporarily?

From the high branch of an apple tree
a robin's evening song.
The first drops of rain.

von Rennenkampff

TIM FITTS
FLIES

While driving my kids home from school, the subject of heartbreak arose. My oldest daughter had been dumped by her boyfriend. We were half a mile up Chapel Road from the school. Frankly, the conversation came as a welcome break. That morning, I had taken a shower, and water must have gotten behind my eardrum, because ever since, it felt like something bulging from the inside, and with every step, the sound of a balloon being tapped inside my head. However, as the day went by, the sound began to happen on its own, building from regular to erratic beats. In my mind, the seriousness of this ranged from inconsequential to grave. It was nice to have a divergent train of thought.

"So?" I said to my daughter.

"So, it *hurts*."

"It hurts who?"

"*Me*."

"On a scale of one to ten, how much does it hurt? To set a baseline, let's say a broken arm is five."

"A broken arm is five."

"Four or five, sure."

"A broken arm is not five."

"What is it then?"

"Nine."

"No way," said. "First, you've never broken your arm. If you had, you'd know it's not that bad. Now, a compound fracture is a completely different thing. When the bone sticks out of your body, then nine is on the table. Do you know why?"

"No, dad."

"Because it's not about the pain anymore. A compound fracture is about the fear. It's about seeing the bone in your arm when you're never supposed to see the bone in your arm. If you are looking at a bone sticking out of your arm, you have every reason to believe that you could lose that arm. You could suffer a bone infection and die within a couple days. You could die of shock. You could die of flipping fright."

"You can't die of fright."

"Shit," I said. "This is the problem with sixth graders. You get straight A's, but none of you have any real idea of what you're talking about. You can certainly die of fright! You can die of fright in the moment or even over the long run. It's probably the cause of every death, basically."

"That's comforting."

"Hey, that's life, pal. Let me ask you this. How much does this heartbreak hurt? Same thing. Scale from one to ten."

"*Nine.*"

As I turned to look at her, I felt a clump of wax fall from my ear, the ear in question. I had hoped that this had signaled some relief in the pressure, but no change in the erratic drumbeats. Maybe there was more to come.

"No way," I told her. "No way does this heartbreak hurt nine."

"How do you know?"

"Because I know. Same thing as the broken arm. You've got no house to split up, no finances to rummage through. No kids to share. Maybe this guy, this fellow has a new girl and has put a picture of them holding hands already on Facebook, or whatever, and has announced his new relationship to everybody. Which, if he has, I'll grant you two more points. Three maybe. Bonus pain. Has he done this?"

"Nobody uses Facebook anymore."

"Yes, they do."

"Yeah, old people who fight each other about politics and vote *dictators* into office."

"What do *young* people use then?"

"They use other things."

"Other things that are going to turn into the same thing."

"No, it won't. People in my generation aren't racists."

"So, I'll give you three. Three points for pain."

"Can I skip school tomorrow?"

I turned on the radio and let her take over the dial. My problem was that I had engaged. If she was going to suffer, she was going to suffer. We drove a few more blocks, and I told her that I was sorry. If it's nine, it's nine. She'll look back and see that it was three after all, but no sense pressing the issue.

The next morning, I awoke, and it was still dark outside. I thought it was happening again, except it felt as if one clump of earwax fell after another. Tumbling, almost. Instead of falling out, though, the clumps were crawling out. In the next moment, I realized it was not wax at all falling from my ear canal, but three flies had crawled out of my earhole. My stomach cooled. Of course, all I could think about was the legion of eggs inside embedded in all of that funk, what with their siblings and ancestry creeping about the gears and drum heads, all of the crannies, and either the good these maggots were doing or the havoc they were wreaking on my flesh. The sun had yet to come up, and when I pressed my fingers against my ears, I could hear the thrumming of wings reverberating inside the space they had found for themselves. All I knew is they were trying to find their way out, but until then, they were laying eggs of their own. Jesus, I thought. How long has this been going on?

ROD FARMER
TADPOLES

Time eats each one of us
so we can become part
of time's energy
below matter
in the subatomic world
we are energy where
everything touches
everything and becomes
everything.
I gladly donated some of
my morning to watching
my first tadpole this spring,
he lives in a six-inch deep
vernal pool and wiggles
past his younger siblings
sill in their frog eggs,
he too will become
everything, his little
black body hopeful energy.

Farmer

ROCKING CHAIRS

Time slithered past me, again,
I spend too much time letting
Everyday time escape,
Now I understand why my
grandparents, in retirement,
Loved to just set in rocking
chairs on the farm's porch,
breathing easy, waiting for
grandchildren to arrive
and energize everyone.

Farmer

PAULA YUP
SOREN THE SEVEN-YEAR-OLD

builds the best train track ever
even has a lovely bridge
and sweet turns
frustrated when one-year-old
Eveline his sister
destroys the track with glee
we call her Baby Godzilla

Yup

AT THE AIRPORT

after the scare
young man with a seizure
wheeled off the plane
at Seatac

I use the bathroom
two-hour layover in Seattle

(cont)

feel hands around
my left thigh

turn to look
a toddler
looks up with recognition
at my Asian face

I say hi little girl
and leave the bathroom
to take the train
to my gate
for the next leg
of my journey

Yup

W ROYCE ADAMS
BLUE POOL

I looked down at the waiting water, at least forty feet. Some say more, some less. Now that I'd climbed up here, I knew for damn sure it was a whole lot of feet down—whatever. Blue Pool looked more like Black Pool. A bit scary, yeah. I looked down at them, small now, eager for me to prove the dare. They don't think I'll do it. Think I'll chicken out. Thing is, though, they hope I will do it. Probably like to see me hit the water and not come up. If I killed myself wouldn't that give them some juicy excitement in their lives. Witnesses to the real thing. Yeah. My name would be added to all the stories about Blue Pool. I'd become another legend attached to this old Mississippi river road quarry pool where we crazies risked swimming to cool off in the summer despite the fence and those skull and crossbones signs all around the place.

One story has the pool bottomless, so deep that an old train boxcar got dumped in the pool, and nobody's ever dived and found it. Probably a bunch of bull, but who really knows? True story I do know, though. Some guy jumped from here a few years back and ended up paralyzed from the neck down. Yeah, lots of stories about Blue Pool. Like, supposedly way back some Indian Chief killed the lover of his daughter because he didn't want the Princess to marry the guy. Broken hearted, she jumped from where I'm now standing and killed herself. Another Indian story had it that she never hit the water. A giant, dragon-like monster known as the Piasa Bird swooped down, caught her in the fall, and flew off with her, never to be seen again. You can still see where the Illini Indians painted the ugly bird creature on the cliff wall near here. Town's people keep it painted. Well, no such bird around this time.

So, here I am. And I'm going to do it. I left my T-shirt and shoes down below and want her to see when I climb out of the water my bare feet all messed up and bleeding from my climb up the scabby shale cliff. I want her to see me jump, even though she doesn't know I'm doing it for her. Well, for her attention. I admit it. That's what I want. And she knows my name now because everybody used it when they called me a fat head for taking the dare. What she doesn't know is how I feel about her. I'm stuck on her. Dream about her. But now she'll take notice. She'll admire me after this.

I tried to spot her in the group below but couldn't see her. She was there when I left to climb up here. I waved to get their attention, her attention. Hey down there! Look at me! She just has to see me do this. Has to. So....

"Here I go," I yelled down.

I jumped way out, waving my arms like wings to get some distance away from the cliff, then crossed my arms across my chest, pulled my feet together, felt the air force my shorts up my crotch, took a deep breath, and closed my eyes....

The first time I saw her, man, I was clobbered and understood what people mean by "love at first sight." At Tri-City Grocery, where I worked in the produce department during the summers, she came in with her old man, both wearing sporty tennis duds I'd only seen in the movies. I immediately understood. Here were people who mattered to the world. Their white outfits brought out their tans, their classiness, their rich distance from me. No one I knew even owned a tennis racket, let alone played the game. Her dad, tall, a touch of grey in his sideburns, looked strong and confident, like an aftershave ad. But it was her that held me captivated. Yeah, she was probably sixteenish, my age, and I'd never seen any one more appealing, more, what's the word—symbolic—of what I wasn't. Something came over me. What was it I was seeing I'd never noticed in people before? Don't know. But she did it.

I had like this peculiar urge—for me, anyway—to run my tongue along her smooth, bare arms and legs colored light caramel by the sun, so smooth, firm and wholesome sleek. And her long, brown hair, bleached blond in spots from the sun, she'd tied back with a violet-blue ribbon the color of her doe-shaped eyes, every feature of her face perfection, deafening me from understanding the words she spoke. Her light voice, an unfamiliar melody, played counterpoint against her handsome father's deep voice as they examined and discussed the produce. At once, I wanted to be wanted by her, wanted to be what they were, to step into their lives, yeah, to be one of them.

Then she asked me something about the oranges. With no understanding, I sort of froze, feared looking for very long into her clear, violet eyes and stammered some thickheaded sounding answer I don't remember, dropped an orange at her feet, bent down to pick it up, never wanting to rise, only to look forever at her clean, white tennis shoes, her long, firm, smooth bronzed legs. Oh, just to touch them!

My life kinda ripped open in that moment with, I don't know, an inferior feeling. Yeah. Can't tell you why. When I dared look up into her laughing face again, those perfect white teeth, I knew in that moment a life existed to which I didn't belong. She was untouchable, unreachable. She didn't know it, but she had passed sentence on me.

I kept my eye on them as they shopped and then followed them out the door to the parking lot. I pretended I was collecting shopping carts as I watched them get into a new, black Mercedes convertible. Yeah, they were rich alright. The top was down and as they drove away, I felt hollow, empty, a nothing, a no thing.

But her image? It stayed to haunt me.

I kept hoping, even praying, they would come back to the store, but if they did, it was never when I was working.

I began to look for her everywhere I went, aching to see her once more. I couldn't help myself; she'd made me her prisoner. How did that old Russ Columbo song go? The one my mom liked? "I'm just a prisoner of love…."

Then, in the fall, the first day of school, I was leaning against my locker talking to my best friend, Tee Jay, when I saw her walking down the hall. I let my knees buckle, and I slid toward the floor. It was a kinda dramatic act on my part, but I wanted Tee to see how flipped out over her I was.

"Hey, you okay?" He grabbed my arm and helped pull me back up.

"It's her. There she is," I barely got the words out.

Tee didn't need to ask me who I was talking about. I'd bored him to death talking about her so much, he'd often start to whistle a tune to drown me out, or just plain tell me to lay off about her. He turned to look.

"The one coming this way?"

"Un-huh." Oh, my god, there she was.

Tee gave her a good look. "Yeah. Okay. What makes her so special?"

I couldn't believe him. "You don't see it?"

"She's okay, I guess." He didn't seem impressed, and it made me want to punch him for lack of good taste. He had to be kidding me.

Then she walked down the hall straight toward us. I froze. She was wearing—I don't remember, but it doesn't matter. Yeah, there she was, my wish come true. Then she was right there. Say something, say something. Quick.

"Hi," I dared.

She smiled. "Hi."

Her velvet eyes. I, me, was in them for a moment.

But then, I watched her walk on.

"That's it?" Tee asked. "You've been mooning over her all summer and all you can say is a mousey 'Hi'?"

"Maybe she didn't hear me. Yeah, my voice was pretty faint."

"I can't believe you." Tee sounded really pissed. "Of course, she heard you, you dunce. She said 'hi' back. Go. Catch her."

But I just stood there, an immoveable force, watching her disappear around the corner.

"You're unbelievable, you know that? You missed your chance, you idiot. Perfect timing. Missed." He shook his head and gave me a-you're-an-idiot smirk.

Normally, I would have said something nasty back, but he was right. I blew it.

Well, come on. What did I expect? She didn't know me. Why would she remember me from the store?

She said "Hi" back. And I think she smiled a little. Yeah.

I held on tight to that while Tee kept telling me what a bonehead I was and that I was never to mention her to him again, or he would personally kill me or do something worse.

Of course, I knew Tee was right. I could've kicked myself for being too afraid to talk her up. Why hadn't I introduced myself, reminded her we'd met. I'd been wishing for this moment and I bombed. Tee's right. I'm a moron, a blockhead, a halfwit, a nincompoop—all the names Tee called me—and more.

I got in a little bit of trouble that first day of school. That's because I was late for every one of my classes. See, in order to find out what classes she was taking, I had to follow her to each of her classes. Unfortunately, she was in none of mine. By the time I followed her, I was late for my own classes. But it didn't matter. I knew where she was every class period, so now I could meet her after school one day, maybe even get up the nerve to talk to her.

All I could think about was how I might approach her. Should I remind her that we had met at Tri City Grocery's? That was a possible entry, but I was so gaga around her that day, stammering and dropping the oranges, she probably thought I was a jerk. More likely, didn't even remember the incident. I needed a plan.

The next day, when the lunch bell rang, I tore out of my classroom and headed for hers, which I knew was upstairs, but by the time I got there she was gone. I searched the halls looking, but didn't see her. I finally gave up and went down to my locker to get my lunch. Tee was there, waiting. We always ate lunch together.

"You're late, birdbrain."

"You're so observant, oh wise one."

I took my lunch from my locker, and we headed outside where we usually sat on the lawn to eat.

"Need I ask why you're late?"

"Do you have such a need?"

"Not really. I'm guessing you didn't find her or you'd be wining and dining with her instead of me."

"God, you're brilliant. How do you stand yourself?"

"What's her name, by the way? I can't keep calling her *her*."

I didn't answer right away.

"Don't know." I hated to admit it, knowing him.

He stopped walking and gave me this you're-in-love-with-this-girl-and-you-don't-even-know-her-name-or-anything-about-her look.

"Don't gimme that. I'll find out."

"Yeah? When? Not at the rate you're moving."

We found our usual eating spot and sat on the grass. We checked out each other's lunches and found nothing to swap.

Right then, I decided what to do.

"I'll follow her around, learn more about her. Find out where she lives. Where she plays tennis. Who her friends are. What her interests are. Stuff like that."

Tee shook his head. "That's your plan? Follow her around? Listen to yourself, numb nuts. You don't even know her name and you're talking about stalking the poor girl."

"No. Not stalking. Just keeping an eye out for her. You know, getting to know more about her."

"Come on, ace. Call it what it is: stalking."

I just shrugged my shoulders. He didn't understand.

"So, what's your first step? Get a disguise? Become her shadow?"

"Shut up, will ya."

I punched him on the shoulder a little harder than I meant and he dropped his peanut butter and jelly sandwich in the dirt. Before I knew it, he grabbed my sandwich and started wolfing it down.

I didn't care. I'd had enough teasing.

"You crack me up, buddy." His words munched together as he chewed.

"Go ahead and laugh. You'll see."

"See what, exactly?"

I didn't answer. I didn't know.

The rest of the school day was torture. I knew I had to get to her last class after the bell rang before she got away again. Before the final bell stopped ringing, I was out in the hall and halfway down the stairs. I got to her classroom just as she was leaving with another girl. Lucky for me I saw Mary Ann, a girl I'd had classes with in the past. I felt pretty sure she'd remember me so I got up the nerve to stop her. It wasn't like we were great friends or anything. We just knew each other from around. She wasn't my type or anything, and I didn't want her to get any wrong ideas. So, I tried to be casual and all.

"Hey, Mary Ann. How are…things?"

She looked surprised I'd stopped her. "Hi. Okay. You?"

"Guess we don't have any classes together this semester."

"Didn't see you in any." She gave a little laugh at the obvious.

"Yeah." I didn't know what else to say, so after a hard swallow I just came out with it.

"Say, do you happen to know the name of that girl over there in the plaid skirt talking with Maureen?" I was pretty sure the girl's name was Maureen.

Mary Ann looked at them. "You mean Grace?"

Grace. The name sang in my brain.

"Uh, yeah. She's new here, huh."

"Yeah. She moved here last summer. Why?"

"Just wonderin'"

"Ah, I get it. Wanna meet her?"

Only more than anything. But what came was, "Ah, no. Just, you know, wondered who she was."

I was so glad Tee wasn't around to hear me lie.

Mary Ann laughed. "And why are you wondering who she is?"

I didn't like the way Mary Ann was making a big deal out of my interest in Grace. And I was worried Grace and Maureen would stop talking and leave. I needed to follow Grace to see where she lived if that's where she was going.

"Nothin' really," I said, digging a deeper hole. "Friend of mine wanted to know who she was, maybe ask her out. Told him I'd see what I could find out."

"Who's the shy friend?"

"Best I don't say. Don't think he'd like it if I told anyone. Anyway, thanks for telling me her name. I'll pass it along."

I turned and started walking away when she yelled, "Bye. I'll let Grace know she has a secret admirer." Then she laughed and I knew she knew the truth. I turned back, hoping Grace hadn't heard Mary Ann yell. But she must have heard her name because she looked our way.

Embarrassed, I turned the corner, and once out of Mary Ann's sight, I ran all the way down the hall and out another side exit. Then I made my way back to the door I knew Grace would come out when she stopped talking with Maureen. I hung back out of sight hoping I hadn't missed her. I didn't have to wait too long before Grace came out—and by herself. Perfect.

The after-school crowd started to thin out and I had to be careful Grace didn't see me following her. I stayed back, following her to the bus stop. She started talking with someone in the waiting crowd. She looked so—I don't know—above them all. Yeah. She kept shuffling the load of books in her arms and I wanted to rush up to her and say, "Here, let me carry those for you."

That's when I realized I'd been in such a hurry to find Grace I'd left my own books on the desk of my last class. Oh, well.

The yellow bus arrived and everybody started piling on. I held back until Grace got in. Then I dashed and made it on just before the doors closed. I knew she was on the bus so I didn't bother to look for her. I didn't want to be noticeable. I slipped into a seat up front and kept looking straight ahead, waiting for Grace to get off. After about four stops and the bus started emptying, Grace got up to get off. She stood so close to me I wanted so bad to reach out and touch her. That's when I wasn't sure what to do. Was I going to get off with her? That could be awkward. If I didn't, then how would I know where she lived, the whole point of my following her?

While I tried to figure out what to do, the bus stopped. Grace was the only one to get off, and the bus started up again.

I thought fast.

I stood next to the driver and gave him my pitch. "Sir, I'm sorry, but I missed my stop. I wasn't paying attention. Could you please stop here?"

"Sorry. Too late. Against the rules. I can only stop at designated stops."

Crap, crap, crap.

"Where's the next stop?"

"Five blocks."

I just stood there, looking at the door handle lever. No. Don't even think it.

"You'll have to sit down," the bus driver said.

I did as told, sure in my heart I'd never make it back to Grace's stop in time to see where she lived.

When the bus finally stopped, I was the first one to get off. As soon as I hit the sidewalk, I started jogging, then running, back from where we just came. Oh, please, please, please, let me find her before she gets home. I knew my chances of seeing her were poor, but I couldn't give up. When I made it to her bus stop, I stopped running hot and sweaty. I looked around, but no one was on the streets. I walked around the tree-lined neighborhood aware I'd never been in this part of the city before. These were some fancy houses I was noticing. Some two and three stories tall. Mostly brick. Some with tall, white columns in front like plantations I'd seen in the movies. Curved driveways leading from the street to the house curved back down to the street. Gardeners working on at least two of the yards I passed.

I was about to give up when luck stepped up to the plate. That black Mercedes convertible pulled up the long driveway of one of the houses. The top was down, so I got a good look at the driver. Grace's dad.

He didn't get out of the car. He just sat there for a few minutes. I hid behind a thick Sycamore tree and watched. He gave a toot on his horn. The front door opened. And there she was. She was still wearing her plaid skirt and said something to her dad I couldn't make out. She got in the car with him, gave him a kiss on the cheek that I wished belonged to me. Then he backed out the driveway and headed in my direction. I inched my way around the tree trunk as they passed so they couldn't see me.

But now I knew where she lived and my heart filled.

Once they left, I took a good look at the house. A two-story brick house with two, I think you call them gables, on either side of the second floor. Five windows faced the front, all trimmed in white wood. The front door was framed white like the windows. Actually, two carved wooden doors, or at least it looked like it. Big old maple trees stood guard on each side of the house. You could play croquet on the lawn it was so big and smooth. Couldn't tell for sure, but I'd bet there was a pool in the backyard. Sure different from my place.

Some woman, I guess Grace's mother, opened the front door and looked at me kinda funny, so I started walking away. After a few steps I realized I didn't know where I was. I forgot to pay attention on the bus. I walked a few blocks checking street signs but nothing sounded familiar. I had a little touch of worry, but I now knew where she lived.

I began walking, hoping I'd see somebody or a store and could ask directions to my neighborhood. And that's what happened. I stopped some guy walking his dog, and he gave me directions to a street I knew would take me toward home. Even though it was a long way back, I mostly walked on air with my thoughts of Grace in her ritzy house.

I called Tee later that evening.

"Hey. I know where she lives."

"Well, whoop-de-do. What now? Gonna pitch a tent on her lawn?"

"Screw you, a-hole. It's a really nice place. Over near the country club."

"That's a far piece from where you live. How you gonna keep tabs on her?"

"Thinkin' about a bike."

"You don't own a bike."

"No, but you do."

"Oh, no. You're not borrowing mine. I don't believe in spying on young girls…or old ones, either."

"Quit calling it spying. I'm just…you know…."

"Spy—ing."

"No, dammit. I just want to know more about her. Hope to get to know her. Come on, Tee, I really like her. A lot."

"Then why not walk up to her and say, "Hi. I like you a lot. I want to get to know you better. What's your favorite hobby?"

"Lay off, will ya. Don't be a smart ass."

"I'm not. Why go through all this mystery stuff? Just introduce yourself. What's she gonna do? Bite you?"

"No, It's just …I'm too shy, that's all. I wouldn't know what to say to her. That's why I want to know what she likes, so I can talk to her about stuff she's interested in."

"I'm tellin' ya. You're goin' about this all wrong, chicken liver. She'd probably be all flutter-bugged at your interest in her, think you're cute or something. I mean, I know you're not, but you can't tell what girls think."

"But what do I say? See, I need to know more so I can talk about things."

"You're the one who's gone ape over this girl. What do you want to say to her? What 'things' are you talking about?"

"Just things! Everything! I don't know! That's my problem!"

"You're your problem."

"And you're no help."

"You're not listening to my wisdom, fathead."

"Are you gonna loan me your bike tomorrow or not?"

"Not. Definitely not."

By Saturday, he gave in and loaned me his old, rusty-red Schwinn with dirty white fat tires. It was hard to pump, the brakes squeaked and there was no chain guard, so I had to be careful not to get my pants caught in the chain. But it beat walking to Grace's. It didn't do me a lot of good though, because almost the minute I got there, I saw her drive away with her dad. I tried to follow them, but I couldn't keep up, plus I didn't want them to see me so I fell behind and lost them. I pedaled around her block about ten thousand times waiting for her to come back, but I gave up and decided to head home.

That's when the right leg of my Levis got caught in the bike chain, and bam, I met concrete. I couldn't get up with my leg stuck under the bike and lay there for a minute, pissed, watching the front tire spin round and round while I went nowhere. To get up, I had to struggle with the bike and ripped my pant cuff trying to get it loose from the chain. Of course, the chain came off the bike's pedal gear and, after too much struggling with a greasy chain, I couldn't get it back on and limp-walked the bike back to Tee's.

The school week dragged by, but nothing much happened. I managed to catch Grace walking the halls, or talking with friends. No boys, just girls. That kept me encouraged. One day, I did catch the bus again just to be around her. Instead, I got off before she did. I ran most of the way and got to her house just as she walked in her front door. I walked up and down her block a few times, but she never came back out, so I hightailed it home.

But Friday at school, I hit it lucky. I happened to overhear some girls asking Grace if she wanted to go with them Saturday up the river road to Blue Pool. They told her it was where a lot of us hung out, picnicked, went swimming. When I heard her say yes, my body felt juiced. This could be my chance.

Saturday, I talked Tee into hiking up to Blue Pool with me in the morning. It was something we did pretty often anyway. I didn't mention that Grace and friends would be coming sometime. I didn't want to get into his stalking-frame-of-mind accusations.

To get to Blue Pool, you walk a dirt road along an old railroad track for a good mile or so out of town, the muddy Mississippi on the left, shale cliffs on the right. Like I said, Blue Pool is part of an abandoned quarry hidden behind some wild shrubbery set back in the cliffs. Once you make your way through the growth and under some rusty barbed-wire fence, you come across a nice sized circular pool of water cleaner than the river. With not much room around the edge of the water, you had to suffer togetherness with whoever was there.

I saw one or two familiar faces, guys, but not Grace and her group. I started to worry they might have changed their minds. But I didn't need to worry. Soon their girl talk could be heard before they came through the bush. Then one by one they popped out like the brush was giving birth to teenage girls. One, two, three, then Grace, and then Mary Ann. When they got closer to me and Tee, Mary Ann waved and yelled a "Hi, guys."

Tee let out, "Ladies! Howdy-do."

I was myself and just waved. All the girls looked at us to see who Mary Ann was greeting. My eyes wouldn't let go of Grace. She wore a man's white dress shirt, hanging loose, sleeves rolled up. The shirttail almost covered her dark blue shorts. I remembered those smooth, tanned legs from that tennis outfit she wore in the store. She had on brown penny loafers, and I wondered why someone hadn't told her to wear better hiking shoes. A couple of the other girls wore men's dress shirts, too. A fad, I guessed.

The moment of truth. What do I do now?

Then Tee jumped the gun. "Hey, Mary Ann. Introduce your friends."

We sort of gathered around and Mary Ann went through the niceties. I half-heard and sort of knew the names of the other girls, a Peggy and a Joyce, don't remember the other one. Just Grace. She looked right at me and I knew she had no idea we'd met at the store or in the hall that first day of school. But she smiled those perfect Pepsident-white teeth and said, "Hi," velvet eyes giving me the once over.

Then, Tee, never one lost for words, asks Grace, knowing full well the answer, if this is her first time coming to Blue Pool.

She gives the answer we all know while I'm pissed because I didn't think of asking.

But it broke the ice, and she explained just about everything I wanted to know: her family had moved here from Chicago in June; her dad was a lawyer-politician type (her father knew the governor); she was an only child; her mother was still getting their house organized after the move; her family just joined the country club, and she wanted to learn how to play golf; she loved tennis; took ballet lessons; so far, she liked the school; hoped to go to Harvard law school like her dad; played the piano and oboe; liked some popular music, but mostly she played classical stuff.

I began to feel very far away from her even though I was now practically sitting next to her.

When she asked what the big deal was about Blue Pool, Tee started to talk, but from somewhere I found myself cutting him off and my usually moth-filled mouth started moving and I blurted out everything I knew about the weird bird myths and the dangers of jumping off the cliff into the pool.

I guess I finished abruptly, 'cause it got quiet for a minute.

Then Mary Ann chimed in. "He's right. It's really dangerous. You could get killed. Nobody wants to jump from up there."

I saw Grace look up at the top of the cliff. Her words still stick in my ears. "That would take a lot of guts."

"I'd do it."

I'm not sure where my words came from, but out they came.

Some laughing followed. "Sure, you would" kind of things.

Grace put an end to the talk. "I dare you. Do it. Right now."

Thinking back, it seemed a long time before I hit the water. Maybe I'm wrong, maybe I'm making this up, but while I was falling...all the lyrics to the song Tee Jay stuck in my head...I think I sang them...falling...falling in love with love...juvenile fancy...playing the fool....

Here's what they tell me 'cause I don't remember it all, especially after all these years. When I popped out of the water, there was blood all over my face and I was what they call semi-conscious. Tee and someone else helped me out of the water. Lots of talk about the blood on me. Must have hit and scraped my face on a rock under water, they said. Then more about the blood and maybe get me to a doctor. They tried to stop the blood over my forehead gash with my tee shirt but it was now all red wet. Mary Ann, surprise, had driven the girls to Blue Pool in her dad's car and volunteered to drive me wherever Tee suggested. Tee said the hospital. I said home. They took me home. Parents took me to the doctor. Stitches. Bad, but not as bad as it looked. Probably a slight concussion. Bed a couple of days. Parental what-were-you-thinking lecture.

Mom wouldn't let me go to school for a week. Tee called a couple of times to see how I was, filled me in on what I didn't remember. Said I'd made a name for myself. Told him I didn't want to know what it was. I thanked him for his help, told him to thank Mary Ann for the ride. No talk of Grace.

And here's the thing. And I can't explain it. But it's like I left or lost those feelings about her back in Blue Pool. It's like as fast as my interest in her hit me, it left just as fast. It's like the dark water baptized me and washed away my…what? Don't know. I just know I came out of Blue Pool on the other side of elsewhere.

R G ZIEMER
I HEARD THEY WERE CLOSING ST. CASIMIR'S

I heard they were closing St. Casimir's.
The convent silent and brooding,
The window-pocked escarpment that ever loomed
Over the flat landscape of Marquette Manor
From prairie
To parish,
City square
To slum.

(cont)

A hundred years of black shod feet
Shuffle into silence,
Sisters in voluminous folds of rustling habit,
Pale perfect faces wimpled,
Worn out from the yowling births
And the howling trauma
And the violent demise of the neighborhood
Under the Holy Cross.

No more
Little blonde Marias learning Lithuanian,
No more
Aves in the garden's cool shadows,
No
Rosaries recited by ancient virgins
In the murky grotto
Where cold water trickled silvery
And the Sisters' whispered prayers
Hung over the shrine like fog.

Once
The Sacred Grove of perfect trees bore fruit—
Sweet slobbery pears and mouth-puckering apples
Once
The garden's nightcrawler earth yielded a savory prize when
Deep in the dusk
We gathered a watermelon
 Green,   round,   and   luscious.
(Cracked it wide in malicious glee—
But the sweet red meat glistened with a jagged hex,
And we passed round a bottle to ward off the curse.)
Once
We wondered mysteries and horrors
When "Pray-the-Lords" tramped past our bungalow.

Were they shaven to the white of their skulls under the cowls,
Those holy wives of Christ?
Breasts bound to their pallid bodies?
Womanhood maimed with no maidenly vestige?
Or did they bear the babies of lecherous priests
*   in secret cellars of the motherhouse?*   (cont)

Now
Gangster bangers and crack whores roam the grounds.
They've tagged the Lugan Monument,
Cracked the chapel's amber glass,
And care not a bit if the
Secrets of St. Casimir's sword,
 the lily and the crown
are lost to history.

Moth-white dust settles over the
Empty rooms and
Mother Maria's Venerable bones
And a busload of brittle old nuns retreats to the suburbs,
 Where they'll bide their slow time
Till the end of mystery.

Ziemer

IVANA MESTROVIC
THE FUR COAT

When my parents went out to a party
my mother wore a black cloth coat
with a large hood and close sleeves
with mink hidden inside.
I would stand with my arms wrapped
around her and smell her Norell perfume
the warm soft skins of dead animals
and jasmine draped around me.
I did not want her to leave—her shining
hair, my father's smooth hand
firm in the cup of her back—
I wanted to be stroked
by those million silky fingers
linger in that muffled, humid darkness.

Mestrovic

SKYE
for ESE

Thirty years ago on Skye
when we had gone as far as we would
north looking for shelter

we found an island that seemed full
of cats, black and teeming
with innocent portent

and so we fled—
I remember the exuberance
of our panic, laughing at our fate

We were so young
We did not know how to navigate
that perilous space

and crossed back
thinking we could escape our luck
a broken-down car

or at worst a broken arm
the limits of our imagination
not the years as they fell

Mestrovic

JULIE GARRISON
AGING IN PLACE

Women lose their value as they age. The day a gynecologist asks a woman, "Are you still laying eggs?" she has been diminished in value. On the food chain of womanliness she is just a notch above a slug. My first impulse when asked the "egg" question was to reply, "Why yes. And I'm selling them, too!"

My grandmother used to say, "Dear, aging is not for the faint of heart." But old age is when hearts are the faintest. Everything about being old is harder. Heart difficulties, high cholesterol, high blood pressure and a myriad of other disorders are endemic to the elderly. Sometimes doctors are patronizing to senior citizens and treat them as if they can't think for themselves. If a senior woman wants to be valued in our youth-oriented, male-dominated society, she must engage in expensive cut-and-paste procedures to eliminate her jowls, turkey neck, and sagging eyelids. A man can just age, but woman is required to nip and tuck. Granted, though, in our society, old age diminishes both men and women alike.

Our society worships the young, especially young women. We are not like the Japanese or the American Indians that revere and find great value in their elders. Now, in business and elsewhere, older people are let go and replaced with younger, cheaper models. The youth-venerating culture of Hollywood, in the words of Goldie Hawn, classifies women in three categories: "Babe, District Attorney and Driving Miss Daisy." The latter says it all.

A snapshot of a grandma in the 1950s consisted of a squishy, overweight woman with silver hair, clothed in a housedress and lace apron. She would be posed, sweetly in her warm kitchen taking chocolate chip cookies from her Deluxe Magic Chef Oven and bottles of whole milk from her Kelvinator refrigerator. Grandpa would be sitting in his overstuffed easy chair smoking his pipe. All would be fuzziness, warmth and lovingness.

Gone are the days when men treated elderly women with genteel respect. A real gentlemen would even walk an old woman across the street. By now all those gentlemen have moved on to the afterlife. Now, if an elder in a crosswalk has the misfortune of falling or being hit by car, an onlooker will film the event and post the video on Facebook. Society lives for dirty laundry. Respect for the elderly has all but evaporated.

Many senior citizens want to "age in place" amid familiar surroundings instead of being shipped off to retirement homes. Sometimes, though, placement is a matter of necessity.

When my mother-in-law was unable medically to stay in our home, we were forced to find a convalescent facility for her. We surged to the challenge of finding a pleasant old folks' home, only to be disappointed at the choices available. We learned from my mother-in-law's geriatric doctor that there hadn't been a new convalescent hospital built in our city in over 30 years. And why is that? The one we ended up placing her in was able to handle her medical needs, but it was a far cry from what we had hoped for. My first impression of the place was, "This is the end of the line—the place of no return."

The rooms were dark and dingy, and the farther into the building you went, the less appealing it got with its stained floors, dark curtains and musty smell. Fresh air hadn't seeped into that place in a long, long time. At the end of the hall adjacent to my mother-in-law's room was a blob splattered on the ceiling that looked to be butterscotch pudding. Sadly, this was the best place we could find that she could afford. In fairness to my mother-in-law, though, she had severe dementia and didn't give a rip about the retirement home's aesthetics. I did tell my husband, though, to kill me before he ever put me in that place.

Seniors are our heritage, and they have so much to teach us. Sadly, though, in much of America's landscape, the elderly are devalued by their appearance and age. Young people blithely exist as though old age is eons away.

When my children were young, I would take them to the local convalescent hospital to visit the residents. I wanted them not to be afraid of the elderly and to experience their wisdom and value. One day as I was standing in the hallway, an ancient gentleman shuffled past me, and on his way by, he pinched me hard on the buttocks. It took a bit for me to wrap my head around what had just happened, and then I laughed to myself thinking, "Well I'll be darned. He may be an old man, but he definitely hasn't lost his spark!" I hope that in my old age, I will still have my spark, too.

BRIAN RIHLMANN
NOTHING YOU CAN DO

there's no remedy
for what truly ails us
life is too often
like the first moments
of a blind date
when she stands
in the doorway
and you recognize her
from the red shoes
she said she'd wear

(cont)

then you take her all in
and are entranced
by her beauty
you soar when she
sees you wave
and walks over
but only briefly—

because though she
smiles and says
so nice to meet you
her eyes have already
clipped your wings

and even worse
when it's you
who wields the shears

nothing you can do
but watch
as she falls

Rihlmann

CECIL MORRIS
IN DADLAND

On Saturday mornings we washed both cars—
a '62 Olds Delta 88 and a '66 Chevy Malibu coupe.
We washed them and wiped them dry
before the rising sun topped our house
and threatened to dry spots on hood or roof.
Then back inside, fingers numbed and ears bright red,
for pancakes and, on best days, marshmallow-topped cocoa
that would warm our hands while we waited for it to cool.
Then we dusted and vacuumed and oiled
all exposed wood—banisters, mantel,
the cheap hollow-core interior doors.
After that Dad freed me to my own fun

(cont)

unless something needed fixing—leaky pipe
under a sink, squeaky belt on the dryer—
then I passed him tools and held the flashlight.
He'd push me with his knee or foot when I
let the beam wander from the target.
On Sunday nights we polished shoes—his, Mom's,
mine. While Disney shows played on TV,
we spread out newspaper, polish tins, and rags
and rubbed the waxy polish into Dad's
wingtips, Mom's pumps, and my own oxfords.
I wore a shoe on one hand as I worked.
And then we buffed and buffed and buffed
until shoes looked almost new, the week's scuff
marks erased, disguised, shoes ready for another
week of work and school and everything back
in shoe shine box, and I was sent to bed.
Not much talk in Dadland when I was growing up,
but we cleaned and washed and burnished and fixed
and kept the world a bright and shiny place.

Morris

OUR DAUGHTER IN HER FOG

Our lost daughter Persephone comes home
in an ambien-oxy stupor, broken bobble head
with her life in a thirty-gallon trash bag.

She pinballs down the hall and collapses
in her old room, more nightmare than dream,
a dankness hovering over her, an anti-aura.

When she wakes, she sleeps still. In zombie trance
she forces two legs into one yoga leg,
falls and flops in tiled hall, where she moans

and rolls, mermaid on the rocks, handicapped,
no siren call, this roll and cry, for legs lost,
for inch and crawl to bath at end of hall.

(cont)

In poly-spandex second skin, in hypno
half sleep, in artificial prisons bound,
Persephone lolls, our damaged nymph.

We find her stranded, sob-shaken. We peel
her legs and help her rise, all white and bare,
where   she   wavers,   unsure,   our   daughter   half   born.

Morris

OUR DAUGHTER RETURNS FROM DEATH

Persephone rises from her underworld
like bubbles billowing up in slow motion—
their swelling retarded by karo syrup,
by molasses, by something almost too thick,
too sticky. She emerges, caul of her sins
clinging, clouding her eyes, making her clumsy
and slow, a stunned newborn shocked by shattered light
and fresh air, or prehistoric sea creature,
the living fossil, with four limb-like lobed fins
our daughter a coelacanth almost ready
to crawl from black abyss of poppy's nectar,
from lightless depths of watery caves, her eyes
wet and squinting, shocked by life's motion and glare.
We see our world's airy ways stun her again
and again, old-fashioned flashbulbs exploding
blue white in her bloated face, blanching her.
She blinks, recoils, searches for dark corners
where she can wrap her chill around herself
and imagine what we can't imagine—
extinction deeper, longer than winter.

Morris

THE THINGS YOU LEFT FOR US

When you died, I found your cache of screws and nails,
pounds and pounds of them in fruit jars and tin cans,
cut down milk cartons, some sorted by size or purpose,

(cont)

some jumbled together, free-for-all of fasteners,
of holders, of things to batten down and keep upright.
They filled shelf after shelf in the garage cupboards
you built, in the movable work bench we helped you make
when I was nine, the one marred by nail heads I pounded
over and crescent moon dimples struck by my errant
hammer blows. The hammers but one are gone to me,
to my brothers, to grandchildren, to distant cousins,
the drivers gone too. You dispersed almost all your tools
but you kept the nails. When we were kids, you walked us
through the wooden skeletons of new subdivisions,
the 2 x 4s, our giant shadows, the evening sun,
all gilded with your attention, and we gathered
the loose nails dropped in the dust, the straight ones,
for projects at home—wood-block cars with clunky wheels,
clumsy boats, small stools, bird feeders, and grown-up stuff, too,
the fixing and building we kids took no interest in.
Though more bender-of-nails and denter-of-good-wood
than expert in things constructed, I think you had
nails enough to hold our home together forever.

Morris

CY HILL
WINNOWING AT THE WATER HOLE

When getting the best-looking girl from a gaggle of strangers was the goal, it was all about appearance and preparation. Vin had the look, and he spent everything on clothes to be the standout in a homogenous musk herd. His two trusty wingmen knew their roles, making small talk, laughing amiably while performing the calculus, subtly scanning, visually stalking prey. They practiced this rite to perfection over the years because Vin's rejections, his leavings, were their meat.

The trio migrated among watering holes on Friday and Saturday nights, never wanting to be tagged anywhere as "regulars" because it was all about the one-time hookup. The lived for the hunt after a week's drudgery at jobs they disliked.

This bar on this night was near a large college campus. Vin calculated three males for every two females. Figuring three-fourths of the males to be non-competitors due to looks, attire, or passivity, he was very confident.

"Happy Birthday, Vin," one of his companions said, and they all clinked glasses across the table.

"You know, I almost forgot," because he wanted to forget the aging process; wanted to forget that he was now thirty-three years of age; but he smiled, nodded, sat up even straighter in his chair.

"Brunette at four o'clock," one of his colleagues half-winked.

"Noted." Because he had seen her, too, nested at the bar.

Chasing *after* a woman in a bar was a perilous game. If you missed, you were done for the night because to chase another was an overt act of desperation. The way Vin and his cohorts worked it was to look cool, act cool, and let the women come to them. Because they always did. And once a woman made that walk across the bar and took a seat at their table, she would not leave. She had made a commitment before all. And the three men had their spiel perfected, polished to the point that she would not want to leave until it was with Vin. One woman frequently attracted more, and if Vin preferred one of the new ones, then so be it. It was understood.

Using his finely honed peripheral vision Vin watched the brunette at the bar checking him out. She had a girlfriend either side of her. He compared and calculated her worth against her feminine competition within the bar. Yes. She would be a prize. This was a conquest worth making and the two friends either side of her would satisfy his pride. Slowly, he turned his head.

He ignored the eagerly nudging knee of one of his wingmen under the table as they made direct eye contact. It was all in her eyes, that need. Startling blunt, this one. He smiled. She smiled. He put everything he had into his smoldering look, urging her to make the walk.

This was the moment that Vin had come to care about most.

Being chosen, this affirmation of *him*, mattered so much more than the sex that had become a bit of a chore. Yes, he could deliver, he took pills to ensure he did, but it was this moment that he relished, the act of being chosen, of being the one selected from amongst the herd.

He smiled as she approached their table, hips rolling dreamily. When she arrived, one of the others would offer her his chair and get another for himself. But not too soon. A few words had to be exchanged first. The hook had to be all the way in. All had to appear unpracticed.

Vin smiled.

She smiled. "Excuse me," she said. With a hand upon his shoulder, she squeezed past him. Her waist was lithe, a breast passed within millimeters of his cheek. "Hi," she said, "I couldn't help but notice you," but she was not saying it to Vin.

—a younger man seated at a table directly behind theirs, flanked by two young males—When had they come in?

Her girlfriends at the bar saw it, Vin's glaring blunder, and they laughed at the timeworn fool. She had never been looking at Vin. She was always looking at the younger man directly behind him.

DIANNE SILVESTRI
IT WAS A SCHOOL DAY

yet we sat in rows in Grandma's
white church, mostly a steeple
on a launchpad of flat farms.

We'd driven hours in the Chevy.
I was eight, in my plaid dress,
beside Dad in the pew.

We sang a hymn. I felt
a jerk. Dad's shoulder shook
with silent sobs, his mouth

(cont)

misshapen, face crumpled red,
shiny with tears, handkerchief
out to catch the storm.

I had never seen Dad cry
before my favorite grandma's
funeral, and never afterwards,

though I saw his chin twitch
the time when, home from college,
I asked him if he loved me.

Silvestri

SARA QUAYLE
SURRENDER

Please, open the envelope for me.
Department of Motor Vehicles…
due to your request for a handicap tag…
surrender your driver's license.
Of course, with this paralysis
I won't be driving the Kia—

the crumb carrier, kid carrier,
kayak carrier, the car that carried
crates to summer camp and college.
No, I won't ever drive to the office
or visit the cemetery alone.
Please bring me my purse.
I remove my license
from the zippered pocket,
that photo of my former self
smiling back at me.
I hand it to you. Mail it in.
Here, take the car keys too.

Quayle

EDWARD BELFAR
ELOPEMENT

The evenings are the worst times. The building in which Raymond Rothman has resided for the past three months has only two stories, one above ground and one below, but sprawls like a spider, its long corridors radiating out from a central reception area on the main floor and bending at sharp angles. With the waning of the sunlight, those pale-yellow corridors grow dim, filling with elongated shadows and fears that have lain dormant all day. Dozens of call buttons are pressed simultaneously, and the resulting cacophony of alarms sends aides and nurses scrambling in all directions. Stella Fortuna, who once sang the role of Tosca at the Met when Maria Callas came down with the flu, wails operatically at the frazzled aide trying to bathe her, "Why are you drowning me? Why are you killing me?" Victor Galinski, who played left guard for the Chicago Bears in the early 1950s and then had a brief second career as a pro wrestling villain, pleads for his mother. Every evening, the spindly Margie Atwater, a mother of seven and grandmother of twenty-two, packs an overnight bag and declares to anyone who will listen that she is going back to her parents' house. She has had enough of being treated like a dog—worse than a dog, really, because dogs get fed better and don't have to wait for some lazy good-for-nothing aide to take them to the toilet. Raymond Rothman's roommate, Hal Wallace, a tall, gaunt man with a grayish complexion, pendulous earlobes, a drooping lower lip, and clumps of white whiskers sprouting like weeds from his chin, rails against his two sons—"the dirty bastards"—who are conspiring to keep him in this place against his will, even as they rob him of all the fruits of the roofing business he toiled so long and so hard to make a success. Often Hal resists the efforts of the staff to put him to bed, screaming and striking out with his fists and his feet. One of the home's few ambulatory patients, the old roofer has attempted to elope four times, through three different exits, causing staff and police to spend hours tracking him down. No one would feel happier if Hal finally succeeded in making his escape than Raymond Rothman.

"It's a madhouse in here," Raymond tells his wife, Gloria, whenever she comes to visit.

Like Hal, Margie, and all the other patients still capable of volition, Raymond, a one-time school principal, fervently wishes to leave. He, too, finds the evening shadows unnerving. He, too, complains about the agonizingly long waits for an aide to "toilet" him; about the inedible meals; about the odors—of canned green beans and lima beans and spoiled milk; of mold, dirty linens, and ammonia—that, at various times of the day and night, separately or in combination, permeate the building.

He suffers some more individual torments as well, the worst being his persecution by a seemingly inanimate but, in his view, actively malevolent piece of beige plastic: the tray attached to his wheelchair that, resisting all his attempts to dislodge it, keeps him confined for most of his waking hours. His projected short-term, post-hospital rehabilitation stay, coming after a series of falls and a mild heart attack, has now dragged on for three months. His only child, Steven, with whom he has had but intermittent contact for several years, has suddenly become a frequent visitor, but those interactions have brought more anxiety than solace. Steven appears to have one overriding concern: the disposition of Raymond's house. He urges Raymond, a little more forcefully with each visit, to sell it to him, for much less than its market value, or transfer over the title outright. "If you don't," Steven warns, "the nursing home will get everything."

At such times, Raymond feels a Hal-like urge to scream and punch and kick and call his son a dirty bastard. He resists it, though. More than death, he fears the loss of his faculties, fears becoming a screamer like Hal and Stella or a babbler like Margie or one of the wax-like figures who sit motionless in their wheelchairs all day long, heads drooping to one side, mouths hanging open. And so, Raymond struggles fiercely to retain whatever shreds of his dignity he can. He insists on shaving and dressing himself each morning, often to the chagrin of his aide, who then has to work at a frenzied pace to get him and her other patients into the dining room in time for breakfast. When Raymond rises from his wheelchair for his twice daily, walker-aided march up and down the corridor, he ignores the occasional warnings of the aide walking by his side not to overexert himself and refuses to stop until he is panting, sweating, dizzy, and aching all over and feels as though he can no longer hold himself up.

Though he bears his trials stoically, one night his reserve breaks down. After dinner, he waits in his room, alone and forgotten, for more than an hour for his aide, Donna Thomas, to take him to the toilet. By the time she does appear, he has soiled himself. A heavy-set woman, prone to surliness when her workload grows unmanageable, as it inevitably does for all the aides at some point during every shift, she scolds him: "Raymond, you have to tell me when you need to go."

"What do you think I've been doing for the last hour-and-a-half? Didn't you hear the call button?"

"You're not the only patient I have, you know."

In manner, gesture, and expression, she flaunts her disgust as she roughly wipes him down, muttering all the while about having to "toilet this whole damn section myself."

Back in his wheelchair, hemmed in again by the tray attachment, gazing inattentively at the television as he waits for the relief of bedtime, Raymond realizes, belatedly, that his son is standing in the doorway, watching him. Before speaking a word, Steven drags a chair from a corner into the middle of the room and places it directly in front of Raymond's wheelchair. When he sits down, the two men's knees nearly touch. The father has on gray sweatpants that belong to another patient and a frayed flannel shirt. The son wears a pinstriped navy suit; a light-blue shirt, sans tie and open at the neck; and a watch with a silver band and a charcoal face that contains, in addition to its silver clock hands and the silver numerals representing the hours, three smaller gauges that serve no readily apparent purpose. Steven has a rounder face than his father but the same thick, wavy black hair that Raymond had before it grew sparse and turned white, and the same straight nose and dark eyes. As Steven turns again to his favorite subject, Raymond experiences the eerie sensation of being hectored by his doppelgänger.

"I don't think you realize what the situation is. Medicare is only going to cover your costs here for another week. After that, you're on your own. Your savings will be gone in no time. They might have lasted a little longer if you had let me invest your money for you instead of keeping it in the bank and having it earn a quarter percent a year, but that's all water under the bridge now. The house is the biggest asset you have, and if you don't protect it, it'll have to be sold to pay the nursing home. Do you want to see Mom thrown out onto the street? Maybe you ought to think of someone other than yourself for once."

"Nobody's throwing her out on the street. I'll be going home soon."

"No, you won't. It's time you faced the truth."

"Who told you this? Or did you decide it yourself?"

Hal Wallace shuffles into the room, followed by the lumbering Donna Thomas and another aide. The latter, Juliette Jean-Louis, is a diminutive, round-eyed young Haitian with straightened hair brushed back from her forehead, high cheekbones, and a pleasant smile. The presence of the two aides enables Raymond to suppress his impulse to slap his middle-aged son.

Steven, however, has no inhibitions about continuing the quarrel in front of them.

"The truth is, you probably won't be going home at all. Ever. Mom can't take care of you anymore. She told me it's killing her."

"Get out! Get out of here now!"

Addressing Steven, Juliet says, with uncharacteristic sharpness, "Visiting hours are over. Mr. Rothman is tired. He needs his rest."

Steven glowers at her.

"I'm his son."

"I know who you are. We've met. Several times. I'm sure you want to do what's best for him, which is to let him get a good night's sleep. You can come back tomorrow."

"Who the hell are you?"

"Nobody. I'm a nobody from a poor, miserable country where a son would never talk to his father the way you do."

Steven jumps to his feet.

"I want to speak to your supervisor."

"She'll be in tomorrow. You can talk to her then." Under her breath, Juliette murmurs, "*Cochon*."

Steven grudgingly leaves, but Raymond's shame lingers. It squeezes his viscera. It causes him to speak gruffly to Juliette: "You didn't have to chase him out. I can handle my son."

"Whatever you say, Mr. Rothman," replied Juliette, rummaging through his dresser in search of his pajamas. "But we can't have people coming in here at bedtime causing disturbances. Nobody will get any rest that way."

Raymond detects a troubling coolness in her tone that he has not heard from her before, and he regrets having snapped at her. Of late, he has become quite fond of the young aide, perhaps even a little infatuated. Having the good fortune to draw Juliette as his designated aide, as opposed to Donna or some of the others, can make for a tolerable day. When Juliette works the day shift and guides him on his daily walk, they carry on a mock flirtation. Raymond employs the scraps of French he still can recall from high school and college, while Juliette corrects his pronunciation and even teaches him a few new words, though he has more difficulty remembering those than the ones he learned sixty-odd years ago.

Unlike Raymond, Hal does not worry himself overmuch about the possibility of giving offense to anyone. He makes no move to don the pajamas that Donna Thomas has placed beside him on his bed, and when she, losing patience, attempts to pull down his trousers, he kicks her in the stomach.

"Get your filthy paws off me, you stinking two-ton whore!" he roars.

Additional kicks follow, accompanied by a torrent of racist slurs, obscenities, and accusations of bestiality. The beleaguered aide retreats from the room, accompanied by Juliette. Both return a few minutes later with a security guard and a nurse, the former to hold Hal down while the latter gives him an injection. Brute strength and pharmacology soon do their work, and Hal's tantrum subsides.

Hours later, while Hal snores peacefully, Raymond, unable to sleep, thrashes about in his bed, reliving the day's indignities. All the noises of the night—the passing footsteps, carts, and gurneys; the keening summons of a call button—sound as though magnified a hundredfold. When he closes his eyes, he sees again the unfathomable hatred in Steven's.

Rolling over onto his side, Raymond stretches out his arm as far as he can and plucks the phone from its base on the night table at the head of his bed. On the eleventh ring, Gloria answers with a groggy "hello?" He knows he has disturbed her sleep, but he feels no remorse. He lashes out at her as though she were the source of all his miseries: "You left me here to rot. You left me here to die. You and that…that…that son of ours whom we should have strangled at birth. You can't wait to be rid of me, can you? Well, I've had enough. I'm going back home. To my house—the house I worked thirty years to pay for. Nobody's taking it from me. Not him, and not you, either."

Before replying, Gloria lets out a long sigh. "Raymond," she says, in the gently cajoling voice that she had employed in her days as a second-grade teacher, "you will be coming home soon. As soon as you're better."

"I'm going home tonight. I cannot stay another day here. You get me out of here tonight."

"Raymond, how can I possibly do that? Please be reasonable."

"Get a taxi. Or call Steven."

"It's 2:30 in the morning.

"You get me out of here or I'll walk home. Do you hear me? I will leave this place and walk all the way home. I don't care if it kills me."

"Raymond, you know you can't walk home from there. It must be at least ten miles."

He repeats his threat, though this time with less conviction, for, as they speak, the sound of her voice begins to dampen his rage and his terror. "I'm losing my mind here," he says more quietly. "If I don't go home soon, I'll go mad."

"You're not losing your mind. You forget things sometimes, but otherwise, you're as sharp as ever. You're going to get better, and you're going to come home. We'll talk about it in the morning, O.K.?"

Raymond meekly assents.

#

Some eight hours later, Gloria enters his room.

Even before she has seated herself, Raymond asks, plaintively, "Have you come to take me home?"

"I…I…Soon," she stammers, her face reddening, her gaze directed at the floor. "As soon as you're better."

"How long are you and that spawn of ours planning to keep me here?" Raymond yells, yanking at the tray that keeps him imprisoned "I can't stand it anymore!"

She reaches for his hand. Her touch calms him. Each day, he observes, she appears older, smaller, more wasted, her posture more stooped, her forehead and cheeks more lined, her eyes more distant. Though she is a visitor here, her complexion has taken on the waxy pallor of the sickest patients, the open-mouthed ones. Her white hair appears unwashed, greasy, disarranged, its waves flattened. Patches of pink scalp show through.

Raymond leans forward and clasps her right hand in both of his. He wants to comfort her, but the words elude him.

#

When the sun goes down, Stella screeches, Victor cries for his mother, Margie packs her bag, Hal rages, and Raymond stoically endures all the tumult, along with a wait of nearly an hour to be taken to the toilet.

The night does bring one small mercy, however: Hal's bedtime tantrum does not rise to the epic level of his previous one. He causes no one any physical harm and drops off to sleep without sedation. Raymond, too, enjoys a restful night—until the lamp on his bedside table switches on, awakening him. He blinks several times, shakes his head, and blinks some more before he can get his eyes to focus. Steven, looming over him at the side of the bed, dressed in a gray suit and crimson tie with a gold bar clip that features a carving of a ship's steering wheel in the center, has a determined look.

"I need to talk to you."

Raymond begins the slow and laborious process of sitting up in bed.

"What do you need to talk to me about in the middle of the night?"

"The middle of the night? It's not even 9:00."

Raymond, still not fully awake, massages his cheekbones.

"It's about the house."

"Of course. What else?"

"Mom has agreed to sell it to me."

"What? Are you both insane?"

"Unlike you, Mom understands the situation. She knows she'll be left with nothing if you don't protect your assets."

"And how much did she agree to sell it to you for?"

"Two-fifty. It's the perfect solution. I can pay cash. Done in a day. It's off your hands. You'll both have peace of mind."

"And where would we live?"

"Mom could stay on if she likes."

"So, we should sell you the house for half of what it's worth and then what? Have you be our landlord?"

"It's not worth anywhere near what you think. The kitchen looks like something from a model house—in 1975. It's not enough that you haven't remodeled; you don't even maintain the place anymore. There are broken shingles on the sides. One of the down spouts has come loose. The porch light is out."

"Get out!"

"No. I can't just walk away. This is a situation that needs to be resolved. Like yesterday. Somebody has to take responsibility for Mom's welfare if you won't. Somebody competent."

The gravity of Steven's tone suits his message; the faint smirk on his lips does not. Clearly, he relishes this unequal combat. Whatever his failings as a father, what, Raymond wonders, could he have done to provoke such hatred in his only child?

"You're saying I'm not competent?"

"You're not. You have early-stage Alzheimer's. Maybe not so early-stage anymore."

"You've determined this? You've diagnosed me? When did you become a doctor?"

In the other bed, Hal Wallace begins to stir.

"I haven't determined anything. It's what the doctor here says. I've seen your chart. Early-stage Alzheimer's, congestive heart failure, diabetes, hypertension, vertigo..." As Steven, grinning openly now, lists the disorders, he counts them off on his fingers.

"The doctor who saw me once for about three minutes when I came in here and whom I haven't seen since? He says I have Alzheimer's? Because I forget a name now and then, that means I have Alzheimer's?"

"It's a lot more than that. Anyone can see it. You call mom up in the middle of the night and scream at her, tell her you're going to walk all the way home from here. You fly off the handle and humiliate me in front of the staff here."

Raymond's laughter is as caustic as the ammonia smell that permeates the building.

Steven, his eyes narrowed, his jaw clenched, replies, "Inappropriate laughter. Babbling. Mom tells me half the time she has no idea what you're talking about when she comes to visit. Incontinence. You're telling me you're competent to make financial decisions when you can't even control your bowels? No court will find you competent."

"You're going to court now to tell them I'm incompetent?"

Feeling a sudden stabbing pain on the left side of his chest, Raymond reaches for his call button, which is attached to a rubber cord fastened to his sheet near the edge of the mattress by means of a metal clasp. He yanks the cord free of the sheet and presses the red button.

"Bastard!" cries Hal Wallace. "All sons are bastards. Nobody should have sons."

"If you continue to be unreasonable, you'll force me to go to court. Mom needs to be protected."

"Protected from me?" bellows Raymond. "Get out of my room! Get out of my sight! And leave your mother alone, do you hear me? You leave her alone!"

"I can't do that. I'm her son, and I have responsibilities."

"Get the hell out of here, you dirty bastard!" roars Hal, rising from his bed. He grabs the two framed photographs of his grandchildren from the table beside his bed and flings them at Steven. Both strike home, the first hitting Steven on the right shoulder blade, the second thwacking against the back of his head.

"You'll be hearing from my lawyer," Steven threatens before beating a hasty retreat.

"Dirty bastard!"

His shame prevents Raymond from expressing the gratitude he feels toward Hal for banishing Steven from the room. He wants only to turn out the overhead light and bury himself beneath his blankets. To reach the light switch on the wall to the right of the door, however, would require of Raymond more effort than he can manage. He lies down again, closes his eyes, and turns over onto his stomach, but the light and the pain in his chest make sleep impossible. Somehow, Hal, so agitated just a moment ago, has already fallen asleep again. Raymond wishes he could sleep the way Hal does.

Suddenly, he becomes aware of a shadow in the doorway.

"Raymond?" he hears Juliette ask in a voice just above a whisper.

He pretends to be asleep, and the light goes out. To his relief, the chest pain gradually subsides. He wonders what commitment, if any, Steven had wrung from Gloria about the house. Briefly, he deliberates over whether to call her, but he decides against it. Just now, he does not want to know.

#

No sooner does Raymond fall asleep again than he is jostled awake. Opening his eyes, he finds Hal Wallace standing over him.

"Raymond! Raymond!" cries Hal, hopping from foot to foot and brushing his right hand repeatedly over his bald crown. "Call the police. They're holding me here against my will. They're gonna kill me."

"Who's going to kill you?"

"They're holding me against my will. They're gonna kill me."

"Go back to sleep, Hal," says Raymond wearily. "There's no need to call the police. Nobody's going to do you any harm. I promise you. I won't allow anyone to hurt you. Go back to sleep, and stop worrying."

For fifteen minutes or more, Raymond repeats these reassurances until Hal, pacified at last, does return to his bed and almost immediately begins to snore. Raymond barely has time to close his own eyes, though, before Hal awakens him again.

"Call the police. We have to get out of here. They're gonna shoot us."

"O.K., Hal," replies Raymond, reaching for the phone. "I'll call the police."

In fact, he dials the nurses' station, while furtively pressing his call button. Nobody answers the telephone, but for Hal's benefit, Raymond speaks into the receiver anyway: "You're coming right away? Good. Good." To Hal he says, "The police will be here right away. They told me to tell you to go back to bed and wait for them. They won't let anyone shoot you."

Hal looks dubious, but he does as Raymond tells him. Raymond falls asleep only to be awakened yet again a short time later by a jangling fire alarm. He hears people shouting and running in the hallway. The overhead light switches on again.

"Raymond," shouts Donna Thomas, "have you seen Hal?"

"What?" replied Raymond, shielding his eyes from the light with his hand.

"Hal. Your roommate. He's gone. He must have eloped again."

Donna departs without turning off the light. From outside comes the sound of police sirens. The room's only window looks out upon the visitors' parking lot. The shade is but half-drawn, and iridescent red and blue police lights flash in the uncovered lower window pane. Someone in the parking lot is calling Hal's name through a bullhorn.

The light and noise become unsupportable. Raymond sits up and slides his body sideways to the foot of his bed. With one hand on the mattress, the other gripping the corner of the dresser, he hoists himself up. Bracing himself against the end table first and then the dresser, he trudges to the door. He stops at the threshold, leaning his left shoulder against the door frame.

The corridor offers no escape from the sensory assault. The night clean-up crew must have passed through not long ago, for the ammonia stench causes Raymond's eyes to tear up.

Far to his right, above the steel fire door at the end of the gloomy hallway, a red light pulsates. The clanging of the fire bell, which seems to emanate from there, provides a disharmonious lower-range accompaniment to the keening of dozens of room alarms. From across the hall, Stella Fortuna, transformed into Tosca once again, discovers anew that Scarpia has betrayed her and had her lover murdered: "Mario! Mario! Morto! Morto!" In the room next door, Victor Galinski pleads, "Mama! Mama! Mama!"

Bewildered by the commotion, Raymond vacillates over what to do next. Go right? Go left? Go back to bed? The din of the alarm bell militates against the first option; the police lights and the bullhorn, against the last; so, he turns leftward, toward the nurses' station. Head down, left hand gripping the rail that runs along the wall, he struggles forward. After ten steps, already panting, he pauses. He advances two steps more, feels a fluttering in his chest, and stops again. His legs begin to wobble, and he pivots toward the wall, grabbing onto the railing with both hands to support himself.

From down the hall, he sees Juliette running toward him.

"Raymond, what you doing?"

He speaks the first words that occur to him: "I'm going home."

Her expression gives away nothing.

"I can't stand it here anymore. I'm going home."

"I see. If you're going home, you need to get dressed and packed. Let me help you back to your room, O.K.?"

"You don't believe me? Well, I am going home."

His voice, however, has lost all conviction. Exhausted by his twelve-step journey, he wants, more than anything, to return to bed.

"Now, listen to me. First, we're going to get you turned around. You're going to put your left arm over my shoulder."

"I can manage by myself," he replies, resisting her, though his legs feel as if they may give way at any moment.

"Raymond, I don't have time for this. You're going to do as I say. Left arm over my shoulder. Good. Now, step back with your left foot. Easy, easy. Keep your right hand on the railing. We'll go slowly. One step at a time."

Though the Earth's gravitational force feels as if it has increased tenfold, somehow, Juliette keeps him upright. He wonders how this tiny woman can bear his weight.

DEBORAH H DOOLITTLE
ADVICE FROM A TYRANNOSAURUS REX

Extinction stinks. It slinks up
on you unawares. Bites you
when you think you're doing all

the biting. It interrupts
your plans for a future, too,
with that proverbial wall

stopping you dead in your tracks.
Make sure you leave some of them;
deep footprints in mud is best

for those who'll come to extract
them later like mining gems
and will treasure your hubris

(cont)

if nothing else. I've but one
regret: my hands were never
big enough, that much is said,

to undo what had been done;
my thoughts were not so clever,
after all, and dead is dead.

Doolittle

LOWELL JAEGER
SURVIVOR

In the movie, he's the sole survivor,
post apocalypse, scavenging rubble-strewn
streets. He owns it all, now, in the fog
of ashen grit, anything left half-standing.

In the char, in the shards, perfect silence
but the cinder-crunch beneath his shoes
as he stumbles like a drunk, like a madman
twisted with confusion. It's the business-like propriety

of those shoes, smudged, a trace of gleam
and laces intact. As I rose and dressed
as usual this morning, I couldn't shake
the drama, ridiculous and fantastic, the dull ache

imagining his shoes could be my own.
And I walked into my day like a man grateful,
awakened from a coma. The steaming kettle
on the stove, open book on the end table,

and through this window the sun streaming
its golden touch. Such unaccountable good fortune.
And…who is this, swaying through the kitchen
with her broom? She laughs

when I pull her tight, hold to her, and won't let go.

Jaeger

NOTE TO AN EARLIER SELF

For a semblance of resolve, let's run the reel back
to that late afternoon on a graveled farm road
through monotonous miles of corn and soy,
an August sun sizzling your shoulders and thighs,
as you pedaled across the heartland, alone,
the longest year of your life,
waiting for a court date, waiting for papers to sign.

Flat horizons of nowhere rose gradually
after crossing a bridge, wooden and decayed,
remember? In the muck below, a muskrat struggled
with a cable-snare, thrashing. Another nearby, slick
with scum, also ensnared, but this one lifeless,
drowned.
        It's like the click of shutter—isn't it? —
the way a simple glance can lodge in the brain,
while so much goes by we let pass . . . as if
behind our eyelids there's no one there.

And there she was, one hand raised head-high,
standing on the front porch of a weathered farmstead.
Truly, she was there, in the flesh, wasn't she? The bib
and skirt of her apron stained crimson. Tomatoes, maybe.
Or blood? You, with only a toehold on the cliffs of what's real,
did you invent this apparition? You waved. You saw blood,
and you kept going, muscling your way blindly forward,
immersed in vapors of guilt and ghosts of worn apprehensions.

Was her hand uplifted
for sake of shielding her eyes from the sun's lowering horizon?
Or was she beckoning to you, and you ignored her call?

Jaeger

GRAHAM C GOFF
THE RED MERCURY

Marty Felker paid for his motel room by the week, as he had been in the habit of doing for several years. The motel staff considered him a permanent resident and reduced his rate. Marty considered himself a temporary visitor; he would leave as soon as he saw Evangeline's red Mercury racing to meet him at the diner. She would show up any day now and they would travel the world and be married just as she promised.

The motel staff had grown quite used to the strange middle-aged man who spent his days in a lawn chair outside his room painting landscape of the same highway every day. The receptionist, Emily, had grown particularly used to him, and for a woman accustomed to a stream of impersonal interactions with worn-out truckers and strung-out junkies, familiarity and affection were necessarily associated.

Emily even hung up one of Marty's landscapes behind her desk. It was not very good. The watercolors bled together on the cheap paper, only vaguely resembling the Texas highway outside her window. Marty had never tried watercolors before his stint at the motel, but it was something to do while looking at the cars, so he painted a landscape a day. They were always of the highway, and the only variation between them were the cars on the road. Sometimes, Marty painted a white Chevrolet. Sometimes a blue Toyota. Never a red Mercury.

Every morning, Marty went to the diner down the road from the motel, just past the scrap yard. The diner doubled as a convenience store with a few shelves of cereal and a refrigerator with sliced ham, cheese, and milk. Every morning, Marty got a cup of coffee from the diner and every Wednesday, he got enough food to feed him for a week, no more because he did not want to have to leave much when Evangeline came for him.

One particular morning, Marty woke up earlier than normal. He had a bad dream that he forgot when he awoke. Marty was not particularly bothered by the day's early start because the diner was open around the clock.

Marty got up and changed into his usual slacks and white dress shirt. The shirt was wrinkled and the collar had been stained for months. Lifting his watercolor palate from the nightstand, Marty left his room, placing it on the lawn chair by the door. When he returned from the diner, he would have to ask Emily for some paper.

It was very early—around 4 AM. The sun was not out yet, but

Marty did not mind because a few of the street lights on the way to the diner still worked. Marty did not mind that most of the street lights did not work because he could find his way without them.

Hobbling down the road with a frailty not justified by his age, Marty sidestepped loose patches of gravel and potholes. He could see the diner's lights from down the road. The diner's sign needed to be repaired. Only the "D" and "E" glowed.

Marty passed the scrap yard. The scrap heap piled high above the corrugated steel fence because the recycling company from Oklahoma was running late on their regularly-scheduled pickup. The pile sprawled across the entire property and a crane with a magnetic disk for a claw loomed idly, waiting for a truck to load. The heap was precariously situated, like a breeze might cause an avalanche of discarded hardware. There were refrigerators and boilers, and atop the pile, almost regal in its desolation, a red Mercury with a bent frame, a shattered windshield, and a mismatched passenger seat door. Marty kept walking, taking no notice of the refrigerators or boilers or the red Mercury with the shattered windshield and mismatched door in the dark.

In the diner, Marty ordered a cup of coffee. His groceries already awaited him by the door in a paper bag. It was Wednesday. He sat by the window and watched the highway for cars. It was too dark to identify them, so he watched the headlights and wondered what a red Mercury's headlights would look like in the dark.

One thousand six hundred forty-two miles away, Evangeline awoke in a panic. She slept through her alarm. It was an hour later where she lived than where Marty lived. Slipping on a bath robe, she descended the stairs and started making breakfast, putting bread in the toaster and pouring milk into glasses. Evangeline went out to get the newspaper from her porch and smoke poured from the toaster. Her daughter's toast was burnt.

JUDITH R ROBINSON
PROMPTS TO SELF

Keep trying to love the world again.

(cont)

Walk each day to clear
the magpies that jabber in the head.

Remember your father's arms, his legs,
the handsome shape of them.

Pity the decent poor kids
who do not beat up the rich kids

For their fancy shoes.

Pity the mail carriers, cheerless
Souls dragging through streets

To deliver piles of detritus
Wasted paper filled with wasted ink

Forests felled to instruct   to plead
Buy this   buy that   buy anything.

Pray for the Jewish people, the Rohingya,
the Uyghurs, the Christians of Sri Lanka,

Those currently struggling to merely exist.

Pray to unfreeze the tears.

Pray for that simple relief

Denied by only God
knows why.

Robinson

AARON FISCHER
ON HIS DEAFNESS

It hasn't taken music yet. It will
in time, degrading what the birds don't say—
open the door, the door, teakettle, teakettle—
(cont)

the ragged rasp of *John the Revelator,*
Blind Willie Johnson's end-time call-and-response,
the slide's jagged scrimshaw incised on bone,

or Spooky Tooth's sustain-and-fuzz homage
to *Sgt. Pepper,* which sounds the way being stoned
on hash feels. My wife and kids are right, I should

do something, but there have been so many doctors:
my heart, my teeth, my eyes, my privates, my mind.
No doubt this failing can wait a little longer,

while I still can hear schoolchildren break and surge
across the street, sandpipers dodging the surf.

Fischer

THANK YOU FOR YOUR SERVICE

It's my beard of course, long and luxuriant as Whitman's
in those cabinet photos he gave to visitors.
More realistically, a Hasid in sneakers
and sweats. Santa, I expected, or Gandalf, not the man

in ShopRite who reached across his cart, with its payload
of bad choices—sausage patties, crinkle-cut fries—
to shake my hand. Or the one in the dry
cleaners, or waiting to pick up my order at Saigon Jade.

Right war—Viet Nam—wrong army, I don't tell them,
keeping it simple: "I'm not a vet," I say with a smile.
It's easy to thank me, a guy with a stringy ponytail
shopping at Home Depot. But which of us will commend

for his service the black man in jungle camo on patrol
in the bus station, or the one crashed out in the toilet stall?

Fischer

FOUND: 15 WALLETS FROM THE 1940S, STOLEN AND STASHED BEHIND A BATHROOM WALL
— CNN News Story

Broke or bored or both — what set off your one-woman
crime wave before you finished high school
in Centralia, Illinois, or it was finished with you,
ditching the billfolds behind a vent in the girls' bathroom?

Were you an honor student in a perky pillbox,
an usherette at the Alhambra Movie Palace on weekends,
or a senior with nothing going for her beyond
a swing shift at the carpet plant?

We're storytelling animals. We trace a dragon, a dog
in the scattershot stars, find the profile of the first president
in an outcrop above the Hudson. That makes you my Midwestern
Artful Dodger, whose touch was deft

and delicate as halo of moths troubling a porch light
left burning by mistake.

Fischer

JANET AMALIA WEINBERG
SOMETHING STINKS

I'd worked late so it was dark when I left the subway, and the
street was deserted.

Two and a half blocks of padlocked warehouses and dimly lit
tenements stood between me and my apartment. I hesitated at the top of
the subway steps, then took a bracing breath and started walking.

There was a punk with pig eyes smoking outside Mooney's
Saloon on the corner. I smelled his sweat and felt his eyes on me like
leaches as I did my speed walk past him. Near the end of the block, I heard
footsteps behind me and thought it was him. I walked faster. So did he.
But when I turned to look, there was no one there.

I made it to my building all right, but couldn't relax yet. Anybody could get into the lobby so I always checked the alcove under the stairs. It reeked of urine but that didn't mean some creep wouldn't hide there. Then I had to stand, visible and unprotected, while I waited for the elevator. At least it was empty when it arrived, and no one got on while I rode up. Finally, I reached my floor and raced to unlock my door. Once inside, I slammed the door shut, turned the dead bolt, secured the safety latch— and only then did I feel safe.

Stale air and radio voices greeted me. I kept the windows locked so no one could climb in from the fire escape and the radio was on to make it seem like someone was home. You can't be too careful when you live in a big city. There were times I wished I had someone to come home to, but even when I was married to Joe, I didn't always feel safe coming home to *him*.

This was the loneliest time of the day, sitting by myself at the big table Joe made when we still thought we were going to have kids. Usually, I just whipped up some eggs or heated something from the freezer, but that night was different. I'd gone for lunch with Sally, she's the only other data analyst at work who's been there as long as me, and she'd ordered a large macaroni and cheese. When it came sizzling from the oven in a brown oval dish, I got one whiff of that cheesy smell and a movie turned on in my head:

I saw a child, maybe three or four years old, propped up in bed in pink pajamas. A woman sat beside her, holding a brown, oval dish of macaroni and cheese. "This one's for Daddy," she said as she shoved a spoonful in the little girl's mouth. The child gagged and made a face. A slime of mucus and noodles oozed down her chin and onto her pink pajama. The woman said, "Poor Baby," wiped up the slop and held out another spoonful. "This one's for Auntie …."

The image evaporated and left me shaken. *What was that all about?* I wondered.

Later, after lunch, Sally handed me her doggy bag and told me to take it. "There's plenty left," she said, "and I won't be home all weekend." So that's what I was having for supper.

While it heated in the oven, I went to the living room for my obligatory, nightly call to Mother. Her television was on loud in the background. She always had the evening soaps on when I phoned. Right off I asked if she used to make macaroni and cheese when I was little.

"Did I?" she said. "That was your favorite. And when you got so sick, I made it all the time. All that milk and cheese, I thought it would be good for you."

"When I got so sick?"

"Oh." She paused as if just realizing what she'd said. "Well, you weren't really sick. You were…nervous. Yes, that's it. Nervous."

"What do you mean, 'nervous?'" I asked.

"Nervous." Her voice screeched the way it did when she got upset. "You know what nervous means. You—"

"I smell burning cheese," I said, then ended the call so I could check the oven.

But the cheese wasn't burning. I shut the oven off anyway. I couldn't eat with that stink in the air. I sniffed around the garbage can and the rest of the kitchen but didn't find the source of the odor. It seemed to vanish and reappear like a phantom. I followed it out of the kitchen and was in the hall, headed towards the living room when I got scared. *Maybe someone's here!* I thought and pictured the neighborhood homeless man, sprawled on my couch in his stiff, unwashed clothes.

I reached for the wall to steady myself and listened. There were outside sounds—a dog, some cars, a distant siren—but the only sound inside was an eerie silence. My door and windows were locked and there was no other way to break into the apartment, but I grabbed the big kitchen knife anyway. Just in case.

With the knife raised and ready, I tiptoed to the living room. No one was on the couch. Or behind the door. But a series of flattened splotches on the rug led from the couch to the bathroom. *Footprints!?* It was one of those velvety carpets that look disheveled if you don't keep the nap smoothed in one direction. If those marks had been there before, I was sure I'd have noticed and brushed them away. But I wasn't a hundred per cent sure.

I followed the trail to the bathroom and peeked in. Empty. That left the bedroom. Nothing seemed out of place there either. Then, just when I was thinking I'd worked myself up over nothing, I caught another whiff of that smell. This time it reminded me of male sweat and cigarettes. *That punk? Impossible. Still….*

There was only one more place to check: the bedroom closet. *He could be in there. Waiting.* I'd imagined creepy stuff like that before and it hadn't come true but maybe this time it might.

My heart was pounding. The whole room was pounding. I felt I was going to explode—

I was already in the living room, frantically calling Mother when I stopped. I knew how that would go. *"Call the police!"* she'd say. *"But I'm not sure anyone is really here,"* I'd say. Then she'd shout something

like, "For heaven's sake Roberta, do it! Before something awful happens."
And her fear would scrape my insides like nails. I put the phone down.

I thought of Joe. Despite his faults, Joe would come if I called. But he lived an hour away. A whole hour!

I knew what I had to do. I had no choice. Before I could stop myself, I walked to the closet and took hold of the knob. My hand went rigid and wouldn't turn but slowly, as if I wasn't doing it, the knob rotated...the door opened...and a nightmare exploded in my face.

A toddler in a yellow pinafore is playing jacks alone in an alcove under some stairs. She bounces the ball, picks up a jack...bounces the ball, picks up another...bounces the ball— From out of nowhere, a massive hand slams into her face and shoves her head down to the cold tile floor. The smell of rancid sweat invades her. She clamps her eyes and mouth shut. Her lips are pried open. Something big, bigger than her mouth, is forced in. It rams her over and over. Then it's gone and a taste like Clorox burns down her throat. She vomits blood and mucus, curls up in the vomit and rocks.

I backed away from the closet but could still see the little girl rocking and coated with slime. *Oh my god,* I thought, *Oh my god....*

That's when I *did* call Mother. "What happened to me when I was little?" I demanded.

"Happened?" I could hear her television in the background. "What should happen?"

"Something bad!"

"Bad?" The television went silent.

"I mean, did a man ever...was I ever...molested?"

"Molested?" She seemed to spit the word back at me. "Why would you think such a thing?"

"Mama, you've *got* to tell me."

"Why?" she screeched. "What good will it do?"

Suddenly I saw myself, saw how stunted and constricted I'd become, and a damn broke inside me. I mourned the self I could have been and screamed with rage and grief. "Why didn't you tell me?!"

"It was too awful." She was crying now. "I wanted to put it behind us."

"So, it could follow me the rest of my life?"

"I thought if you knew, you'd be scared of men."

"But I *am* scared of men."

"You are?" She sounded genuinely surprised. In a way, so was I.

Then I was crying too. "Who was it?" I yelled between sobs.

"Who!?"

"Poor baby." She tried to soothe me the way she must have done when I was little. "You're too upset. Why don't you have some of that nice macaroni and cheese and we can talk about it later?"

I cut her off, stormed into the kitchen and dumped the whole stinking mess into the garbage, brown dish and all. Everything I believed and felt about myself—about my whole life, was shifting and falling apart....

I must have gone into some kind of a stupor. After I don't know how long, I became aware of myself leaning against the kitchen table, staring out the window. And that stink! It was still there, permeating the kitchen, permeating *me* with every breath. The thought of it inside me made me gag.

I rushed to the window, struggled with the damn lock and stuck frame and finally heaved it open. For a long moment, I took what felt like a deep, lifesaving breath of fresh air then re-shut the window and locked it.

No! I thought, *I've lived in a PTSD world long enough.* I knew I wasn't going to change overnight, but I could start by unlocking the window.

The night air was cool and calming and if I looked between the buildings across the street, I could see all the way to the river. I even left the window open to air the place out. And yes, it did occur to me that some guy could climb in from the fire escape, but I told myself it wasn't very likely.

MARC KAMINSKY
HANDFAST
to Maddy

Giant cranes invade the sky around us.
Jaws of earth-moving machines harrow the ground,
dig holes deeper than the surrounding houses are high.

Clouds of debris, the tat-tat-tat of jackhammers. Rats
fleeing vast construction sites infest our backyard.
The six years separating our ages multiply

(cont)

as the time of changes speeds up. Streams
stained by the red dust of brownstones
run down the length of our street. Floor

by floor slabs of marble go up, blocking the sun.
Soon, soon we will live in the shadow of luxury
condos, high-rise hotels. We will be strangers

here. Come winter, the rats will seek shelter inside
our home. When we moved in thirty years ago,
our neighbors were born and died in the same

house over three generations. The new owners
do gut renovations. Every day cards and letters
from developers offer us a small fortune: they

want to buy our building and flip it. How long
will we hold out? Where will we go?
You spend more and more time in the country.

There, you take pleasure in hiking up the side
of a mountain, sitting by the fire and watching
the sky change colors as the night comes on.

I enjoy solitary week-ends, and step carefully down
the two flights of stairs to our kitchen, boil
water for tea, and carry it carefully back to my study.

In your absence, I travel by way of stories I read
to places that can't be reached by foot, and close
the book and drift back into your presence.

In my reverie, we are walking together
through these impermanent streets.
At every corner where the curb is steep,

I see your watchfulness grow an outstretched
arm, you reach for my hand and take it
lightly, sending wave upon wave of

well-being along my skin, your caring mind
pours though my body. This is more
than I ever expected to know: gratitude

(cont)

that I live permanently inside you
as you live in me. Mortality has begun
unraveling me at the joints, between

grinding bones, on arthritic knees, I step
across the blood-red river at the curb, and
you are with me, helping me cross over.

Kaminsky

YVETTE A SCHNOEKER-SHORB
THE STATE OF MY TOWN

In my town there is confusion
over the First Amendment
and the Second. We love
to express ourselves
in charged assembly—
Black Lives, Blue Lives,
Fetal Lives all matter,
but what matters most
are rights, rifles, masks,
and individuals obsessed
with a need for consistency;
either we all comply or we don't.

Freedom is found in flying flags
tied to trucks, protest signs
gripped by shaking fists,
handguns held like security
blankets, and streets occupied
by quiet vigils for the planet,
for justice, for a just world
that doesn't seem ready for it.

(cont)

It's all muddled, red and angry,
messy, misdirected, fear-
infected, and I can't discern
which direction drives the danger
when armed guards patrol
to enforce peace amidst
this pandemic—our angst
has gone viral. But in my town
we resist anything, everything
resembling civility;
addicted to adrenaline
peddled by the zeitgeist,
we now take comfort offered
by conforming to our tribes.

Schnoeker-Shorb

MATTHEW FEENEY
THE SECOND COMING (OUT)

My first week in prison, my name got called over the P.A. for a visit and I was stunned when the entire cell block started chanting "HO-MO! HO-MO! HO-MO!" It was just like those classic prison movies right before a riot breaks out: loud, scary and intimidating as hell. Shaken, I went to my visit and shared the experience with my parents. I told them I didn't know how I had been outed as a gay man to the entire cell block, but I remember naively stating my profound relief that "at least they don't know I'm a sex offender."

Two hours later I returned to my cell block to learn everyone had actually been chanting, "CHO-MO," prison slang for a child molester. Thus began my six-year prison sentence for criminal sexual conduct with a seventeen-year-old male and his younger teenage brother.

Remarkably, I survived and served my entire prison sentence, the maximum allowed by law, I am now serving a new "indeterminate" (defacto life) sentence in a state mental asylum under Minnesota's draconic civil commitment laws for the exact same crimes for which I served my prison time.

I am attracted to males and have been all my life. Back when I was growing up, this wasn't just socially unacceptable, homosexuality was actually illegal and a diagnosable mental illness. The severe homophobia of the Catholic Church taught me my sexual attraction towards my male classmates meant I was "intrinsically flawed." I was encouraged to "love the sinner but hate the sin." It was bad enough to hear masturbation was morally wrong, but as a teenager with an active imagination, I was petrified to learn even thinking sexual thoughts was as sinful as committing the act itself. I was screwed. So, I buried my secret attractions deep, and fought like hell to hide and deny my homosexuality. I tried dating females in college and even explored becoming a priest as a valid, if not noble, explanation as to why I was still single and a virgin.

The American Psychiatric Association eventually dropped homosexuality as a mental disorder, but I never got the memo. I struggled with loving myself and never really got over the shame of my homosexuality. I was a damaged man with low self-esteem, embarrassed by my lack of sexual experience, and I tried to find acceptance with younger males.

I admit I screwed up. I broke the law. I pled guilty without any plea agreement and I served the maximum sentence allowable under state law. While incarcerated, I underwent three years of intensive sex offender therapy under the infamous Minnesota Sex Offender Program (MSOP). Within this program homophobia ran rampant, as evidenced by the fact gay men were given polygraphs asking about sexually acting out while straight offenders were asked about selling Ramen noodles. I had ample opportunities to have consensual sexual activity with attractive inmates, some who humorously self-identified as "gay for the stay, but straight at the gate," but I chose not to. Despite being unable to act upon it, my circle of physical attraction has been enlarged while in prison. Knowing the possibility of civil commitment was looming over my head, I knew that any sexual activity while in prison would be used against me as evidence during my trial; not of me being cured, but rather of me being unable to control my deviant sexual desires even when under intense supervision.

As my six-year prison sentence was nearing completion, I was informed that the State of Minnesota was pursuing me for civil commitment, so instead of releasing me, they scheduled me for another trial, this time in civil court. They used the same facts and criminal history that precipitated my original prison sentence to claim I now had a mental disorder and needed to be locked up for the rest of my life in a secure mental hospital. Several of the homophobic actuarial tools used to assess potential targets for civil commitment raise your risk score if you provide an affirmative answer to "has at least one male victim." As a gay man, my crimes involved post-adolescent minor males and obviously any sexual activity with age-appropriate adults was not a crime, so there's no record of such legal activity. My only current mental diagnosis is that I am attracted to post-pubescent males.

Of course, the MSOP civil commitment "treatment" program is a joke, a facade to provide the required legality to an otherwise unconstitutional civil commitment program. Like the Catholic Church, MSOP prefers to promote total abstinence and the program specifically prohibits any healthy sexual activity of any kind between clients, some who have been civilly committed for 28 years. Since I've been locked up, same-sex marriage has become legal in Minnesota. While MSOP policy has to now officially allow two clients to get legally married, the married couple is still subject to the same "no touch" restrictions and are moved to separate living units and not allowed any physical contact or display of affection. Married or not, anyone caught violating these policies is locked up in segregation, written up with multiple BERs ("Behavioral Expectation Reports") and punished with room restrictions, loss of privileges and having to do additional "treatment assignments" connecting their current "acting out" to their original offending behavior.

It's ominously comfortable for this recovering Catholic to once again be living in such a homophobic environment where I'm being constantly watched and reminded how any & all sexual activity is bad and needs to be kept as a dirty little secret because we'll get punished if we get caught. No wonder no one ever completes this "treatment" program when healthy same-sex sexuality is punished and used against us in court as further evidence of our deviancy and need for further confinement. This program makes the old fashioned "ex-gay conversion therapy" seem like summer camp.

So here I am, an openly gay man, spending the rest of my life in a mental hospital which is pretending to provide "treatment" for a homosexual who already served an entire prison sentence for having sexual relations with a minor, while prohibiting him from engaging in any age-appropriate same-sex relationships... at the cost of $398 a day.

J ELIZA WALL
UNIT

When you are in a relationship
You move as a unit—
Lots of heavy breathing—
Lots of shuffling of feet—
Lots of pulling the other along.
The excess weight.
You take turns being
Awake and asleep—
Shifts.
I carry you one night,
You carry me the next.

Wall

JEANINE STEVENS
SANCTUARY

The linden's branches form a dense canopy.
Low sun illuminates the small Buddha,

once bright verdigris, now peeling from frost
and rain. Patches of amber light shimmer,

outline a young face. The blotchy surface,
like a relic from a forgotten Cambodian temple,

a camouflage in this miniature jungle of dark
mint, wild garlic and variegated ivy. Mottled,

he remains slim, serene with plaited hair, no
pot belly, not bald but much as he first appeared

on a tidal wave with no wind. I recognize my
own wiry hair, thinner bones. Sitting on the deck,

(cont)

a sprig of sweet woodruff floats in May wine,
sun edges toward solstice and summer thunder.

A terra cotta St. Francis holds a flimsy dove's nest.
A peaceful sanctuary: one tree, one god, one saint.

Stevens

LEE GROSSMAN
WAITING FOR WHATSISNAME

A play in one act

Cast of Characters:
Sheldon, an old man
Bernie, an old man
Esther, an old woman

Scene I

Daylight. A park bench in a large city, in the present day.

> *The curtain rises to find SHELDON sitting on the bench, facing the audience. He has a container on his lap for sorting pills by the day of the week. He opens all the flaps on the container. BERNIE enters, stage right. He sits next to SHELDON. They don't acknowledge each other but they know each other. BERNIE takes out a similar pill container, and opens every flap.*

BERNIE: Got any Lipitor? I'm out.
SHELDON: Nah. *(He looks through his pills, picks one up.)* I got Detrol.
BERNIE: Okay. *(He takes the pill and swallows it.)* You waiting for Whatsisname, you know, the guy with the thing? *(He gestures vaguely in the direction of his face.)*
SHELDON: Yep.
BERNIE: Haven't seen him lately. *(He takes out a pill).* Want a Dulcolax?
SHELDON: Sure. *(He takes the pill from SHELDON and swallows it.)*
BERNIE: Maybe he's dead.

SHELDON: Nah. We would've heard.

> *(ESTHER enters, stage left. She uses a walker, which has a shelf built into it.)*

ESTHER: Hi, gents. *(They nod and grunt greetings.)*

> *(ESTHER sits next to SHELDON and arranges the walker in front of her so she can use the shelf. She takes a pill holder similar to the other two out of her bag and sets it on the shelf. She opens all the flaps. She takes out a pill and throws it in front of her to the pigeons.)*

They love the blue ones.

BERNIE: Hey Esther, got any Lipitor?

ESTHER *(looking)*: No, sorry. *(She picks up a pill)*. Want a Flomax?

BERNIE: Okay. *(He takes it and swallows it.)*

SHELDON: How come you have Flomax? That's for prostate.

ESTHER: My Max, may he rest in the peace he never gave me, had prostate. He also had a young nurse, which is why he had Viagra. Which I found after he passed. *(She throws another pill to the pigeons).* Always the blue ones. *(She shouts to the pigeons).* Watch him, honey! He's probably got a robin bigbreast on the side! *(To the men:)* You want some?

> *(They both shake their heads emphatically, embarrassed.)* You waiting for Whatsisname, with the —? *(She makes a vague gesture toward her face)*.

BERNIE: Yes.

SHELDON: Bernie thinks he's dead.

BERNIE: I didn't say I thought. I said maybe.

ESTHER: Haven't seen him lately.

SHELDON: We would've heard.

BERNIE: He took a lot of pills, I remember. *(The others nod.)* Anybody want a Halcion?

(The others raise their hands. He passes them out, they swallow them).

SHELDON *(holding out his palm)***:** Anybody know what these are? I've got three of them.

> *(The others look.)*

ESTHER: Nope.

BERNIE: Nope.

> *(They each take one and swallow it.)*

> (To ESTHER) What else did Max have?

ESTHER: Arthritis. *(She holds out pills and they all take one.)*

SHELDON: What else?

ESTHER: High blood pressure. *(She passes out another round of pills. They swallow.)*
SHELDON: And?
ESTHER: Gout. *(Another round of pills as before.)*
BERNIE *(looks in his pillbox)*: Uh oh. Thursday's empty.
SHELDON: I got plenty of Thursday. *(He passes a handful of pills to BERNIE.)*
ESTHER: What day is today, anyway?
BERNIE: Who cares?
ESTHER: I got things to do.
     (The men look at her as if she were crazy.)
BERNIE: Like what?
ESTHER: Things.
SHELDON: What things? You got a little something going? *(He leers suggestively.)*
ESTHER: You got a dirty mind.
BERNIE *(to SHELDON)*: Maybe she's meeting Whatsisname with the thing.
SHELDON: Where is he anyway?
BERNIE: He's always late.
ESTHER: Maybe he's dead.
SHELDON: Then he's the late Whatsisname.
BERNIE: We would've heard.
ESTHER *(rising)*: I'm going. *(The men rise.)*
BERNIE: We might as well go too.
SHELDON: See you tomorrow.
     The men exit stage right, ESTHER exits stage left. BLACKOUT.

Scene II
The same bench the next day. Lights come up on SHELDON, BERNIE and ESTHER already seated, pillboxes open. ESTHER is now in the middle.

BERNIE: You know Whatsisname? With the thing? *(He gestures toward his face.)*
ESTHER: Yeah.
SHELDON: Sure.
BERNIE: He's dead.
ESTHER: We heard.
BERNIE: I always wondered.

ESTHER: What?

BERNIE: Do you think he knew about the thing?

SHELDON: Of course, he knew about the thing. You don't go through life with a thing like that without knowing.

BERNIE: I just wondered. *(long pause).* Did he ever say anything?

ESTHER: About the thing?

SHELDON: No. No, he didn't.

ESTHER: A person with a thing doesn't talk about it. If I had a thing, I wouldn't talk about it.

SHELDON: But he knew about it.

ESTHER: He must've known about it. *(She throws some pills to the pigeons.)* They always go for the blue ones first.

BERNIE: Do you think he took anything for it?

SHELDON: Who, Whatsisname?

BERNIE: Yeah.

ESTHER: I miss him.

SHELDON: Me too.

BERNIE: I could use a Zoloft *(takes a pill.)*

ESTHER: Prozac. *(takes a pill with the same motion.)*

SHELDON: Lexapro. *(takes a pill with the same motion.)*
     (They all sit quietly, looking straight ahead.)

BERNIE: Anybody else die?

ESTHER: My Max.

BERNIE: Right. My Evvie went right after she broke her hip.

SHELDON: When was that?

BERNIE: When? *(pause)* Bush was president.

SHELDON: Which one?

BERNIE: The dumb one.

SHELDON: Ah.

ESTHER: Anyone care for a Fosamax? *(They each take one from her and swallow it.)*

SHELDON: I lost my Flora during Obama.

BERNIE: I got Lasix. *(holds it up.)*

SHELDON: I got Neurontin. *(they trade and swallow the pills).*

BERNIE: So, who's left?

ESTHER: Us.

SHELDON: Oy vey.

CURTAIN.

SHIRLEY HILTON
RISK

for Ben

The Internet drops me on a random street
in Kuala Lumpur, so musical the sound of this place
I might not know if not for the board game
we played on those days when I needed to know
what was inside your young mind, your father
having shipped off your sister to live with a mother
neither of you knew. If you missed her, you never
said, though you clung to me and violently pushed
your father far from our protective circle.

I never really understood the game of Risk
but then, there are so many things I never
understood. I didn't know, for example,
that the step in my parent name meant, step
up when things get tough and messy, when
a child needs a friend, an ear, a hug,
but step away from any rights to decide
what's best for the child when those who created him
wage war on each other and on the step.

When you conquered all my countries and we tired
of Risk, we retired to your room that I'd decorated
in a jungle theme, a surprise for you. Remember?
Reclined on that comforter of leopard spots, you
read me parts of the Potter stories. We were always,
it seems, looking for an escape to another world
where there was the possibility of magic and a happy
ending. I keep the newspaper clipping with the picture
of you winning the bookstore contest for the latest title.

I keep all your pictures, in a box in the basement
where they can't hurt me, where I can pretend
our years together never happened. Then suddenly
today without warning I find myself on a palm-lined
avenue in Kuala Lumpur. And there you are again.
I search the cloud and find you have a daughter.
You look happy. It's a risk, you know, to love someone.

(cont)

They may be taken away, or they may walk away.
But they come back again and again. At least, you do to me.

Hilton

HUNGER

The bird feeder in the back yard is empty
again this morning. My neighbor complains
the deer come at night to feast
on seeds intended for the birds. I smile,
tell her I don't mind. Lately it seems
that every living thing is hungry.

Across a continent and an ocean and
a continent my friend is suffering. She calls.
She cries. Her husband is unfaithful.
She is preparing a whole red snapper
for his dinner hoping to please him. He
sends a message, *I'll be late*. Alone
in her garden she fingers the scarlet bracts
of her poinsettias, remembers when she
dared such flamboyance. Oh, to bloom again!

Here, over coffee, Howard drones on and on
'splaining me the many ways to discourage
the deer. I pour him a second cup and nod
but hardly hear, something about the scent
of human hair instilling fear, a scarecrow,
wind chimes or motion lights. Perhaps
he didn't hear or doesn't care
I've no desire to scare the deer. Once
upon a time, we listened to each other.

Mother watched from her deck the last days
of her cancer. It wasn't deer but squirrels
that haunted her. I delighted in their antics,
though she waved her arms and shouted "No!"
which didn't deter their hunger, nor had it ever mine.
Now I will never know the answer, why she
would feed one soul and starve another. Perhaps
a life of scarcity did that to her? On brittle winter
grass I cross the yard to fill the feeder.

Hilton

GWENN A NUSBAUM
COLORING SUBURBIA, 1967

i.

New development,
rows of white houses
slope down the hill
of St. Mary's Drive.
Black, yellow, red, brown
painted on shutters,
doors.

ii.

A Black family moves
into the neighborhood,
fire set to their lawn.
Something burning.
Cross?

Kids careen on bikes
through sky opened bluely—
halt to witness this.

Bewildered indelibly,
they ride silently
through haze gray
as an honest pencil.

iii.

Across the street,
another family's red
Cadillac top down.
Sunlit shrubs soaked
in green, Mountain ash,
flowering white clusters.
Flagpole—golden glint
of American bald eagle.

Nusbaum

MICHAEL ESTABROOK
THE BIG BANG

Lean back
gaze up through
the darkness
at the stars glowing above.

What if time isn't time
at all
never has been
and everything that ever happened everywhere
in the existence of the universe happened
at the exact same instant
so there was no past present or future
no beginnings middles or ends
to anything
no clocks or calendars
ticking off seconds minutes hours
days weeks months
years decades centuries . . .
no history or future prognostications
but instead
only a simple explosion of everythingness
everything ever created
time space matter energy all of it smushed
together existing together
in the selfsame moment
formed into one gigantic amorphous stew
and all that matters to any of us ever
is this moment now period.

Estabrook

JONATHAN B FERRINI
THE PICNIC BASKET

I raced home from work to my wilderness paradise, looking
forward to a weekend of catching up on sleep, gardening, and enjoying my

spacious home. My realtor arranged an "Open House" for Saturday and Sunday, in hopes of attracting a large buyer turnout. I've worked my entire career in healthcare, and, nearing retirement, rose to the position of Executive Vice President of a nationwide medical provider. I hoped this would be the weekend the home sold, and I would be freed from the grind of my prominent position, daily commute, and embrace the specter of retirement.

I never married, had no children, and relished my life of travel, treating myself to a beautiful wardrobe, and owning a gorgeous, 5000-square-foot, southwestern-inspired home, on a 6-acre lot. The majority of my property consists of hills, sagebrush, boulders, but home to snakes, bobcats, coyotes, and rabbits. It's located in a remote, sparsely populated section of southeast Riverside County, east of Los Angeles, but not far from the interstate freeway.

I live in a gated community with neighbors situated far enough away to provide me with privacy and quiet. We enter our neighborhood through an automatic gate, opened by a four-digit code changed every month. As the iron gate opened, I spied our gardeners, a kindly, father and son, leaving with a load of vegetation, tightly concealed under a black tarp covering the back of their pickup truck. The common areas of our neighborhood consist of drought-tolerant gardens requiring minimal maintenance, but, on occasion, the gardeners make extra money by removing sagebrush, weeds, and trees on property owners' lots. I was happy to see they picked up a side job filling their pickup bed. We waved to each other as they left for the day.

Our neighborhood borders expansive, county-owned, wilderness land. The terrain is treacherous, and access is so difficult, I never saw county officials enter or exit this wilderness. The HOA members joke the county-owned wilderness is ideal for outlaw marijuana grows.

Although my home includes a state-of-the-art security system, the alarm was seldom triggered, only by animals or birds. It is a neighborhood I could leave the door open without fear. I am proud of my interior design of western-inspired, leather and mahogany furniture. My landscaping requires little, if no irrigation.

I wouldn't be able afford the upkeep of my home after retirement. I placed the home on the market for sale, but the real estate market was "soft," and, I hadn't seen a single visit from a prospect since listing it with the realtor six months previously. The proceeds from the sale of my home were necessary for a comfortable retirement; I set my sights on retiring to Spain or Greece.

The next morning, I walked about my yard, assuring it was in tip-top condition for the open house, placing the flags and "Open House" sign in the front yard. Across the street, I noticed a wicker picnic basket placed atop a hill, partially camouflaged by sagebrush, as if "hiding in plain sight." I had the open house on my mind, and gave it no further thought.

There were no prospects to see the house all day, and I walked outside to remove the flags and open house sign for the evening. I noticed the basket was still there. I sent an email to the HOA notifying all homeowners of the basket, and prepared to settle in for the night.

The following morning, after placing the flags and open house sign, I noticed the basket was still on the hill. I checked my email but no response from the HOA. I became concerned about the basket. Could it contain abandoned puppies or kittens? I retrieved the basket, and, just as I was approaching my door, our gardener's truck passed slowly by my home. The gardener and his son, caught a glimpse of me with the basket. I thought it odd the gardeners would be working on Sunday.

As I carried the basket, it appeared full, and fortunately, no cries or whimpers from abandoned animals, if still alive! I placed the basket on the kitchen counter. It was locked, so, I retrieved a screwdriver, hammer, and broke the lock open. I carefully opened the basket to find it full of neatly stacked, crisp, new, one hundred-dollar bills. It didn't take me long to count the bundled stacks of cash amounting to $100,000.

I was faced with the decision to report it to the police, and be swept up in a lengthy investigation, I wanted no part of, but what bothered me the most, was the possibility of a criminal expecting to retrieve the basket from the hillside. Complicating my decision further, if I kept the money, I knew a $100,000 cash deposit into my bank account may trigger Treasury or DEA scrutiny, and, I'd face tax liability on the deposit. I decided to place the money in a safe deposit box until the owners revealed themselves, or I figured out the prudent course of action.

No prospects visited my home all day. After dinner and a movie, I settled into bed with a book. I heard a car park, and was afraid to peek out the window. I heard car doors open, muffled sounds of men speaking about a missing item, followed by the closing of car doors, and the vehicle driving off. I surmised the basket belonged to these men, and regretted bringing it into my home.

Minutes later, I received a call marked "Unknown Caller" on my cellphone. Assuming a "robocall," I let it go to voice mail. My curiosity demanded that I listen to the voice mail. I heard some ruckus and incomprehensible talking in the background, heavy breathing, then a disconnect without a voice message. Shortly, thereafter, I received a text message from my realtor informing me of a prospect wishing to tour my home the following evening. I texted a confirmation of the showing to my realtor.

Marco was a distinguished looking man with an undiscernible accent. His salt and pepper hair was combed back, and he wore a bespoke, black suit, and white, silk shirt. I noticed his shoes were adorned with the distinctive "Gucci" horse bit. He was followed by three men, likely in their twenties, wearing stylish clothing, and beautiful, leather dress boots, who said nothing.

"This is a beautiful home and suits my entertainment and home business needs. It's gated, country location, without nearby neighbors, and quick access to the interstate connecting me to Riverside, San Diego, San Bernardino, and Los Angeles counties, is ideal! Let's sit, and I give you my offer."

My realtor's face lit up and was quick to reply,

"Certainly, Sir. Allow me to take us into the dining room where we may sit."

I offered my guests refreshments, but everybody declined wanting to "get down to business."

"My appraiser informs me the home is fairly offered at $500,000, but tells me it's been on the market for 180 days with no showings or offers! I pay you $400,000, cash, and close immediately without contingencies!

"You have twenty-four hours to accept my offer. The longer you wait, the greater the home may 'depreciate,' if you "know what I mean." Good day, ladies."

Marco and his men stood, and walked to the door as I followed. Before letting themselves out, Marco turned to me,

"I want $100,000, cash, of your $400,000 sale proceeds. And by the way, my offer includes everything! You leave with only the clothes on your back and your vehicle.

"My staff will keep you company here until escrow confirms the transfer of the property, and you hand my men the cash and the keys. It will be a quick and seamless ending for you."

Marco and his "staff" let themselves out. I watched a black Bentley drive away.

I knew Marco wanted the $100,000 from the basket returned, and the $100,000 from my sale proceeds, in addition to my furniture, clothing, and everything else in my home, was my "punishment" for interfering with his "business."

I returned to the realtor who was anxious to discuss the offer,

"In my twenty years of selling homes, Melody, I've learned its common for cash buyers to drive hard bargains. I suggest you counter them at $490,000, testing their motivation. Even in this soft market, $400,000 is a 'low ball' offer."

My realtor didn't know the offering price was "take it or leave it," and included everything in the house!

"Allow me the twenty-four hours to consider the offer, Rose, and I'll phone you with my decision."

"I understand Melody, but remember, don't 'look a gift horse in the mouth!'"

After the realtor left, I thought about the Gucci shoes with the trademark horse bit, and thought how ironic the term "gift horse" was to my dilemma. Under different circumstances, I'd find Marco attractive; he was handsome, and I admired his opportunistic, "go for the throat," negotiating prowess. If I accepted his offer, Marco's gains amounted to $300,000; $100,000 off my asking price, $100,000 cash out of my pocket, and the $100,000 within the basket.

I trembled at rejecting the offer from a dispassionate, ruthless, negotiator like Marco. I couldn't eat, and I resorted to alcohol to calm my nerves. I knew if I rejected Marco's offer, I could be harmed or killed. I believed the $100,000 loss from the fair market value of my home may be a tax write off, but the $100,000 cash payment was an "out of pocket" expense with no tax deduction. $200,000 was a major portion of my retirement income; its loss, forcing a reconsideration of my retirement lifestyle. I regretted my decision to retrieve the basket.

After midnight, I was awoken to the sound of a car parking outside my home which was uncommon. Suddenly, the car's audio speakers barked the lyrics,

"These boots are made for walking, and that's just what they'll do, one of these days these boots are gonna walk all over you."

The car sped off and I contemplated the Nancy Sinatra lyrics which warned me to accept Marco's offer. I pulled the blankets up over my head, and trembled, alone, in my large, dark home, fearing the alarm system might be triggered by assassins. I could be murdered and buried within my six-acre lot with little chance of ever being found. My gated community providing security, now felt like a prison, offering me no choice but to acquiesce to Marco's demands.

I heard the cry of a lone coyote, possibly, warning me not to reject

Marco's offer.

I tossed and turned all night, managing only a few hours of sleep. I crawled out of bed, fearful, but managed to complete my morning routine as I prepared for work. I skipped breakfast, loaded the basket full of cash into my car, and my first stop was to be at the front door of my bank when it opened for business, eager to place the cash into my safe deposit box. Upon leaving the bank, I'd text my realtor to accept Marco's offer and prepare the purchase contract, including all of Marco's terms.

As was my custom, I entered my attached garage from home, started the car, and pushed the button to open the garage door. I placed the car into reverse, pulled back into my expansive driveway, closed the garage door, placed the car into drive, and proceeded to exist my driveway. Suddenly, the HOA gardeners' truck pulled into my driveway, boxing me in.

The kindly old gardener and his son, exited their truck, removed their caps and approached my car. I exited my car, but left the engine on in case I needed to sequester myself inside the car, and attempt an escape, blowing the car horn like an "SOS" signal.

"What's the meaning of this? I'm not aware of any scheduled appointment? I'll be late for work!"

The father spoke; his son's eyes were fixed on the wicker picnic basket in the passenger seat of my car while holding a razor-sharp machete which glistened in the morning sun,

'Ma'am, we've come for the picnic basket."

"Did you receive the email I sent to the HOA?"

"We're aware of it, but we saw you, and you saw us, after you retrieved the basket from the hillside. Please give it to us. It will solve your problem."

"How do I know it's your basket? Can you tell me its contents?"

"Ma'am, the basket contains one hundred thousand dollars."

"I was visited by a very frightening man, named Marco, who claimed ownership. How do you figure into all of this?"

"Ma'am, the less you know the better, but we completed a "harvest" for Marco, and the basket includes our pay. We were to retrieve it Friday evening, but our rig broke down, and weren't able to come for it until Sunday. We told Marco about the situation after seeing you with the basket. He's very angry with us. I'm aware of his visit, and the threats made against you, but I pleaded with Marco not to intercede if I could retrieve the basket. I told him you're an honest woman who attempted to find the rightful owner by notifying the HOA. Marco agreed to give us one last chance to retrieve our pay, so, please give us the basket."

"How do I know if I give you basket, Marco will leave me alone?"

"Do you have your cellphone with you, Ma'am?"

"Yes, I do."

The father pulled his cellphone from his shirt pocket and completed a short text message. Within seconds, my cellphone rang, showing, "Unknown Caller." I hesitated to answer, fearful of speaking with Marco.

"Please answer the call, ma'am."

I answered the call, and recognized Marco's voice,

"Give them the money, and the deal is off! You should consider whether I would have permitted you to leave the property after its transfer to me, knowing, at any time, you might notify the authorities. You own a large lot with many holes to plant your corpse."

Marco hung up. I reached into my car, retrieved the basket, and placed it on the driveway in front of me. The gardener's son stepped forward, picked up the basket, removed the lid, and quickly counted the money, assuring himself the $100,000 was inside, and walked back to his father, joining him inside the truck. The truck rolled forward, and I feared they would run me over, but the father leaned outside the window,

"Thank you, ma'am. You won't be seeing us anymore."

They drove off.

I stood next to my car, heart racing, and looked at the beautiful wilderness terrain surrounding my home, realizing my fear of Marco would never permit me to enjoy my home again.

I texted my realtor,

"I'm rejecting Marco's offer. Reduce the price and include the term, 'Motivated Seller.' Schedule weekly open houses until the place sells! Place a lock box on the front door as I'll be moving out immediately, and renting until the home is sold."

I looked up at the hillside where I found the basket, and a coyote, perhaps the one from the night before, emerged from the sagebrush, looking down upon me as if to say,

"It's better to 'leave well enough alone!'"

PAUL HOSTOVSKY

LAUGHING IN THE FACE OF FEAR

I'm too chicken
to laugh in the face of fear.
But after
the fear has passed
I've been known to laugh
at fear's back.
Like when it's behind me
and I'm looking back at it
sauntering off,
growing smaller and smaller
until it's so tiny
it's laughable. Like the time
I thought that lump
was a tumor, but it was just
a bug-bite.
Or the time I went to the urologist
who said it was just
the asparagus,
and I practically peed
from laughing so hard.
If I could only
make fear turn around
when I'm laughing at fear's
back like that,
then I'd be laughing
in the face of fear.
Or maybe that's just
wordplay. For some of us,
words are all we have, though,
finally. Scary thought.

Hostovsky

TO THE PEOPLE WHO DON'T WRITE BACK

Maybe you haven't written because
you're still reading
and rereading what I sent you,
giving it the kind of close read it deserves,
the kind a lover gives a love letter,
a Sumerian scholar gives a cuneiform tablet,
a reader of poetry gives a poem she doesn't
totally get but can't get enough of.

Or maybe you haven't written because
you're still writing, still
agonizing over the right words,
deleting the superfluous poignancies,
rethinking the commas,
looking for better verbs, discarding
sentences, whole paragraphs, then starting
all over again. Then again,

maybe you haven't written because
people don't write anymore,
let alone read. Letter writing has gone the way of
candlelight. They're shouting "short-form copy"
from the rooftops and the laptops. The mailboxes
are disappearing. And so are all the letter writers.
And all the English majors. And the English language itself
is shrinking at the same time it's expanding

not unlike the universe. Plus, the children
no longer collect stamps, nor even know
in which corner of the envelope to affix them.
Maybe you haven't written because
there is death in the world. And evil and email
in the universe. Maybe you're dead.
Or maybe I haven't heard from you because
I'm dead. And just don't know it yet.

Hostovsky

LUCKIER

Praise the man
who lives on the corner of 109 and Lake
and hasn't mowed his lawn
in years—
all those flowering weeds,
untamed shrubs,
hegemony of ivies
claiming that yard like
a promised land,
not to mention the grass
he has let grow so long
that the leaves—
the leaves of grass—
could hide the girth of a man
as large as Whitman
if he lay down there
and looked up at the clouds,
a blade of grass in his teeth.
I don't know who he is
but I know the neighbors
are calling his yard an eyesore,
they're calling it obscene—
the way Whitman,
the father of free verse,
was called obscene in his day
for his overt sensuality. But I say
praise the man with the sensual lawn,
the epic lawn going onward
and outward on the corner of Lake
and 109, praise his genius
for freedom, so American, so
ahead of its time, transcending
all the manicured, boxy work
of his unimaginative contemporaries.

Hostovsky

CHAMBER POT

When first they learned about Paul Revere
in their 6th grade classroom—his famous ride,
the advancing British troops, the Longfellow poem
("One, if by land, and two, if by sea") they were
unimpressed. And now on the field trip
to Boston's North End, crowded together inside
the tiny 300-year-old Paul Revere House,
the docent pointing out the original hearth,
wainscot, beams and ceiling joists, they are still
unimpressed. Then out of nowhere, a chamber pot
changes everything: One of the children notices it
under the four-poster, raises his hand and asks
what it is. "A chamber pot," says the docent. "For pooping
and peeing." Titters, gasps, giggles and groans go up,
and up go the hands, the follow-up questions buzzing
around the master bedroom of Paul and Sarah Revere,
the children more interested now than they ever were
for any part of the patriot's story, or the country's.
"Didn't they have bathrooms?" "What about
toilet paper?" "What about privacy?" "What about
the smell?" "Where did they empty it?" The class
is all ears now, and the docent is hitting her stride
because this is interesting stuff, this is important historical
stuff: "Bathrooms were invented much later," she says,
"in the 19th century. Here it was either the chamber pot
or a long cold walk to the outhouse in the middle
of the night. They emptied them in the street—everyone did.
They didn't know about hygiene. They didn't yet know
about germ theory. The smell was hideous. People got sick.
They died young. Paul Revere had sixteen children,
but only nine survived." And now the class is learning.
They're rapt. Engaged. Impressed! And all because poops
and pees are basic. The stuff of life, of history. The stuff of poetry.

Hostovsky

A SPIRITUAL EXPERIENCE

Clifford threw his back out
while sitting in his car
in traffic. "Don't tell anyone," he said
when I asked him how it happened.
"I won't," I said but I didn't say I wouldn't
write a poem about it. He'd had to pee
bad. And the traffic was going nowhere.
And he had an empty peanut butter jar
that he kept in the glove compartment
for just such occasions—this was not
his first time. He twisted it open, twisted
himself into position, and it was right there
in the twisting that he somehow ruptured
a disc. And where is the poem in all this
you're probably wondering? It's here
in the movement, the passion, the sequence
of twists that a man maneuvering to pee
in a small space in a small cup
performs while seated, the terrible need
to relieve himself a kind of passion,
the holding it in a kind of compression,
the letting it go finally a kind of pleasure
that gives way to a kind of wisdom
that washes over and comforts the afflicted
Clifford. "But which came first," I asked him,
"the pain of the slipped disc or the pleasure
of the peeing?" I needed to know for my own sake
and the sake of the poem. "It was a merging,"
he said, "a conflation of pleasure and pain, sorrow
and joy." It was ultimately what you would call
a spiritual experience, Clifford penultimately moaning
with the epiphany of it, his cup running over.

Hostovsky

PT

She knows the names of all the muscles.
"This here's your supraspinatus,
and this is your infraspinatus,
and here's your teres minor and your
subscapularis," she says, massaging
all around my rotator cuff. I love it when
she talks like that. We've been meeting here
every week for almost a month
and I have a little crush on her. I try my hand
at the new vocabulary: "Is my
subscapularis underneath my scapula?"
"No," she says, "more like in front," then traces
the triangle of it with two very strong index fingers,
and I wince a little. "It actually attaches here
to the anterior surface of your scapula," she says,
"but originates here at the fossa." Her fingers
arrive at the same time that her voice does. I nod
thoughtfully, as if she's telling me something that I can
take home and remember to cherish when
we've gone our separate ways. "It transitions to a tendon
here," she says with a demonstrative jab that hurts
so good. Then with a long, complicated caress
she adds, "It inserts itself on the lesser tubercle
of the humerus, in front of the joining capsule. Here."

Hostovsky

M A PHILLIPS
THE WOMAN'S LOT

"She'll come out of there soon," I said to my father. "Mom can't stay in that shed forever. You know she always comes out eventually."

Dad said to. me, "You're wrong. You're too optimistic. You don't know her nearly as well as I do. I'm sorry, but you don't. Your mother can go for weeks without food. I mean it. I've seen her do it. And she took her canteen, right? You saw that, right.?"

I said, "At least we know she has water."

Dad said, "That may just be mice we hear in there. She may not be moving at all. It's amazing how long she can hold perfectly still."

"I don't think so, I said. "There was too much noise for it to have just been mice."

Dad said, "It could be rats."

"I don" think so," I said. "It would have to be awfully big rats for that much noise."

"I hope enough warmth's sneaking under the door," he said.

"She took her heavy coat," I said. "She remembered more than just water. It's good she wasn't in that much of a hurry this time."

"I'll bust out that window if she doesn't come out soon," my father said.

"Bad idea," I said. "Forget that. She'll board up the window if she thinks you're going to bust it out."

He said, "So you just. stood there, watching her take her stuff in there?"

"What was I supposed to do?" I said.

"You could have come got me," he said, "for one thing."

"I didn't have time for that," I said. "I didn't even know where you were."

"You could have called for me," he said.

"If she heard me calling, she'd have just moved faster," I said. "Or not taken her coat. You know when she gets something into her head there's no stopping her. It makes it worse if you try."

"Boy, do I know *that*," Dad said.

I said, "We're disturbing her, I think, she's probably trying not to listen to us, but she can hear us through the door. We're probably just prolonging the amount of time she's going to stay in there."

Dad said, "I can't just go work now."

"That fence has to be fixed," I said. "We don't want to be chasing cattle in the rain again."

Dad said, "I got it mostly fixed already. They'd have trouble getting out the way it is now."

"I'll come help you," I said.

"No," Dad said. "You stay here. Your mom might need

something. Or she might want to talk. That happens sometimes. I'll have the fence fixed in a couple hours, probably. You can handle this all by yourself, right? Your mom might even be more likely to come out if I go away. She'll hear me leaving. She might even see me through the window, if she doesn't board it. up first." He said that last part louder.

We assumed there were limits to what Mom would do, but we didn't know what those limits were. I was sure it had a lot to do with being a woman. Dad and I knew Mom was better inside than we are. We both knew that. We had to admit it. Dad said it's like comparing peaches with horseshoes. But still a comparison like that can be made. For example, few can resist a peach.

Even Sylvie, the young woman who lives on the next property…. I wish I could see her more. It takes about half a day to get there, and then, of course the same to get back, and her father doesn't want you spending the night.

I know my mother's getting back inside her head in there, to the place she was before she came out here to be in the middle of nowhere with Dad. She's probably playing her piano inside her own head. Dad told her he would like to be able to get a piano out here for her. She never tries to pressure him or anything. Of course, she can't always keep the yearning out of her eyes. She doesn't even always try to anymore.

It does frighten us when Mom hides out in the shed like this. Once she stayed in there for nearly a week. Really. Dad says sometimes he's sorry he put the window in there. He said she wouldn't stay in there so long then. But I think she would. She might even stay longer just to show him.

At least she has enough room to lie down. Nights are pretty warm still. We don't have many rats out here since we figured out how to keep our food away from them.

At least she doesn't seem to be crying in there. That's the worst. You want to call to her, ask her what's wrong, but you know she doesn't want that. She only cries when she can't help it. She might be thinking life really isn't worth it. That's what. scares you.

Sylvie told me something about that once. She said you shouldn't try to get too involved when a person is crying. I knew partly what she meant. I mean, in a way it's nice when a girl cries about you. But I think part of it is Sylvie wishes she had more boys to choose from. It's not that we don't like each other. We share a lot of things most people wouldn't. We like to go inside our heads to faraway places, for example. We like the way snow makes the world stop.

Sylvie talks about death sometimes. I know she doesn't believe in heaven and hell, or any of that. She says of course you're not really dead. You're not anything then. Death isn't something you can experience. That's why it's stupid to worry about it. This is the kind of thing she says.

I don't think Sylvie wants to be dead though. She just has a funny way of saying things sometimes. She's smarter than me. I know that. She is a year older, but still Mom told me girls grow up faster than boys. She told me I'll catch up. But women know something men can't. I'm sure of that. I don't think we know anything they can't. This makes us afraid of them.

Mom likes Sylvie. She wishes Sylvie was her daughter. I'm pretty sure of that. It *would* be nice for Mom to have a daughter, as well as me. It must be hard for her to be with only men. Women become impatient with men. Men seem slow to them. Women have an easier time talking than men do.

Then it's sometimes right. after Sylvie and her family have been with us that Mom seems most sad. Sylvie's mom is okay. I like her okay— we all like her. But Sylvie is the one Mom is drawn to. Sometimes I wonder if she feels she should warn Sylvie she's too good for me. I can't help thinking that sometimes.

I'll be fifteen soon. This winter. It won't be that much longer before I'll be fit to marry.

The problem is Sylvie could be someone who could easily wrap me around her little finger. I've seen men like that, and it makes me sick. No man looks more pathetic than he does wrapped around a woman's little finger.

Mom and Dad pretty much stand on the same level at least. Neither one of them is on the mountain looking down at the other. One is better at some things, and the other better at others. So, it more or less balances out, I guess. I don't think I have enough to balance out with Sylvie. Maybe in a marriage one always loves more than the other, and maybe it's better to be the one who loves more.

But still…I suppose it could be a misery.

When I try to talk to Dad about all this, he'll just say something like, "Don't think about it so much. You're like a woman when you get like this."

But I know he'd like me to marry Sylvie, at least so the two pieces of land would sort of be joined together.

I remember something Sylvie said to me once when we were

alone. I think about it a lot, still. She said, "Don't trust anybody. You can't trust anybody. You can only trust anybody only so far. Remember that. Don't ever forget that."

This is frightening. It wouldn't scare you so much if you didn't know it's probably true. In your heart you know you're alone. That's what, she was saying.

She once said, "Take comfort in it. Every time you learn a truth there's comfort in it."

But she can make a game out of things like this. That makes it even worse.

She says things like, "Everybody's always playing."

I know it probably means she's always dancing circles around me.

Like Mom in the shed. Playing with us. Especially with Dad. Twisting him around her little finger. Or trying to. People say women are kept down by men, and that's why they're always trying to find ways to get power. Women aren't even allowed to vote. Men are stupid not to allow them to. Men pay a heavy price for denying them that. They don't even know what a heavy price they're paying, Sylvie said. But she seemed like she was enjoying making us pay.

We're not stupid," I said.

She laughed, and said, "You can't even count the stars up in the sky."

I said, "You're wrong. I just counted all of them, while listening to your boring ideas.

"So, how many are there?"

"Don't you know?" I said. "How will you know if I say the right number?"

"That's what I mean. Only a man would be dumb enough to count the stars . That's my point. Men spend their time counting stars"

I waited a minute, then said, "Why do you do that? Why do you have to be trying to put yourself above me? It makes you look stupid if you have to be always trying to prove how smart you are."

"That was pretty good," she said. "That was really pretty good, for you." She laughed.

"There: you just did it again," I said. "Aren't you clever!"

She waited a minute herself, then said, "I'm a city girl inside, stuck out here in the middle of nowhere.''

I said, "You've never even been to a city. What would you do in a city? You have no idea what a city is like"

She said, "I can feel the city inside of me.''

I said, "That's your problem. All you want is to be in a dream."

"Right," she said. "You're right."

I think about that a lot. I think about how dangerous it would be for me to be with someone who wants to be inside a dream all the time. Someone like that would be bitching and complaining all the time about the real world. A man might be willing to put up with it when a woman is young and pretty, but I've seen old bags nagging their husbands to death, never satisfied. Women act like they got dragged out here. Even some of the mail-order brides, when they see what it's really like here. At least the whores accept their fate. Maybe I'll satisfy myself with whores all my life. I'll have my favorite. Someone who would know exactly what I like.

"Mom" I called again. "Why don't you come out now? You've been in there long enough. This is getting pretty tiresome."

Sometimes it seems like she does this just to make us sit around and think about her.

I remember once I said to Sylvie, "Do you think life is a mistake? No, really. Look at all the crap it makes us go through all the time—with love and romance and all that—just to get the children made—so they can go through the same shit What's it for? Most of life is boring. Love is like a flame we move toward, like stupid moths."

She said, "You're a good guy. You really are."

"Don't always talk down to me, please, " I said. "You'll drive me crazy. I'm not stupid. Not everything I say is stupid."

"Mom!" I called again. "This is really getting to be a pain in the ass."

It was starting to get pretty late. Dad would be home soon. He'd be sad, at least, if she hasn't come out yet.

"C'mon, Mom, "I said. "Dad will be back soon."

That didn't sound quite right.

"We love you," I tried.

That sounded worse.

So, I said, "Alright, stay in there. What do we care? stay in there as long as you have to."

Then I said, "You think the world would be better if women were in charge." Then said, "Maybe you're in charge already."

That sounded even worse.

So, I said. "Dad got your piano. It's waiting out here for you right now. He said if you don't come out by nightfall, he's sending it back."

Then I said, "I'm not good enough for you, am I? Dad isn't good enough either, is he? You should leave us. We'd probably be better off without you. Oh, we'd miss you for a while…but we'd get over your shit soon enough. You're sickening. You feel special because you're the only woman here—that makes you feel all unique and everything. Women make me sick. I hope you stay in there forever."

"What's going on?" Dad said, coming up behind me.

Swiveling in my chair, I said, "You let her drag you around like a dog. That's what the problem is."

Dad just stood there watching me. Finally, he said, "You're right Don't ever get married. Find yourself a good, reliable, clean whore. They're cheaper than this shit That woman in there is the most expensive whore I've ever had."

"Shh…she can hear you" I said.

Dad said, in a loud voice, "I'm glad she's in there so I can finally say these things to her, and she keeps her mouth shut'. She's made me into a coward whimpering after her all the time. I've had enough of it."

Then he said, "You tell her I'm going to beat that door down, or set that fucking shed on fire."

"She hears you," I said.

All of a sudden, we heard Mom laughing in there, hysterically, out-of-control.

PAUL RABINOWITZ
CITRUS HONEY CAKE

I don't have a fancy name or moniker
no one calls me spirit child
only what my father gave me,
and what his father gave him

Once I asked my grandfather
if he ever listened to Brian Wilson's arrangements on Pet Sounds
Watch the setting sun from a sandy beach

(cont)

Only a rich man has time for that, he said

But recall a story he told my father, about a customer
who sang in the night club across from his tailor shop

The way her voice transported him to springtime in the old country
Wished he had the words to tell her all this in English

Instead, he offered her a cup of his fresh-brewed Rumanian coffee
And cut an extra-large slice of citrus honey cake he made from scratch

Rabinowitz

ZACK ROGOW
"WE MIGHT HAVE MET WHEN WE WERE SEVENTEEN..."

We might have met when we were seventeen,
when we didn't even know how it felt
to touch a body unlike our own.
We could've snuck from the floral sofa
to your bedroom
while the parents were snoring
and spent the whole night
exploring
new lands and landscapes.

Or we could have met after college
when bosses and mortgages
were our treasured worries.
We might have made a child then
with your azurite eyes
and the soft, wiry brown hair
I still had in those years.

Or we could have encountered each other
right after our divorces
when our kids were puzzling
over algebraic expressions
or practicing jazz trombone.

(cont)

We happened to meet now,
when the children have
scattered to their own homes,
when more about me is wrinkled
than my sheets, when our bodies still glow
with a beauty that once blazed.

But without having lived
through love gone
sour, would we have understood
how rare our meeting is,
like finding a beach studded with scallop shells,
all split, chipped, cracked, crushed,
and then lifting one complete one
out of the sand,
and rinsing it in a clear sheet of water.

Rogow

ROD MARTINEZ
DADDY'S GIRL

He was never a good father. Thinking back through the years I don't think I ever remember hearing those three words every kid wanted to hear. No, not "I Love you," but "Proud of You." I don't think it was in his vocabulary.

Mom suffered the worst from his actions, not physically—though he would distribute his rage by punching the door, wall, stove or even the glass shower door—but she suffered the silent treatment he would hand out after a hard day of work. If not that we'd hear the fullness of anger in his seething high shrilled voice. My sister and I would run to our rooms and hope the door would stay closed. We were kids, we didn't know.

He was born during the Great Depression, the smallest of three kids, it was rough. Then he served in World War II, came from the generation that we Americans have known to call the greatest. At seventeen, he was the youngest of his family to enlist. He lost both brothers due to the war, then eventually his mother who suffered through bouts of depression after her two oldest sons never came home. Dad was all they had left.

We don't hear stories about his upbringing, his father left—at a time when that seemed a crime in American society. He grew up alone with a bitter mother who seemed to miss his brothers who were dead instead of appreciating the one that came home, though he came home with an issue. He lost one eye in the war. That—we were told—was where the rage started.

Coming home wasn't the pleasant return he had hoped for, so he moved away—far away from the only life he knew, all the way across the country from California to Florida, to start anew.

That's when Mom came into play. In a small town called Weeki Wachee, my father the ex-Navy man was told that another navy man had decided to start a business using of all things...mermaids. It would be an attraction to die for. Mom was a mermaid, a young woman with great lungs who could stay underwater for more than it seemed possible to entertain visitors who would watch them swim. Dad was smitten at the red-headed mermaid.

A quick courtship turned to marriage and she was no longer holding her breath under the clear waters of Weeki Wachee Spring, instead she was folding diapers and ironing school uniforms. First my sister's then mine.

Dad ran the house like a strict disciplinarian who showed no love. Mom was the silent nurturer. At eighteen, my sister quickly married and was gone; that left me and Mom to fend for ourselves when the mood hit. Sometimes he'd throw stuff, other times he'd threaten to kill her, other times he'd take the belt to me just because I sneezed wrong. This was back then parents didn't get in trouble for "punishing" their child, for sparing the rod—it was the accepted norm.

His best friend David LaRucho was a constant visitor to our small home. One day he came by while Dad was still at work. He said he needed to get something from the garage and bring it to Dad—who was working as a mechanic in a large shop. He asked how I was doing. Uncle David always treated me the way I wish dad would. He smiled, he called me cute names like "Pumpkin", "Princess' or "Daisy Flower"—I liked that one best. I asked him why my dad was such an angry man, what happened in his life to make him the way he was.

"Your dad had a rough life Buttercup, his dad left him, his mother ignored him. He looked for love and found your mother."

"But it sure don't seem like he loves her, Uncle David."

"Oh, he loves Rose, Dumplin'; trust me he loves her."

"Well, what about me?"

I was ten years old when we had that talk, he bent down to me and kissed my forehead, "Sugar, you are the reason he lives and breathes."

He rose and walked out of the garage whistling a tune I had never heard of before, could have been Sinatra, Dad used to love him.

"He sure has a strange way of showing it." I mumbled to myself.

Soon enough, before I knew it, I was eighteen and moving out with my new husband. The poor sap had no idea I said yes just get away from Dad. I was grown, I figured, and my new husband would give me a good life. Within a year we had our only child, the girl I had prayed for. I swore I would be a better parent than my dad, I promised it to my daughter while she was still inside me. Then my husband changed, the once loving, smiling, happy twenty-one-year-old that I had exchanged vows with, slowly turned into my dad. Anger, rage, physical confrontation became the norm. I couldn't figure it out, were all men like this? My sister's husband turned into the same person. I had assured myself that he would change, that it was a phase. But one day he threw a plate and missed my daughter by a few inches. That was the last straw. I called my mother, asked what I should do; her reply was not one I was ready for or would accept.

"He's your husband, you married for better or for worse."

"Hell with that, Mom, I'm not going to waste my life on a miserable excuse like you did. I don't know why you didn't divorce Dad, but this jerk's going to be served papers."

Months later I was looking for a place to move and at the same time my sister called. We didn't talk much since moving out, so those three words were not ones I was ready to swallow.

"I'm getting divorced."

"Join the club." I chopped back.

We became roommates, it was almost like childhood except we had my child in the mix. We made up for lost years and became fast friends. Truthfully, we never really got to know each other growing up; she was bookish and I was a tomboy. Those years brought us close together until she found another guy who eventually proposed. I was maid of honor.

The second time around seemed to do the trick for her. I wondered if I'd have that luck. I did. The brother of a coworker turned into the stepfather of my baby girl and we had a happy family. Love, laughter, happiness finally.

Years passed.

My sister was still married, Mom was still miserable—and I was divorced again. This time it wasn't anger issues; it was a young administrative assistant who edited his work at the job. I never saw it coming.

I met up with mom for coffee after my daughter moved out with her boyfriend. She wore the years of strife on her face with a silent pride that I could never understand.

"Honey, I have cancer."

My heart dropped. Mom? Cancer?

"I have maybe six months; your dad doesn't know, neither does your sister."

Together we held each other in that coffee shop drenched in years of mutual tears.

"Mom," I asked, "why didn't you ever divorce dad? I believe all the years of torture is what's helped make you sick."

"Our generation doesn't divorce; we are in it for life."

"Mom, that doesn't make sense, he tortured all of us, all you had to do was leave."

"He wouldn't know what to do with himself."

"Really? He'd just find another slave to iron his shirts and cook his food! You were a fool all these years and now look at you!"

Mom bit her lip, I sat back, guilt took hold.

"I'm sorry Mom, I love you, I just think you could have done so much better with your life."

"As have you, Honey."

Three months later I stood at her grave. My sister paid her last respects and drove away with her husband and kids. My daughter kissed my cheek and walked away with her new husband. Uncle David walked over to me, balancing on his cane.

"Buttercup, you know the care of your father will have to fall on you."

Tears filled my eyes, I turned to my father, sitting in his wheelchair across the grave from me.

"I don't want to take care of him, Uncle David. He reminds me of a horrid childhood and the suffering Mom went through all those years."

He leaned his head against mine, placed a soft kiss on my forehead, "Dumplin', you are the only one he wants to take care of him. You are his favorite, you know?"

"Favorite what, punching bag?"

"Daisy Flower, you know all your life he bragged about you. When all of us guys, the old gang, hung out at the garage playing checkers, he'd go on and on about his baby girl, how he was so proud of her."

"Uncle David, Dad never said those words, why are you trying to butter me up, so I don't send him to a nursing home?"

His soft frail hand cupped my chin and I looked into his watery gray eyes.

"Honey, I have never lied to you and it's not the time to start doing it now. Go on, you know what you need to do."

The staring contest between us seemed to last for hours but I knew it was mere seconds. We both turned and glanced at the old man on the wheelchair. He was holding a rose in his hand and to my surprise, crying.

I glared back up at Uncle David, the old caring constant in my life. He was right, he never lied to me. He patted my shoulder, winked and turned and walked away.

I fought myself, inside there was a battle of epic proportion. I'd rather roll the wheelchair into that hole so he could be with Mom forever. I walked over placed both hands on the bars of the chair.

"Come on Dad, let's go home."

He's ninety-two now. Just the two of us, living in the small house I grew up in. Every room reminds me of strife, anger, remorse. I wasn't sure how long I could be here, truthfully, every time he cursed because he couldn't open a jar of peanut butter, or because he couldn't put his socks on or because he couldn't get up in time to go to the bathroom. It reminded me of the grunts and the swearing he would utter just before slamming a chair against the glass door. Except this time, I wasn't going to jump in fear—instead I would race toward him and ask him what his problem was. Toxic, that's the best word to describe us. How Mom did it I have no idea, but I am a stronger woman than she was, and I won't take it.

Last night we sat at the table, I asked him to tell me about his father.

"I don't want to talk about him; he was a jerk."

"Why?"

"Because he left us when we were little, what father does that? Leave your wife during the Great Depression, with kids and just disappear. What kind of man does that?" The rage surfaced, it seethed through his fake teeth. The frown grew more, he slammed his fist on the table and the coffee cup rattled, spilling droplets of the hot drink on the white tablecloth in front of him.

"You see what you made me do?" he motioned to get up but lost balance and fell back in the seat.

I watched his face, he felt defeated. He wasn't the same man who would get up and take off his belt. He didn't even wear a belt anymore, he stayed home all day and walked around in his underwear, and they covered his Depends.

I stood, picked up the cup and walked to the sink to empty and wash it. He took his spoon and tossed it on the floor under a series of profane barks.

I dropped the cup into the sink and turned to him in instant rage.

"Are you done? Are you finished having your tantrum? Mommy isn't here to cower away, and I'm not going to run to my room just because you want to give your show, so are you done with this act, Mr. Hollywood?" I got in his face, "*are you!*?"

I was close enough that he could have slapped me, but instead he backed away and lowered his head, and to my surprise burst out in tears.

Taken by this sudden change, I didn't quite know where to move or what to do. I had never heard a man cry like this. It was like telling your kid, on the way to Orlando, "No we are *not* going to Disney."

He collected himself, wiped his good eye of the last tear. I stood, still frozen at the sight in front of me, my once all-powerful dad, now a feeble crouched old man fragile enough to fall off his chair if he stood too quickly.

He cleared his throat.

"I'm…I'm sorry."

My eyes ballooned at what I thought I heard.

"I'm sorry for how I treated you, for what I did all those years. Honey, I'm so sorry. I swore to myself that I would not turn into my father, and I think I did worse than he did. I don't know that you or your sister could ever," he choked again, "forgive me for all those years. I didn't want to be him, and I turned into him…even though I never left. I turned into him. Your mother was so, so caring, so loving…she was so forgiving, and I just played on with this power and authority…and I felt I lost your respect for it."

He did, though I never told him so.

"I'm truly sorry, Baby."

Anger wanted to set in, oh yes, rage was at the door, all the words I heard him scream all those years at us were at the tip of my lips ready to shoot out like swords and pin him against the wall.

He looked up at me.

"Would you forgive me?"

In that split second, the little girl in ponytails emerged out of me.

That was my daddy sitting there. My World War II hero daddy, the one who lost his eye in the service fighting for our freedoms. The man who fell in love with a mermaid. Uncle David's best friend.

I knelt to him and held him in a long soft hug.

"I love you, Daddy."

ROGER SINGER
GRAVEDIGGERS

soft dirt foot print
on a fresh grave,
a deathbed
of brown earth
and a few
small stones,

shovels lean
on a wooden shed
where inside
two men play cards,

soiled fingers
sweaty shirts
the odor of work
in their hair,
they snort
and spit
rising slowly
cursing the heat
and the dead.

Singer

RENT LOST OR WHISKEY FULL

candlelit shadows
collide
as hands reach
and then withdraw
in the room upstairs
soaked with
comfortable aromas
and layers of dust
where men with
rough shirts
and weathered hands
toss dice
at the crease of
wall and floor
smoking cigarettes
speaking softly
when the dice
bite back
or cast a smile
when luck
rises for a
moment

Singer

LESLEY L LAMBRIGHT
DURING THE PANDEMIC

We drive up the Thumb of Michigan
three weeks after the election
where Biden and Harris won by more than six million votes
and still we watch as Trump flags fly defiantly

It's the day after Thanksgiving, eight million souls have COVID in America
and seventy-four million voted for "him" knowing full well the truth
but not caring, loving bravado and chaos more than life itself
crying fraud and hoax as trained, believing in a false messiah   (cont)

We are in search of beauty in this time of death and isolation
holiday setting for two and the specter of Christmas looms lonely
One daughter down with COVID, the other watching over her and very exposed
so off we travel up the coast to the tip of the Thumb

Helpless to be of help, desperate for reprieve and renewal
following the lake and seeing how close it has cut the shoreline
up to Port Austin where the Art Barns dwell, created by Detroit artists
linking the rural to city, seeing the parallels and hoping for community

A bridge in the form of an Ark, old falling barn wood repurposed
in the shape of a ship to safe harbor; another barn now exhibits a pie slice
exposing sky and field beyond, while the wind makes music when within
 the cut's angular womb; the third barn painted with a piquant pigeon

The other side a mural homage to American Gothic but sporting gas masks
families having sold out to agribusiness and chemical companies
meanwhile the sun settles beside the barn amongst harvested Dow corn stalks
and the full moon can be seen in broad daylight just above a chain of wind turbines

The beauty is breathtaking despite its implications and complications
we begin the return journey, traveling the middle of the Thumb down
through farmer's fields and endless humming wind machines
only to enter the coastal road in time to witness three hundred snow geese
resting for the night on Lake Huron, their plaintive weary cries the final dark beauty

Lambright

BRUCE OVERBY
FRUIT STANDS

"I'm sorry, Lynn," he says.

"Just go, Simon. And only one soda, okay. The dentist is finding cavities all over the place." She slaps a pillow and puts it in place. Simon digs through a drawer for socks.

The bed made, she turns to him. "If you leave, when will you go?"

He focuses on a pair of tube socks in the drawer. "I didn't say I definitely need to leave, Lynn," he says.

"But if you do, when will you go? Two weeks? One? Tomorrow?"

"Let's talk more tonight, Lynn," he says, and he picks up his shoes and goes out.

* * *

An hour later, he steers the station wagon down Monterey Road, the four-lane expressway that links the Santa Clara Valley to points south. It's a run to the fruit stands, something Simon does with the kids two or three times each summer. Towering eucalyptus trees line the road, filtering the morning sun, interrupted every mile or two by a stand, typically just a few sheets of plywood and a flimsy frame of two-by-fours, purely makeshift but somehow holding up year after year. A farm family works inside, sheltered from the sun and surrounded by stacks of crates, the top one always tilted forward as a display. Beyond, fields and orchards stretch to brown hills dotted with ancient oaks. The valley gets smaller here, the gray of buildings and commerce giving way to the greens and ambers of the landscape, the hills on either side growing nearer and nearer as Simon drives on and the children chatter around him.

"You do too like her," Frances says to Chris.

"Oh, shut up," says Chris.

"She got in trouble with Sister Mary Clement for her uniform skirt."

"She did not."

"She tucks it up around the waist to make it short like that, you know."

"God, will you *shut up,* Frannie!"

"Frances, leave your brother alone."

While Chris grouses out the window, Frances, sitting between them on the front seat, shoots Simon a mischievous grin. He thinks of his own sister Clara, and a scene that plays often in his mind. It is winter in the 1940s and Clara is saying to him, "It's all right, Simon. Let's say the rosary until they get back." They're in a '36 Ford—his father loved that old car—huddled in the back in their Sunday clothes and wool coats, Simon's worn through at the right elbow. It is snowing and Simon can clearly see the curves of the seats, the steering wheel, the horn, and the dashboard glowing blue in the half-light.

"I don't remember the prayers," he says to Clara.

"I'll help you. Wipe your eyes." He feels her kerchief against his face, the sting just under his eyes. "We'll pray the joyful mysteries, Simon," she says.

Those words—*joyful mysteries*—and the way she would say them, the freckles under her large blue eyes wrinkling into a little smile, wisps of white-blonde hair flipping out from under the knit cap drawn tightly around her ears. She would say the same thing all through the season. "We'll pray the joyful mysteries, Simon." And Simon would feel release, stillness, happiness even.

"Hold the crucifix with me, Simon," she would say. "In the name of the Father, and of the Son, and of the Holy Spirit…" She would lead him in the sign of the cross, moving the crucifix first to his head, then to his breast, then to the left, then right shoulder. "…Amen."

"You have to cross, too," he remembers saying, and the process would be repeated on Clara, to the head, then to the breast, then to the left, then right shoulder. And they would pray the joyful mysteries, moving their joined hands from bead to bead, repeating, "Hail Mary, full of grace," and "Our Father, who art in heaven," leaning in close to one another in the darkness, sinking deeper into the large seat of the big Ford, occasionally glancing out at the Wisconsin snow gathering on the windshield.

And then his parents would return, just out of the local tavern across the lot, opening the car doors in a rush of cold and laughter.

"Oh George," his mother would say. "Look." The laughter would cease and his mother's smile would soften. Her eyes were deep, dark brown, and glistening. Turning to his father, he would see another glistening pair of eyes, these blue, and a smile that wasn't really a smile, but rather an expression of regret and searching.

As the memory breaks off, he sees Frances gazing absently out the window, her eyes not unlike Simon's mother's, her cheekbones not unlike his sister's.

* * *

The cool of the morning gives way to the summer heat, and Simon rolls his window down a crack. "How's summer school going?" he says to

Chris.

"Okay, I guess. I got a report due next Friday."

"Want me to take a look at it for you?"

Chris looks at him, incredulous. "What?" Simon says. Frances giggles, and Simon sees that she's covering her mouth, and in the rearview mirror he sees that Mark and Patrick are also giggling in the back seat. "What?" he says again. "I used to look over your homework all the time."

"I still got a lot to do on it, Dad," Chris says, "but thanks anyway."

"I used to look over your homework all the time," Simon says again.

"He's taking Language Arts class, Dad," Frances says, and Simon is in on the joke. He long ago established his ineptitude with grammar and spelling, and Lynn and the kids had some fun with it when he did. He vaguely remembers Chris, at age nine, correcting a spelling error in a note he wrote for him.

"Besides, Chris is a big brain-o," Mark says.

"Shut up, Mark," Chris says. "At least I'm not a big dunce-o like you."

"Okay, guys, that's enough."

"Chris has straight A's since the third grade," says Frances, suddenly a wealth of information.

"Second," Chris says. Then, after a pause, "Thanks anyway, though, Dad."

Looking at Chris, Simon's mind wanders to Sunday Mass, Father Samuels speaking directly, defiantly. "We have great minds in high positions in this country, and what God and the people need now are great ideas and great compassion, not an endless cycle of aggression and ignorance." Simon is haunted by a vision of Chris, five years from now, naked and muscled, his floppy brown hair reduced to skin and stubble, his eyes stone still with panic and contempt. "Willful ignorance is a sin," Father Samuels said. "God will not charge the sins of Indochina to the foot soldiers, but to the leaders who sent them there against their will."

Simon and Lynn have been happier at St. Agnes of Assisi, having left the stodgy St. Jude's, where the children attend school, and embraced the enlightened thinking of Father Samuels. Lynn is now on birth control and for a while the late nights had been filled with the rich tang of tastes and smells Simon had not explored for years, heat and wetness both coarse and smooth, all of it enhanced at first by the weight of their exhaustion. It was love with abandon for those glorious weeks, and afterwards their sleep was heavy and final, broken only by the most insistent rattle of an alarm clock or the door knock of a frightened child. But in time, both knew it couldn't last, the desperate need for sleep rearing its head more and more. "You forgot your purse, Mommy." "I thought we were going to the hardware store, Dad." "Mommy, Chris said he can make a pizza if you want to rest some more."

And as broad-minded as Father Samuels is, St. Agnes is still the middle of the road choice. It isn't St. Jude's, but it isn't the tiny St. Bernadette's either. There a young priest celebrates Mass in jeans to a congregation seated on pillows and folding chairs. Buses gather to ferry parishioners to protest marches. Hippies blend with families, ponytails and beards alongside white button-down shirts. Smiles of contentment attend action against injustice. Most of the marchers are similar in age to Simon and Lynn, who married in their teens and spent their twenties having babies.

* * *

Annie and the little girls, Colleen and Katy, sit in the very back of the car, in the small seat facing backwards. Annie tries to read over her little sisters' constant chatter. They notice some horses in a pasture.

"That one's making a doodie!" Colleen says.

"Eeeewwww!"

Katy's voice grabs Simon's attention. He remembers the doubts he had the year she was born: Bobby Kennedy and Martin Luther King killed, body counts from Indochina on the news, no end in sight, not another child. But that was long before the switch to St. Agnes, and looking back now, it's just a blur.

"Annie, will you take us to see the horses at Lee's tomorrow?" Colleen says, pestering her older sister as she often does.

"If Mom'll let us."

"Why does Lee have such lousy horses?"

"They're not lousy, they're just old."

"But why does he have them?"

"I don't know, Leenie!"

Colleen has been a light sleeper since starting kindergarten, so Simon can't even poke his head in anymore after night classes. Colleen wakes up, then Katy is awake, and Lynn glares. "Come on, Simon, it took me most of an hour to get them down."

He'd spent an hour himself, years ago, getting Chris and Frances and Annie down. But then he got the first night job teaching at city college. Things got better, so he got a second one. But when he got the third one, he started missing out: Mark's first steps, Patrick's first tooth, Leenie's first words. He pictures all of them older and less fragile, maybe running to the car to greet him on a warm Saturday morning like this one.

* * *

He considers Frances and Chris, next to him on the vinyl bench seat, two kids who might have to grow up a lot in the coming months. At ten, Frances is already a beauty. Annie is a bit of a tomboy, and Katy and Leenie are little more than babies, but Frances is something else altogether, sure to be the envy of all of them in the vanity of their teens.

"Mark and Patrick and me went to the pool yesterday, Daddy," she says to him.

Chris turns to his sister. Mark and Patrick hear their names and break off their conversation to listen in.

"Pool? What pool?"

"At Walt Whitman school. They have free swim."

Simon remembers Lynn telling him about this. Twenty-five cents per child, and she'd been letting some of them go two or three times a week.

"It was really fun," she says.

"Really fun?"

"Yeah." She says this matter-of-factly and adjusts the hem of her t-shirt.

Mark and Patrick are staring directly into the back of her. "They have races there, Dad," Mark says.

Chris looks at his sister now, his brow line set. "Frannie's a really fast swimmer, Dad," he says. "She always wins the races at the pool."

"She wins the races by a lot," Patrick says. Simon can't remember the last time Patrick spoke a kind word toward Frances. Annie, too, from her place in the back of the car, is looking on.

Frances is the center of attention, even as she stares blankly at the road ahead of them.

"She wants to join a swimming team, Dad," Chris says. Frances turns to him, and something like fear comes into the boy's eyes.

"She's really good, Dad!" Mark says.

The first fruit stand comes into view. Simon pulls the car to the side of the road and finds a patch of shade to park in. Katy puts her hands to the back window, waiting for Simon to open it. "Aren't we going, Daddy," Colleen says, but Simon barely hears her. The rest of the car is silent. Frances's bell-bottoms catch his eye, paisley fabric sewn on to extend the length. He recognizes the sneakers she wears, hand-me-downs from Lynn. Mark opens the side door.

"Let me talk to your mom, Frannie," Simon says.

"Thanks, Dad," she says.

Simon looks in the rearview mirror and sees Annie, Mark and Patrick smiling at him. As they open doors and scurry out, he considers a talk with Lynn about a swimming team for Frances, a talk that might happen now on the phone, on a Saturday visit, maybe in the kitchen with a new man standing by. A breeze sweeps out of the orchard carrying the aroma of leaves and wet soil. It is a sickly smell. He considers mornings for Lynn without him, moping children, rebellion, the weight of it. And as he closes the car door and begins walking, he thinks of Frances as an athlete, perhaps a winner, but certainly a teammate, a part of something larger than herself or her family. He absently kicks a stone, hitting it squarely.

* * *

Sometimes, there would be an hour. A whole hour. Simon would be ready to leave the office, his lesson plans and handouts for the following day's courses in order, and he would know that, with traffic, he'd be able to drive to his night class with an hour to spare. And he always knew where he'd go. Near the old town center of Campbell, just off the main drag, there was an old rail yard surrounded by dilapidated cannery buildings. The gray of the wood, stripped clean by the years and the weather, the evenness and harmony of it would still Simon's thoughts and ease his neck and shoulders. The gray buildings, loading platforms, and railroad ties. He would park the car facing the yard. He'd get out and sit on the ground in front of the car, lean back against its square chrome bumper, take in the warmth of the aging asphalt curb and the glistening chrome. And he would listen to the quiet, feel the breeze if there was one, and let his eyes drift across the landscape before him, the wash of gray, broken here and there by the gray-green leaves of an ancient oak or the red-gray rust of iron and steel rail lines, gate hinges, pulley blocks and hooks. And he would imagine the place in the not-so-distant past—perhaps twenty years, perhaps ten, the year Frances was born—when it was a clamor of enterprise, fruit trucks bearing crates and baskets rolling in, and trains loaded with boxes of cans rolling out. And workers in hats and denim coveralls everywhere, some weathered and tanned from outdoor work, others fair and perspiring from the cannery.

And the thoughts of work and bustle would lead him to thoughts of a very different Lynn, one without all the children, with only her mind and her sense of purpose. After the days of passion about Kennedy and the future, and the years of inconceivable tragedy that followed, he feels a pang as he imagines her, donning a sweater and flashing him a timid smile, leaving him to the house and charging out into the protests with a placard. She knew so much from her books and magazines, and if things had been different, a very different troupe of friends would have taught her even more, and Simon may not have mattered at all.

* * *

"Cherries!" Katy says. She takes one of Annie's hands and Colleen takes the other, and their straight hair bounces behind them as they skip and trot toward the stand.

"Look at the strawberries, Daddy," Annie says, and he goes to her.

"Those look pretty good," he says.

The old farmer manning the stand moves closer. "Those came out of the field yesterday," he says.

Simon smiles and scans the berries. "We'll be coming back through," he says. "Don't want berries bouncing around in the car all day."

The farmer nods, then flashes a grin at Annie, who looks up at him over the wooden boxes. Annie is Simon's most plain-looking daughter, with fair skin, small blue eyes, and fine straight hair. But her plainness seems to charm people somehow. He grabs a small paper bag and plunges his hand into the cherries.

"Daddy," Annie says. "Did Mom tell you about Lee?"

"What's that, honey?"

"Did Mom tell you about Lee?"

"Lee? The man with the horses?" Simon continues filling the bag.

"Yeah. Did Mom say anything about him?"

"No, honey, your mother didn't say anything. Is something wrong?" Annie is looking at Katy and Colleen, who are on the other side of the stand pointing and laughing at the squash.

"He's leaving," she says.

Simon turns to her. "What's that?"

"He told me last week he's giving up the ranch and leaving." Her eyes remain fixed on Katy and Colleen. "Mom was supposed to tell Katy and Leenie, but I don't think she did." She turns to him, squinting against the sun. Her mouth is pressed shut, her jaw set, and her lip is starting to quiver.

"Annie?" he says. He lowers himself and puts an arm around her waist. He knows the girls love horses, but why would Annie be crying? What do they do at Lee's? Do they ride? Clean out stalls? Feed the horses?

Annie shudders and sniffs. "Can you tell Katy and Leenie, Daddy?" she says.

"Of course, I can, honey." She presses her face to his shoulder, and he feels the warmth of her tears through his shirt.

The old farmer appears and hands Simon a paper towel. "Everything all right, sir?"

"Yeah, I think we're okay, thanks." Simon hands him the bag. "We'll take these." He hands Annie the paper towel. "You okay, honey?"

She blows her nose, nodding.

"I'll talk to Katy and Leenie before we get home," he says. "Your mom must have forgotten." She nods again, still holding the paper towel to her face. "The next stand is Mr. Tanaka's," Simon says, and Annie slowly manages a tentative smile.

The farmer takes the bag to the scale. "Six bits," he says. Simon finds three quarters in his change and hands them over. He and Annie walk over to the car, where Patrick and Mark are sitting on the hood. Katy and Colleen have settled into the shady ground.

"Cher*rieees!*" Katy says, opening her arms as if to hug them. Simon reaches into the bag and grabs a few, then hands the bag to Katy. "Careful of the pits, now, honey," he says. "And share those with your sister."

* * *

Driving toward the next stand, Simon looks into the rearview mirror. Annie sits reading her book and solving the occasional mystery for her younger sisters. In his mind, he sees her with the old and stooped Mr. Tanaka, a Japanese internee during World War II. The old man is smiling and reaching a hand out to his jumping, spinning terrier, Kazu. Annie's love of animals and open spaces seems to spark the old man.

The vinyl of the station wagon's dashboard is a dark, smoky blue, polished to a shine last week by the boys. At the end of the passenger side, a small patch is cracked and discolored. When Simon bought the car, the used car salesman had no explanation for this blemish in the otherwise spotless interior, and it had never spread, had never gotten any worse.

Lynn's words from last night reverberate in his ears: "What do you want from me now, Simon?" Glancing in the rearview mirror, he thinks about telling the children. Annie is his deepest concern. She's the third oldest, behind Chris and Frances, who certainly must be told if he decides to go through with it. Just as certainly, Katy and Colleen can be spared, at least for now, and probably Mark and Patrick as well. But Annie's a tough one. She'll take it personally either way: by hearing the news, or by being left out.

They park and walk toward Mr. Tanaka's stand, and Simon scans the prices on the plywood signs.

"Where's Mr. Tanaka?" he hears Annie say. A young Caucasian man is in the stand holding a crate of strawberries, a puzzled look on his face. There is panic in Annie's eyes. "Where's Mr. Tanaka, Daddy?"

"What?" the young man says.

"The farmer. Mr. Tanaka," Simon says. "Is he here today?"

"Who's Mr. Tanaka?" Katy says, and Simon realizes she would be too young to remember him.

"Just a minute, honey," he says to her.

"You mean the Japanese guy who used to own the place?" the young man says.

"Used to?" Simon says. Annie is frowning now.

"Yeah," the man says. "He sold out last month."

"Who's Mr. Tanaka?" Katy says again.

"Katy!" Simon says, turning to her. "I said, just a minute."

"They're building something here," the young man says. "My brother and me are looking after things until they break ground. Then all this stuff gets plowed under." He gestures to the fields behind them. "Kind of a shame, really. Darn nice farm."

"Is Kazu still here, Daddy?" Colleen asks.

"God, Leenie, you are so dumb sometimes," Annie says, and she stalks toward the car.

"Annie!" Simon calls after her. "Annie, I want you to apologize to your sister!" But Annie just keeps walking, past the car and into a grove of trees beyond. "Annie, come back here!" No use.

The young man is still there, holding the crate of strawberries and looking on. "She was sort of attached to Mr. Tanaka," Simon says. He feels a tug at his pant leg.

"Daddy," Katy says. "Who's Mr. Tanaka?"

Simon lowers himself and puts an arm around her. "He's a nice man who used to own this stand, honey," he says. "You remember? He had a little black dog, and we played fetch with him last time?" Katy just looks around at the stand, and at the young man, her brow furrowed against the bright sun.

* * *

Simon sends the kids to the gas station for sodas, then walks into the grove and finds Annie under a tree facing the strawberry fields. Cars pass by on Monterey Road, interrupting the quiet sound of the wind through the branches. Annie hugs her knees, and her face is set in a severe frown.

"Annie," he says. "You're going to have to apologize to Leenie."
She glances up at him.

"Come on, honey. Chris is getting sodas. Let's go back."
She mumbles something into her knees.

"What's that?" Simon says.

"I don't want a soda," she says, lifting her chin just high enough
to get it out.

He sits on the ground next to her and gazes out at the sun-drenched
field.

"Why is everybody leaving, Daddy?" Annie asks him.

He wants wisdom, to tell his daughter in some wise and believable
way—some way that reaches into her young life for signposts and symbols
and language she can understand—that people change, places change, and
life is not all that cruel when you get right down to it. But all he can do is
stare out at these green, glistening fields and think of last night, of his talk
with Lynn.

"Yes, Simon," she'd said in an even tone, "I realize you work
seventy hours a week. So what? That's the hand we drew."

"I just want you to know what's on my mind, Lynn, that's all."

"So, what is it you want from me?"

"I just want you to know about it, Lynn. I just want you to listen
to me."

"And what does that do to me? What does it do to me when you
tell me you're feeling trapped? That you need to find yourself? Of course,
you're feeling trapped, Simon. We've got seven children and you've got
three jobs. There's no fix for that. That's the way it is."

Annie is still looking at him. "I don't know," he says to her finally.
"I just don't know."

"Dad!" Chris is running toward them. "Katy swallowed a pit!
She's choking!" They run, following Chris to where the kids are gathered
around Katy. She is holding her throat, convulsing, her eyes pressed shut
and her mouth jutting out, red and O-shaped. Simon takes her by the
shoulder and claps her on the back. No change. He claps her again, harder
this time. He claps a third time, even harder.

"You're hurting her, Daddy!" Annie cries. He hits her again,
feeling the size and weight of his hand on her tiny ribs.

"Man, what are you doing?" It comes from behind him, the young
man from the fruit stand. Simon pauses. "Call an ambulance, you idiot!"
he screams. He pulls his hand back further now—there is no way he can
hit his baby any harder than this, no way he'll be able to dislodge the thing

if it means hitting her harder than this—he claps her a fifth time, feeling the air release from her tiny lungs. She hacks louder now, bends forward, and ejects the half-masticated cherry, black and blood red in a stream of pinkish saliva. Simon watches it land and roll in the fine gravel.

Katy is coughing violently now, taking in as much air as she can between hacks. Gently, very gently now, Simon pats her on the back. "Easy, honey," he says. "Easy now." Colleen smiles and wipes away tears with grubby fists. As Katy's coughing fit subsides, she cries out and starts weeping loudly. She inhales deeply between sobs, and it is the sweetest sound Simon has ever heard. Frances takes her sister in her arms, absorbs the sobs, strokes the little girl's straight blonde hair. Mark puts a hand on Katy's shoulder, and Simon's hand ceases patting, slides down Katy's back and off. "You're okay now, Katy," Mark says. She just keeps on crying. Her eyes do not go to Simon. They are flooded with tears, but not closed, and they only look at the ground in front of her.

All the children are gathered around Katy now, each reaching through to lay a gentle hand on, except Annie, whose eyes are locked on Simon, wet and stinging with tears and anger. "You hit her," she says.

"I had to, Annie," Simon says.

"You hit her too hard! She's hurt now."

"Annie, I had to, she was going to—" He stopped himself from saying it. "Annie, she was choking."

"He had to, Annie," Chris says. "Don't be such a stupid."

"I am not a stupid! He hit her too hard!"

"He did not! You want her to choke to death!"

"Will you kids knock it off!" Simon feels a cold sweat come over him. "Just knock it off!"

The kids fall silent. Even Katy has quieted, her sobs reduced to short, rhythmic breaths. Simon does not meet the children's eyes. The cherry lies in the gravel, trampled, now just a brownish purple mass with the light ball of the pit poking out its center. "Just knock it off," he says again, quietly now. They hear a siren, and they all turn.

* * *

Katy is next to Simon now as they all drive back up Monterey Road, back toward home. He is imagining the sixth slap on her back, and the seventh. Frances is also in the front seat, and Katy has curled up to her, fetal and silent under her wing. On either side of the road, the valley is widening, the orchards and fields stretching further to the distant hills. The three boys are in the back seat, and in the very back of the car, in the seat facing backwards, Colleen watches out the window for horses, and Annie sits low in her seat, just the top of her head visible.

In 1963, when Lynn was still carrying Annie in her womb, they sat in a neighbor's yard surrounded by the little children, both theirs and the neighbors'. And Lynn and the neighbor man argued about Martin Luther King and the meaning of the big speech he had made. Simon was chatting with the neighbor woman about insurance and property taxes when he saw Lynn lean forward and lay her hand on the man's forearm. With quiet resolve, she was making a point, but the man just shook his head, got up, and asked Simon if he wanted a beer. Simon muttered a response, then his eyes met Lynn's, and he could see that she had gone somewhere, somewhere far away from him. And he wonders, in that moment, with the road passing under his wheels, if he can go there too, if he can ever find her.

SARAMANDA SWIGART
SESTINA: A WOMAN'S WORK

One hand holding the door handle
I trip—oops!—over the spindly dining chair
between my teeth, a mechanical pencil
begriming my face with leaden dirt
glass of milk, overturned on the table, pools
across the top of my work's printed page

I'll wipe down and reprint this page
while more work accrues than I can handle
I curse the English department's part-time pool
though she does what she can, our Chair
assigns us each semester's dregs and dirt
the wait intensifies homeschooling penance, a pencil

lolls in spilled milk, and this pencil
hasn't once touched the homework page
I grab a dishrag (I notice too late it's covered in dirt)
wipe the milk still holding the handle
of this pot of mac and cheese. I push the chair
in with my leg, while my son's tears pool

(cont)

The work isn't hard, but his interests pool
elsewhere—the tree outside, lost friends, this pencil
that he feeds thin lead—while he cries in his chair
for books he wants to write, for a different page
full of pictures he'd draw, characters' names (handles
like "The Great," "The Forgotten"), and the dirt

On his lip I've ignored for four hours. Dishing dirt
with friends, drinking drinks by some pool
used to be real (didn't it?). Memories I handle
carefully as good china—he throws down his pencil
on a scribbled-on, scratched-up page
with maximum noise he scrapes back his chair

And leaves, so I sit in the boy-warm chair
set the mac and cheese in the dirty
milk, dull to piles of laundry, mountains of dishes, empty pages
while the work—domestic, professional—pools
around me so I break leaden nibs off the pencil
and say, "Come on: This is nothing I can't handle."

I need to get a handle on this shitshow, sit in this chair
grab my trusty pencil, dig my way out of all this mental dirt
pool my resources, and finally—face this life, face this page.

Swigart

MARGARET H WAGNER
FLOW

There's mastery in spreading honey.
Turning the open notches of the wooden dipper,
first right, then left, waiting for honey
to flow onto a piece of perfect toast
in remembrance of bees.

Wagner

HE WORE SPURS

You dragged your spurs on the wood deck near the screen door.
Spurs with rope dust and horse hair,
an extension of your livelihood,
your badge of courage.

You held the door for me
at that mom-and-pop restaurant
in the middle of the Wyoming town
where horses were tied and dogs ran free.

Questions remained on my tongue:
    "Did you grow up in these parts?"
    "How large is your ranch?"
    "Do you have a wife, children?"
    "Would you carry me into the sunset?"

Amid the hum of customers, you waited your turn,
hoping for some chicken. "Nope," the ladies said, "we just ran out,
but wait a second, we'll put more on the grill for you.
How many pounds do you want?"

I left the cowboy in the hub of a community where nothing was too
much trouble.
Back on the road, I drove through ranch fields burning orange in the
setting sun,
those spurs branded in my memory,
saying *giddy-up, giddy-up, giddy-up.*

Wagner

CHRIS VINER
STALKER

    As the golden autumn leaves tumbled along the cobbled ground
near the stone walls, which meandered up the hill towards the rose-pink

café on the corner, Warren noticed how Montmartre appeared less busy than it had done just a few days ago. He liked it this way. The sky a more concentrated grey and the crowds all but dispersed from the notorious district. He was able to absorb it now—its quiet, alluring charm. He could breathe better too, without all the noise. Black birds carved ovals across the chimney-plotted landscape, which slopped and beveled with an organic composition, like a beautiful, misshapen fruit; it felt good, to be able to walk through such a fine part of Paris without the usual hoorah of tourism.

As he turned a corner, descending a narrow street, the moisture in the air suddenly sprinkled fresh specks of rain across the dark trees and the roads ahead. Rain possessed such a freedom, Warren thought. It was everywhere, not imprisoned in a body like humans and animals. It was liberty incarnate, bursting from nowhere and out into every corner and crevice of the old world. And it could follow anything or anyone it liked. Although desire was probably not something with which rain concerned itself. It had better things to do. Like paint Paris in its wash of archaic color, as it skittered across rooftops and pavements, washing down turfed-out gullies and boulevards. Rain cleared things, cleared the air, the streets, the buildings, the restless knots and entanglements of a life. Even the homeless avoided it, opting for resident enclosures and empty porches, rather than the customary roll of cardboard under rows of streetlamps.

He liked to go walking in the popular districts, when they were just quiet enough for their real, romantic charms to start brightly festooning into existence. It was humdrum enough for that mysterious moody color to come hovering over the night lights, and across the waiter fixing the table in the café under the blue, early evening sky. The time when wind had swept away the pastiche, and when the cold had kept the narrow avenues clear enough to walk by without a knock from the shoulder of a stranger.

As he strode up the hill, foot by foot, with the smell of smoke and alcohol stirring through the oily, embalmed air, he thought about the first time he had come here. He was young, very young then—still in school. He thought about how he'd scaled the steps up to the Sacre Coeur and a man had chained a beaded bracelet around his wrist. How he'd panicked. "He wants money—give him some euros," his friend Luke had said at the time, Warren's French being under par, was unable to speak. The man had gripped on to the string of the bracelet. "Pour Vouz. Cinq Euro," the man had repeated, following Warren, with a calm yet menacing determination. The swirl of foreignness around him, the thick alien tongue in the heat of the solstice, striking him as blunt and harsh. Warren, his head meekly bowed, finally offered the man a scrap of coinage, and the man had released his grip.

That seemed like so long ago now. And although it really wasn't very long ago at all, his perception of Paris had almost entirely altered. Back then, it had quite firmly terrified him. Now, as his face had deepened, and an understanding had shaped around experience, he'd earned an appreciation for its heavy, oneiric smells, developed a strong affection for its ritual, its food and wine, and its rickety, appealing balance between Bohemianism and aristocracy. Although he was not much of a part of its social life, he could admire it now from a distance. He dreamed of it too, romanticized it, hoping, one day, he too might be a silhouette in its shining, elusive window.

When he reached the summit of the district, Warren noticed a small, empty café in the square. Was it open? There didn't seem to be anyone around. His calves ached from walking up the steep hill and the chairs were out, so he decided to sit down to catch his breath. He looked out onto the patio: pigeons grazed at morsels, a few strangers passed over the curve of the square and out into the foggy distance. There were no berets or chalk faces in sight, nobody's relative was being distorted into a caricature, which brought an unusual and serene peace to the environment. Warren listened to the rain drift and sputter down the gutter spouts and skim across the paving stones, and almost, for a moment, lost where he was.

"Tu vu quelque chose?"

Warren turned and saw a young lady leaning on a beam in a black apron. Her arms were folded and she struck a cheerful demeanor.

"Vouz avez la menu?"

"I'll get you a menu," she smiled when she detected his accent.

The smile was an affectionately mocking one, since Warren's French was too English sounding to be taken seriously. Warren hadn't gathered this, however—all he saw was a classic, pretty face, and, perhaps, most especially, blunt, ruby lips, which being so striking in the wetness of the landscape appeared to stain the air—even as she turned nonchalantly on the beam to whisk herself back into the kitchen—like a smudge, a stamped rose on the impeccable scene, stuck in the visual portage of Warren's guileless, dumbfounded mind.

The young lady returned and Warren glanced at the menu.

"I'll get a coffee—un allonger?" Warren said, a half question, causing the young lady to curl the side of her lip again. "And the onion soup."

"Well, alright!" Her face was bright now, twinkling with a novelistic enjoyment of his earnest character.

She scribbled down his order on a small pad, and to Warren's surprise, she remained leaning on the beam. The young lady asked him how long he'd been in Paris, and he told her of the aunt he was staying with for the autumn season. It became apparent to Warren that the young lady harnessed an unusual sense of comfort around him. She began to complain, thrashing her arms into the air, staring at the rain-soaked square melodramatically, as she groused about tiny rooms and extortionate rents, torrential summers, and stuffy tourist traffic in a snail-shell of a city.

"It's expensive—there're a lot of people here. And…it's small," he said, trying to think of what to say next. And then there was that smile again, which reassured Warren. After all, a smile could almost only mean she liked him. This, to his mind, was affirmed by what she said next: "Don't worry. You're not one of the tourists I hate. At least not yet!" Was she blushing? He wasn't sure, the reflected pools of rain often exposed uncommon colors in things this time of evening. "Donc. I'll go and place your order."

When the young lady returned, she placed a steaming bowl of onion soup, then one hot coffee, in front of Warren, and introduced herself as Chloe.

She leant on the beam and lit a cigarette, the smoke mingling into the dank air, before wafting under a canopy and out into the open.

"So have you been learning French very long?"

"Well, actually, yes—you could say that I have."

Chloe's lips pursed into a smile. She let him continue, not feeling the same gravity in the pause to which Warren had become unusually sensitized: "I mean…if you count the lessons at school, and the preparation I did for this trip—that's a long time! Although it probably doesn't seem like it!"

"French is hard—you'll get there," Chloe said. She breathed smoke into the air, bored by her own response.

"Yeah…I'm not sure if I will actually."

Chloe unearthed a cackle, instinctively putting her white cloth to her mouth to smother it. "So, you are staying with your aunt? You are close with her?" Chloe asked, feigning interest.

"I am—but she's a funny character. A bit of a religious fanatic you could say…."

"Ah, we have had a lot of those here. Not all of them good."

Chloe's complexion suddenly became cold. Color withdrew from her cheeks, causing Warren to lose the small slice of confidence he had uncharacteristically forged. "No, I suppose…."

"Excuse me, I have to check on something," Chloe said, flicking her cigarette into a puddle and rushing to the kitchen.

For a moment Warren thought he'd really blown it, that he'd offended her with his stupid, insensitive remarks. He was, after all, fairly new to the culture. The French, surely, were different to the English. To be so different, and yet separated by such a slim channel of water.…Warren's foggy, bleak thoughts dispelled, however, when Chloe returned. This time, with a brighter smile on her face. Perhaps he hadn't offended her. With her arms folded, and her weight leant on the beam, she stared out into the misty rain and began to talk of her life, her voice different now, her tone more somber, yet truer, as though she were reining in to some inner focus. It seemed then that Chloe were as close to him as any other important person in her world, as if she trusted him. "My parents are English. They were Bohemian, so when Thatcher came into power, they moved here without a second's thought."

Warren savored the drawn out, atypical phonetics of Chloe's phrasing. The way "here," was delivered to sound like "ear," for example, how the pronunciation of Thatcher came out as a rough, textualized "err" at the end of that name.

"They cut off everybody and started this new life," Chloe said.

"It was that easy, huh?"

"Much easier then, actually—believe it or not. We think ourselves freer now with the internet and such things, when in fact they slow us down, keep us tied together with people we don't really care about…."

"Is that weird for you?"

"How do you mean?"

"Like, you know, living here. You know, having parents from England…you seem so ingrained, sort of, in the whole…."

She smiled, and Warren noticed her teeth were a stained, tobacco smoker's yellow, that her hands were not as clean as he had first perceived, that the black varnish of her nails was chipped, all of which had the strange effect of relaxing him around her a little more than before.

"Well, yes. But I've been here since I was a baby, so…and anyway, you don't have to be here very long before you start to feel Parisian. Look at you right now, for instance, with your cup of coffee, your French, your onion soup!" Her eyes brightened. "You see, it doesn't take long at all!" Chloe pulled out another cigarette, lit the end and took a deep drag. "Besides, my parents…they made a rule when they moved here. Never speak English. Never look back. So that's why…why…my English is quite bad, yes…hup!" She shrugged her shoulders and tapped some ash into the air, which blew the flakes into nothing.

"No, it's not necessarily that…it's just…."

"I should let you eat…bon appetite, my friend!" She smiled and her eyes seemed to glimmer like a pair of beautiful dark stones.

Warren did not take that 'friend' lightly. Did she refer to every customer as her 'friend'? He doubted it very much. He, therefore, must have been special to her, she must have felt the connection he had felt—Warren was sure of it. 'Friend' could have all kinds of connotations, especially in France, and in Paris!—well…who knows what she may have been subtly, but surely, signaling. Warren turned his head and admired her angular, waify frame, her dark complexion, the way her scruffy hair hung down from her shoulders, as she set a table in the back. He noticed the ridged line of her nose. Her misshapen nose and large brown eyes made him think of a Renaissance portrait, the dark background, the unusually intimate gaze of the subject. So familiar and penetrating, and yet so incomprehensibly far away.

The next day, Warren decided he would crawl up the hill again to the same café in the hope of finding Chloe. The weather had cleared and the district was busier now. People jammed through trails of Montmartre and caught themselves in the nets of melodramatic painters and mime artists, which made the area seem lacking in its truer mysteries living beneath the façade. It had lost its oneiric quality and the walk seemed to Warren sobering rather than romantic or dreamy, as it had done only yesterday. It almost appeared to him as a different place, the atmosphere was so changed. But he knew that it wasn't. A cold breeze blew across his face and refreshed him. In the shop of local paintings with the yellow walls, he watched an elder lady pridefully hang up a small framed piece out the front—a Van Gogh style mustard landscape with a thick blue sky—and Warren thought to himself that things weren't so bad. He walked the long way, through narrower avenues, around the backs of flats and bistros, where men in grey one-piece suits moved furniture along ramps from a building, and odorous heaps of steam pummeled out from the open windows. Warren's hair was still wet from the shower and he felt the morning sun through the pale trees on the other side of the road beginning to dry the roots as he walked. The quieter way had led him straight to a bustling metro station, where suddenly he was sifting through crowds and feeling that familiar yet unusual collective loneliness, as he felt the fabric of stranger's clothes brush past him, until finally he reached the café at the top of the hill.

He approached and then paused outside the café. He noticed Chloe serving coffees and putting bill trays on tables. The place was busier now—and the café seemed to overflow from the rafters on to the cobbled street with an older, financial type. Chloe, in turn, noticed Warren, but—contrary to how he'd imagined on his way up the hill—she did not smile, or wave, nor, indeed, did she present any indication to him that she at all knew of who he was, which was a bizarre and troubling disposition with which to be greeted. A greeting which, by degrees, was true, of course—they did not really know each other—and so he sat down at one of the empty brown tables, like any ordinary customer, and looked out sadly at the detail of the winding district beneath the rising sun. He waited, a little longer than he'd expected for Chloe to come over. When finally she appeared, hovering over his rickety, street-side table, Warren found the initial feel of stoicism that had formed—at having not been acknowledged in the way he expected—had stiffened, hardened into a firmer barrier, which, not wanting to appear sinister—or sensitive—he tried to shake off, but was unsuccessful by the time she approached.

"Hey," Warren found himself saying, a little deeper in the throat, and a touch more severe than intended.

"Bonjour!" Chloe exclaimed, lightly and with an air of affirmed distance. One thing was clear: she'd retained some of her brightness. The color in her cheeks, the soft transient glow in her eyes, as though even during the waking day a portion of her were lounging on the couch of a dream. Still, something was off, something not quite there that had been. Warren wanted to find a way to get it back, to destroy the wedge that time had driven between them. Just then, he noticed how she held the notepad high, how the pen in her hand sat readily on the page, how the voices of the crowds seemed to shake the day turbulently forwards. He anxiously looked at the menu and tried to translate before quickly giving up.

"What would you like, sir?" Chloe smiled—and although there was life in it, the smile was not the same as the day before.

"I'll get the…yeah…I'll just get the same as yesterday, thanks."

"And what was that?" He couldn't help but frown.

"Uh, the onion soup…the…the coffee?"

"And that is all?"

"Yes. I…I think that's all." His eyelid involuntarily trembled. "For now."

"D'accord," Chloe took the menu with an impossible

graciousness, and before Warren could think of what to say she was gone. But something else, too, had disappeared: the spirit of yesterday, its sense of possibility, its magic. Now the dry sunny weather blew things along, and the customers yammered away about their problems as usual, drawing shapes in the air with their hands, and so it seemed something important was lost. It was like their perceptions of one another had recalibrated. The awkward, fuzzy energy between them now stifled Warren with a sense of betrayal. And although there was anger, this was mostly aimed at himself: for having allowed room in the midst of a mere passing day, for the glimmer of intimacy and trust, to have spread its wings and come swooping down into the next morning.

But days are so different, Warren thought. If a day changes, if the weather and energy of a city changes, if the planets move from one position to another, why do we presume a person stays the same? The sky was just an idea. But things—feelings—they were constantly in flux.

When Chloe returned to Warren's table, she surprised him. "What are you doing today?" she asked, as she set the onion soup and the coffee in front of him. When he didn't answer immediately, she folded her arms. She was smiling and he felt a familiar tingle in his stomach beginning to stir like a cocktail of hormones. As he looked at her smile, her dark eyes, it seemed they were sharing in something almost akin to what had been shared before, as though just for a moment, the doors of yesterday had opened and all its faint, lightheaded promises lay once again ajar. He'd almost forgotten she had asked him a question.

"I…actually, I might have to go and revise at one of the libraries. I'm trying to get into this university for Art History."

Chloe didn't say anything back, but rather simply held her smile, comfortable in the ring of silence fattening between them.

"Then my aunt wants to see some opera. She's crazy my aunt. She loves that kind of thing."

"Oh, opera's not crazy," Chloe said softly.

"No, it's not," Warren replied, feeling a sharp pang of stupidity.

"Well, enjoy your day—and the opera!" she said, lifting her eyebrows.

Warren watched her glide over to another table and hand out menus to new customers. He could just about make out the quick startle of her soft voice mingling with the birds in the pale trees on the other side of the road, and watched at how the customers moved and startled as they spoke, and the world itself seemed to move and startle.

Warren wasn't sure why he climbed the steps to the Sacre-Coeur the next day, only that he seemed to be pulled there by some invisible luster of gravity. As he marched each step in a half-daze, nobody bothered him, not the lost tourists with their maps and phones, not the accordion players with their blazed smiles, nor the men parked at each turn, hanging colorful wristbands from their hands. He let himself be carried to the church, as though no other route could have been picked that morning. When he pushed the heavy door open, and let it glide back in place, a pious silence washed over him. People seemed almost to tiptoe around the interior, gently meandering around statues and paintings of saints and the famous theological scenes. There was a chill in the air, and a distinct musky Damascus smell, stirring off the dark marble and the ancient construction of the building. The weather was slanted, mystical and grey through the stained glass, and he felt once again a strange spark of possibility.

That was when he saw her: Chloe, kneeling beneath a painting of Mary and Jesus. The darkness of the oily shadows in the background caused the faces of the figures to appear stark and eerie, the way the curvature of the bones in the expression of the Jesus figure was sallow, how the eyes of Mary were bloodshot with an apocalyptic fear. Chloe put some coins in the donation box and lit a candle with a match, sitting back reverently on the bench, her thighs somehow effusing sublime energies. The fire cast a red glow across her face and for the first time Warren saw in her a different temperament. He knew that it was just a collection of forces—the atmosphere, the lighting, the silence—but from where he stood, she looked almost holy, as though she belonged there, as though it were impossible to distinguish her from the oily canvases upon which she set her eyes and prayed.

Warren didn't want to disturb Chloe, so he sat on one of the chairs diagonally behind her, a few yards away, where he could still make out the solemn expressions at the side of her face, the movements of her delicate, spidery hands. Was he doing anything wrong? He didn't feel like he was, their crossing was, after all, coincidental. Or fatalistic, depending on how one saw the world. There were a few things he could have done then: he could have left, of course, or else disturb the ritual in which she was clearly wholesomely engaged, and which was obviously deeply important to her, even as he sensed a detachment within her motions of that ritual. Neither of those options seemed right somehow. It was only proper, then, to wait, and watch. Of course, it was. A few seconds went by in stillness and silence. Then Warren observed closely, as Chloe's hand arose, followed by a sweeping movement which he couldn't discern. Perhaps she was making the cross symbol above her chest. But no, it appeared then that she was pulling a note from somewhere. Suddenly, he had a sense, like an electrical tingle running down his spine, that he should remove himself from the situation, that—as she placed the note somewhere on the shrine and a faint tear rolled jaggedly across her cheek—what he was watching was simply too private. He shifted his weight as if about to leave; he imagined himself walking away, past the candles, the Baroque canvases, and out the door into the cool, chaotic throb of Montmartre. And yet he couldn't. It was like some insurmountable weight of gravity had kept him there, bound to his chair, bound to the sight of Chloe. And so he watched. He waited. And he saw what she was about to do next, like a witness to a holy parable.

MEGHAN ADLER
TEACHABLE MOMENT

I only feel pain in my left foot and a sliver of it in my head,
my fourth-grade student says in his high-pitched voice

after our school counselor taught us that sad feelings
can live in our bodies. *That's a poem.*

He laughs. *You think everything is a poem.*
I nod, silently hoping he will transform future shards.

That his solidarity for double-digit division, root words,
and Jolly Ranchers adds up to more than accomplishment.

I want him to know he will always be a poet.
Fourth grade was the last good year I believed my father

could teach me everything and my mom
would always be home.

Our nuclear family would explode.
I made topical maps out of pizza dough

and when I was finished,
I was ready to eat the wide world.

(cont)

Soccer teams without tryouts! No grades!
No divorces! No moved to other states!

My fourth-grade teacher, who wore bright red clogs,
(like the ones I have on now) and soaked our fallen

teeth in Coke to show us how sugar can rot anything,
told me I was a poet.

Gavin asks, *Where do you feel sad, Ms. Adler?*
So, I answer like a teacher,

I feel a twinge of pain in my fingers
when my students have writer's block.

My hips hurt if I see no one passing
the soccer ball to the girls at recess.

And then, as if I am reassuring myself,
a lot of the time, I don't feel any pain,

especially when I see hummingbirds attempt to drink
from dark purple hydrangeas.

I say the word *attempt* a bit too loud.
He's too young to understand that I never wanted anything

to change. I was thrust into pain everywhere in my body.
And that my attempts to lessen it all paid off.

I'm still a poet, and in this poem, I believe
challenges will strengthen his future self,

future pains in his left foot and head.
I want to teach him the root word of *attempt* is Latin,

attemptare, to seek, to not give up, to make an effort.
Teach him the word in Spanish, *atentar,*

which means to try, to move towards
something, to move towards anything.

Adler

BRUCE L BENNETT
PRISON AND TV

The penitentiary, 1993:
I was a young man
When my family gifted me
A brand new TV
Its 12" screen
(15" squared body)
Quite a bulky thing
In my small prison cell—
But, what peace it brings:
A mental escape from hell,
My late-night rendezvous with
SNL, Beavis and Butthead,
And, occasionally,
Reruns of *Kids In The Hall*.
Though my days be filled
With clamoring caged noises
Of prison bars racking, obscene
Violent jokes cracking, and
Voices of angry, aggressive
Men jostling amidst primitive,
Instinctual hierarchies—
Abstract mimicries
Of wildlife programs
On my TV—
I click, click, click,
Through options
Available to me.
Spending my nights with
Rosanne and David Letterman,
The months pass, scarring
My body with tattoos of
Devils and skulls
And doom. Years
Envelop me with
Fighting and rioting
While I desperately cling

(cont)

To an A.M. nostalgia
Of childhood *Looney Toons*.
My TV brings to me
A world of movies on
That amazing 12" screen:
The Postman (as no mail is
Delivered to me) *Braveheart*,
Goodfellas, *Training Day* (as my
Family fades away) *Six Days,
Seven Nights*, and *Donny
Brasco* (as I fall in love with
The beautiful Anne Hache). Decades
Gone behind. I've earned a college
Degree, but now need glasses
To see my TV's flickering,
Hazy grey screen—
Its images dulling,
Buttons malfunctioning
(My bones have begun aching,
My fatigued mind
Reminiscing—regretting—)
A world once so clear,
Now so difficult to see.
Though I still recall *Clerks*,
Mall Rats, *Pulp Fiction*, and
Reservoir Dogs, I've come to settle
More on CSPAN, TVW, and local
Evening news: I nearly cry,
But instead just sigh,
At reports of
Forests and trees becoming
Grey buildings and blacktopped
Streets nowhere for camping
Without paying fees—oh,
You ol' TV, revealing the
World awaiting me. Though
I still visit old friends,
In *South Park* now and then,
My mind and heart are tangled,
Seemingly strangled,

(cont)

By the images pouring
From my faithful TV: raging
Wars and civil unrest,
Iraq, Afghanistan, The Arab Spring
Homeland riots and protests
(Not so unlike Hong Kong)
WTO, BLM, The U.S. Senate,
All amidst a global pandemic—
My release date is drawing near.
My anxious mind contemplates
This thing, this TV—
How many Superbowls have
I seen (Elway, Manning,
Mahomes, and Brady—again?)
How many societal rifts?
Paradigm shifts?
Other prisoners (Black, white, brown)
See my old TV and ask,
"Man, how long you been down?"
I chuckle, yeah,
My ol' "bubble" television
Ain't no flat screen—
Like me, it's a relic
On a dying leg. Oh,
You ol' TV, if you'll please
Last just one more year,
From there, oh please,
From there, I'll soon be free—
Just one month away
From 2023....

Bennett

PAUL WATSKY
NOT MOTHER'S CUP O' TEA

Mostly a river of rocks and brush
after three mega-dry winters,

(cont)

the South Fork of the Trinity
this July gurgles baby-mild

against the undercut far bank,
a narrow channel isolated

by its broad morainic margin.
Noon heat crouches me

into mitigating shade beneath low
mulberry branches. Nature!

Mother's worst-hated enemy,
cornucopia of disease and injury,

mega-predator, perverse goddess,
male three-in-one whose middle tine

she dubbed *Creeping Jesus,*
two weeks before her century

all of them finally battered
that superannuated survivor down

for a final count and left her to die
of nothing special, after she'd repelled,

uncrippled, every overt assault
mounted by her heavily weaponized nineties:

two hips broken, one femur, three
endoscopies for an immense stone

lodged in her common bile duct,
followed by metastatic bowel cancer,

without post-resection chemo
or radiation because—Hah!—

(cont)

they deemed her too frail.
A five-year follow-up disclosed

no malignant cells anywhere
in so toxic a human petri dish,

let alone rebounding tumors, but
the wilds intimidated her. Busybodies

warned me I'd miss Mother if
I lived long enough to see an afterward.

Yet eight years past her grudging fade-out
(splendidly timed to ruin Thanksgiving),

Nature and I are doing fine,
at peace on this unimproved,

deserted inland beach, a place
she'd indubitably have loathed

for its disorderly, introverted rocks,
its unaccommodating attitude.

Watsky

TRISH ANNESE
AUNT CICELY…WHO KNITS

Aunt Cicely had a frame that Abigail loved to watch, and at the same time made her anxious as it wasn't just a body but also a curve of sinuous silk ribbon, at least, that is, when she closed her eyes and tried to picture Aunt Cicely arranged piquantly on a present or attached, fluttering, to a flagpole, which is where it seemed she belonged. Naturally, of course, you can become disoriented if you look at your aunt and there is a person standing there with blood and heart and bone instead of the insouciant and colorful banderole you've been imagining.

People who found it necessary to observe familial likeness insisted that Abigail and Aunt Cicely were two peas in a pod, which pleased Abigail, but when she looked in the mirror she didn't always recognize—or trust—their impressions, for Abigail was soft where Cicely was lean; all Abigail saw in the glass were her curves, and it was self-evident that Aunt Cicely did not have them.

Aside from these fleeting considerations, however, Aunt Cicely was just Aunt Cicely, someone Abigail loved and thought exciting and tended to follow from room to room when her aunt was in the mood for that sort of attention. Her mother always said Aunt Cicely was too exciting for her own good, and while she might have been right, Abigail thought she was probably just jealous of her husband's sometimes wayward youngest sister.

Aunt Cicely still worked at the same department store where she'd first been hired as a part-time salesclerk in high school. She began as a gift-wrap girl, creating lavishly styled bows customers adored until she was chastised for being wasteful, and moved to the jewelry counter where she stacked bracelets up her bare arms and layered necklaces in glimmering metal cowls at her throat. Finally, management assigned her to the children's department; there, she dressed the toy bears in charming but pricey children's ensembles. The night manager yelled until he realized customers bought the costumed creatures and relented. Eventually, she was paid a little bit extra to arrange in-store and window displays. When she graduated high school, she took on a full-time schedule until she became a manager and more recently, a buyer in the women's wear shop, injecting a shot of Bohemian style into the usually tired collections of pants with elastic bands and empire-waisted blouses with twee daisy bric-a-brac along their seams designed to secure and camouflage middle-aged bellies.

She'd been salaried and had just been made a buyer when the American mall began its inevitable decline, and stores that had been anchors in all of the good ways started going under. When the store where she'd worked half her life hosted its going-out-of-business sales, she moved from smaller retail chain to smaller retail chain until she was hired at a high-end boutique in the city, buying quirkily designed T-shirts that sold for one-tenth of the rent she paid for a studio apartment the size of our den. "It's good for Cicely to work," intoned her mother, and her father nodded in agreement, for what else could he do? Her mother went on: "Let's be honest; even if most of her pay goes toward rent and food, it's not as if she has anything better to do."

Aunt Cicely had been gone for almost six months, and Abigail's mother and father and Abigail herself moved around the old duplex in their established patterns, without Aunt Cicely to distract or entertain them. Abigail had slowly resigned herself to Aunt Cicely's absence, bidding solemn farewells to all the things they used to do together: toenail painting parties where her aunt lined up bottles of color on the dining room table and filled a plastic tub with warm water and flower petals and essential oils and called it a spa; front-step sits on warm summer nights where Aunt Cicely gestured with a cigarette poised between her forefingers, pointing out all of the little spaces that were just right for faeries to pass; late-night baking stunts in the kitchen where Cicely experimented with sprinkles and candied fruits and food coloring, leaving racks of cookies to cool and dry out on the counter, a riotously pink drink embellished with skewers of fruit and a brightly colored paper umbrella left half-finished as she snored on the living room couch. But then one evening, Cicely was standing under the light outside the front door with a screwed-up smile and a large purple suitcase—different from the one she'd left with—in her hand and she said:

"Knock, knock?"

"Who's there?" Abigail shrieked, making for her aunt before her mother could stop her.

"Owls say," Cicely replied.

"Owls say who?"

"Yes, they doooooooo!" cried Cicely as Abigail flung herself into her aunt's arms while her mother stood just inside the front hall, grimacing.

"Lights too bright, city too big," Cicely alluded to a favorite book with a shrug before heading up the stairs to the room that used to be hers. She'd had a drink or two; Abigail could smell it almost immediately.

They were all three so surprised by Cicely's sudden appearance they never got round to asking about anything but what was in the suitcase Cicely had abandoned at the bottom of the stairs. When it turned out it was full of craft beer and honey candies and pickled cauliflower and carrots and screen-printed T-shirts from the Brooklyn Flea, her mother invited the neighbors in the duplex next door to come over, and they crowded around the table in the kitchenette like hungry little piglets rooting for a teat. It was a small space, so the children lingered in the background while the adults sat around the table drinking bitter IPAs from the mason jars that had come wrapped in the T-shirts to deliberate over what had happened, as adults were wont to do. Of course, her mother had her ideas, and she wasn't shy about sharing them.

"You know, Cicely, they call it work for a reason. You don't apply for *a play*; you apply for a *job*," said her mother, and the room fell so silent you could hear the cicadas out the kitchen's screen door. It was such an incessant pulse that no one had noticed it until that moment. Outside loomed the lavender twilight of May where the breeze shushed through the burgeoning buds of forsythias and crab apple trees. Abigail sat with her back pressed against the heat of the dishwasher, the worn linoleum floor warm beneath her bare thighs; it had been a day hot enough for shorts. She had a honey stick in one hand, but she dared not slurp it, stilled as she was by the steel in her mother's tone.

Why someone would apply for a play was anyone's guess; it had to be an idea her mother had coined and thought clever, for her mother thought she was very clever indeed. At any rate, whatever her mother had meant by that portion of her observation, it was eminently apparent what her intention had been from her supercilious tone, and Abigail could see the mix of aggravation and shame competing for claiming rights on the landscape of Aunt Cicely's face. Its intensity was visceral, for Abigail could feel herself succumbing to its mix of resentment and humiliation; she had to shake herself as a reminder that her mother was not speaking to her.

"At least someone in this family knows how to have fun," Aunt Cicely pronounced, but her voice wavered and her eyes, which usually glittered, smoldered darkly as she finished her beer. "Good night, everyone," she announced and left the room. They thought she was headed to bed, but she had made her way into the backyard to smoke, letting the screen door slap closed behind her.

Her mother stood clenching her empty glass, but no one looked at her, and certainly no one had anything to say, so she barked at Abigail's father to wipe the table and directed Abigail to unload the dishwasher before retreating to the bathroom. Abigail knew she would wash her face with Noxzema and apply her Pond's lotion like it was 1978 before "gathering her chi" as she did every night. "Don't eat any more sweets," she barked at Abigail as an afterthought. Abigail and her father did as they were told. You would have thought they might speak to one another, but they never did, caught as they were in their own private recriminations. Abigail couldn't help but wonder how her father, a mild-mannered gentleman, had attached himself to her mother, but she had seen her mother's picture when she was a girl, so she didn't really have to guess; she also knew that the dances of adults were well beyond her ken—she'd read enough YA romance to know that relationships could be complicated.

Her mother worked as an administrative assistant in the travel agency downtown, processing paperwork for a ruggedly handsome supervisor named Joshua who trafficked in casual harassment that he shrugged off by ending every off-color observation or question with a guffaw and a "Just joshing you, right? Just *Joshing*." Her mother complained about him on days when she was especially incensed by his careless hands and loose tongue, but most of the time she seemed to like it and often reported that *Joshua* had promised her a raise, or *Joshua* had guaranteed her a promotion, or *Joshua* was planning on having her represent the company at a conference in some exotic locale. And though Abigail was young enough for her father to be sure she didn't understand a thing, she did understand that her mother was never going to receive any of the things she'd been promised, and she wondered if a price got paid in pursuit of their possibility. Almost immediately, her mother tried to convince Aunt Cicely to apply for a job at the agency's branch across town, but to no avail; Aunt Cicely was patently disinterested in her sister-in-law's life, even though she fully inhabited it. Naturally, there was no end to the muttering her mother did about this particular irony.

Instead, Aunt Cicely whiled away a handful of months in her room, staring blankly at her phone, texting with friends on occasion, and smoking out her window above the front porch where Abigail, on her way up the driveway after getting off the school bus, sometimes noticed her eyeing the handsome mailman from time to time. Sometimes, after dinner was finished and the dishes had been put away, and her mother and father and Abigail were in the TV room watching *Jeopardy*, they could hear Aunt Cicely exit the front door without saying goodbye, leaving the relentlessly fresh scent of a perfume she had mixed herself in her wake. It smelled of lemons, ginger, and something Aunt Cicely called "ylang-ylang." She would come home long after Abigail had turned off her light for the night, banging up the stairs, clattering into the bathroom, stumbling down the hall, before returning to her room where Abigail could hear Japanese pop music that Aunt Cicely explained to her was an homage to George Harrison circa "after the breakup."

One afternoon in September, Abigail arrived home after school to find Aunt Cicely sitting on the couch, clutching knitting needles and staring raptly at a video on her phone. Soon, roughly knit items appeared in the house in various colors, patterns, and styles: scarves came first, then afghans, then socks. Baby booties and blankets, winter hats, lightweight summer shawls, cowls, and skimpy knit halters. When Aunt Cicely learned to crochet, she added little animals with button eyes and funny outfits to her repertoire. She applied for and was accepted to an artist's fair where she sold out most of what she'd created by the end of the weekend, so she went home and made more. She joined a knitting circle where she made friends with other women and the occasional man who knit as voraciously as she did, and she spent less time in her room. Her mother rolled her eyes, but she couldn't complain because sometimes Aunt Cicely brought home groceries or vacuumed the living room carpet, humming. Her father was pleased, and although he knew enough not to let on, sometimes Abigail caught him watching Aunt Cicely magic her yarn with a mix of relief and delight. Aunt Cicely taught Abigail to crochet as well, and sometimes the two of them would sit and laugh and watch movies, and Abigail thought it felt like before and for quite some time, it was quite good.

Eventually, Cicely opened an online shop where she sold her creations—patterns and kits she put together herself, sitting on the floor in the tiny dining room, winding little balls of yarn left over from her own projects that she added to the mini collections she assembled for others. She taught online classes and tutorials and took on private students she coached at the dining room table, an enormous hutch Cicely had assembled from recycled wood pallets rising behind her, stuffed to the brim with yarn and needles and knickknacks. It occupied space in the dining room where the nail polish used to go for spa days, and one of the cats was always pulling at a loose end and gleefully unravelling it. In what seemed no time at all, the little duplex had become a hub of activity, and Abigail found herself resenting the gaggle of girls and young women who gathered to listen to podcasts and eat in her living room two, sometimes three nights a week. For the first time, Abigail felt a creeping solidarity with her mother.

At first, it had been fun to have a new hat for fall and a specially made scarf for winter, especially when Abigail could dictate the colors and the stitch and go to school and claim it was "bespoke" if classmates complimented her. But there are only so many knit items a school-age girl needs, and soon her inventory of clothing assembled from the industry of Cicely's obsession felt intrusive, expanding inside her closet to the exclusion of other items like the high-waisted jeans and crop tops Abigail had noticed her classmates wearing. One Friday morning, one of the girls at school noticed the third knit poncho Abigail had worn that week and whispered behind her hand to the boy whose locker was next to hers; both classmates erupted in laughter, grinning at her with barely concealed derision and carelessly knocking her shoulder when they passed into the classroom. Abigail had had enough.

When Cicely asked her if Abigail wanted her to crochet a cropped sweater for her for Christmas, Abigail politely declined, and inside she could feel a shift that she had previously thought impossible and couldn't quite name. Cicely looked hurt, but recovered quickly, laying herself out like a luxuriant stretch of velvet ribbon across the back of the couch as she reached for her knitting satchel. "Oh, but I've already started, Abigail," she exclaimed. She rummaged in her bag, extricating a delicately knotted blush confection that would have burnished Abigail's complexion beautifully had she worn it. "What can I say, Abigail? I'm a woman who knits!"

"I know," Abigail said deliberately. "You're a woman who knits."

And even though she was still very small despite being already in the sixth grade, her voice was so deep with disdain that at first Cicely thought she was teasing and giggled until it became clear she was alone in her laughter. Cicely stilled and sat upright, staring at her niece. Then, without another word, she pulled the garment to her, removed the delicate metallic hook from its finely executed loops and unraveled each stitch with a steady repetitive pull, not once taking her eyes from Abigail, who bolted from the room, both furious and afraid.

RED HAWK
WHAT WAS LEFT

When the White men came to slaughter
the Buffalo, they only took the tongues and fur,
left behind the rest to rot in the weather.

The old wizened Indian women who came
upon this scene of desolation were ashamed
at what they saw, at the bloody remains

rotting, and the Wolves and Crows circling.
They picked through what was left,
took horn and teeth and bone, dug out

the organ meats, the last to rot,
and sang the thanking songs,
and sprinkled corpse with sage

(cont)

and dust when no corn meal was left,
and they smoked the Woman-pipe
and when it was their time to starve

they stripped naked like the Buffalo
and lay down barren in the snow;
this was their sacred letting go.

With what was left of breath,
they sang the tremolo
to honor the Lord of Death.

(historical footnote: This poem is a compilation of many such events which occurred during the U.S. Army's genocidal campaign against the native tribal nations, part of which aimed to exterminate the Buffalo as a food source, thus starving the combatants. The sacraments described here were common to many tribes, though it was the Whitehead Society of the Lakota—the old crones—who were the pipeholders of the Woman-Pipe).

Red Hawk

THE DIFFERENCE BETWEEN A WOLF AND A DOG

A dog will fetch a thrown stick;
a wolf will turn to see who threw it,
will bare its fangs, and come for you
on the dead run, the wind in its coat.
On command a dog will do a trick;
under pain of death a wolf won't do it,
won't obey your commands, but will ignore you
then go for your throat.

A dog won't bite the hand from which it feeds;
a wolf will fight until it bleeds
to death in order to remain free,
will chew through its leg when caught in a trap,
drag itself to heal beneath some distant tree,
and on 3 legs then, forage for carrion scrap.
A dog will wear a collar and answer to a name.
Some scholar will write a history affixing blame

for the extinction of the wolf, why it was not saved,
while dogs are just one more thing humans have enslaved.

Red Hawk

RUBY BONNELL HAWKINS
WE ARE SURVIVORS

Grandma is blind, she rocks the babies
And places vinegar paper on mama's head
When she has a headache
We get by
We walk to the school bus and it's cold
Mama is a wreck and it's no wonder
Kids and a blind mother trying to keep
Body and soul together
We live on grandma's old-age pension
And the few dollars daddy gives us
Mama screams and curses
Holds a knife to her throat and
Threatens to kill herself
She's a crazy woman but she's all we have
And we get by
When the bean pot is empty and potato bin bare
I walk the trail to daddy's house
When his wife leaves the room
I ask him for money
Most of the time he gives me a few dollars
I walk up the trail to Robert Bridges' store
And buy pinto beans, mama will go later for potatoes
They're too heavy for me to carry
But we get by
It's bad at home but it's where I want to be
Relatives visit and ask me to go home with them
I don't want to but I go
To leave more food for the others
When I'm fourteen I meet a nice young man
He asks mama if I can marry him
And I do to have a safe home, because I love him
And to leave more food for the others
Mama married again and had one more child
Mama raised all six of her children
Then lived alone in her little house for many years

(cont)

She died at age eighty-seven
We all went home every year for the holidays
And on mama's birthday
As her children grew up mama became calmer
When her last child married, she worked as a nursemaid
To old ladies and came home every weekend
Our childhood was hurtful
But we got by
Mama did it, raised all her children and saw them married
Saw grandchildren and great-grandchildren grow up
She loved us all
She lived in the same house for sixty years
She met no strangers, everyone loved mama
Our daddy died at age fifty-two
Mama's youngest child retires this year
We're all alive and kicking
Our childhood made us strong
We are survivors

Hawkins

THE SMOOTH BROWN PATH

I still can see the crooked path
From kitchen door to creek
Where every evening after school
My boys took their trek
On doubled arms the baby rode
Safe in his brothers keep
To see the creek go rushing by
And all the things which round it thrived

The minnows swimming by in droves
Green frogs plopping off the logs
Dragonflies soloing by
Hawks gliding across the sky
These are few among the gifts
My children gave to me
To hold within my heart for all eternity
They give my life a special spark
That lights my way when days are dark

Hawkins

DEMONS

I've battled demons all my life
Lost almost every round
A mother good with gentle tongue
Is all I wished to be
But words as swift as arrows came
To bruise young tender souls
And I would battle every day
And cry such bitter tears
I stood as tall as I could stand
I fought so hard and long
Always to be beaten down
The demons are so strong
And now my sons are grown up men
And have lives of their own
They look at me with loving eyes
In spite of all I've done
And yet I see the tender spots
Where hateful words have flown
And I can never call them back
Tho I would give my soul
My head is bowed and bloodied
I'm beaten to the ground
I wish I would not rise again
These demons in me always win
They are so very strong

Hawkins

DON STOLL
QUARANTINE

Cora tried to strike a balance between the desire for affection from the detainees and the knowledge that their affection would complicate her work. The first smile or the first tender touch by a detainee would put her in mind of a long-ago February morning. On that morning, a songbird's trill had shocked her out of the trance induced by the shuffling of her boots—ill-fitting hand-me-downs from a cousin she hoped she would never see again—through the snow's gray melt. Looking up, she had seen a blur as the bird took wing from its perch on a leafless branch. For Cora, the dark nakedness of the branch had evoked her great-grandmother as she struggled to claw her way out of the bathtub. Without Cora's help, she would have died there. The sky had sagged like the old woman's flesh and with the same color of defeat as the snow. The bird's vividness had been startling against the background. The first cardinal of the year meant that spring was coming. But it was a long way off.

Cora did her best to be understanding of the detainees who never showed affection. She knew that none of them were happy there. She also knew that a person's unhappiness tends to spill out onto other people. But most of the detainees understood that this wasn't her dream job. They also knew that she'd had nothing to do with putting them there. For these reasons, she thought, most of them tried to limit the spillover of their misery onto her. They looked at her as being almost in the same boat with them: a fellow sufferer deserving, if not affection, at least a modicum of respect. Or tolerance, coming from the detainees who felt so defeated that they couldn't muster respect.

Toward those who showed affection, she strove for a professional approach. She would remind them that affection was natural since they had no one else. But she would also point out that even if they had no one else, for her there were fifteen others, so they would do well to fight their natural impulses.

She was assigned to 113 through 128. 117 had a tendency to become extremely affectionate. She hated doing it, but when he got like that, she would tell him about the man in 115 and the other one in 120. Neither was as affectionate as 117, but close enough for her to make the point. 117 would weep and apologize and Cora would console him.

Every time she consoled him, she ran the risk that her kindness would strengthen his attachment to her. She would rest a hand on his shoulder. She would caress it just enough to be reminded that he'd had all the time in the world to do pushups and build muscle, but—she hoped—not long enough to give him the idea that she liked the way it felt. He would have time to build a lot more muscle. There wasn't much else he could do with himself. She would watch for him to reach up for her hand so that she could pull away in time.

But as time passed, she felt herself becoming increasingly adept at reading all the ones she was assigned to and at calibrating her responses to them. What she saw in 117 was not the gradual strengthening of his attachment that she had worried about in the beginning. Instead, she saw an ebb and flow. And because 117 was fundamentally a good man, she thought, his ebb never went as far as hostility, or even coolness. It would stop at respectful. Respectful seemed to her ideal under the circumstances. It didn't mean that respectful was ideal, period. Her absolute ideal was something more. But to seek it in these circumstances would have been foolish.

Under the circumstances she considered herself lucky to have been assigned to 113 through 128. Conversation with her co-workers was discouraged, and getting caught associating with any of them outside of work would have cost her the job. But in the few moments they had together just before and just after work, there was time to pass back and forth not only cigarettes, but the odd remark. The man assigned to 193 through 208 was an emotional wreck because more than half of his were like 117 and he had a hard time detaching himself from their feelings. The woman assigned to 481 through 496 had it nearly as bad. For Cora, the only problems like those two had were with 115, 117, 120, and—a little— 127, so she couldn't complain.

On the other hand, there was 124. She never spoke to her co-workers about 124. She preferred to listen in the hope of hearing that one of them had someone similar. But she never heard of anything like it. There were of course many instances of violence. Cora had never experienced one of these. Perhaps oddly, she gave little thought to the certainty that, if she kept the job long enough, one day she would. But she couldn't see why she ought to worry since the resources put into observation were such that the violence could never go far. Whenever a detainee turned violent, the guards would react instantly. Within seconds they would seize the offender for permanent removal.

Cora did not like thinking about what would happen to the detainee after that. She thought the guards acted more harshly than they needed to—because they enjoyed it, it seemed to her—and she worried that, wherever the offender was being taken, once he got there the treatment would be even worse. She wasn't sure that anyone deserved that. But at least the vigilance of the guards meant that she didn't need to worry about serious injury.

124 wasn't that kind of problem, anyway. She had never thought that 124 might turn violent. However, 124's spite was such that Cora thought maybe she ought to act spiteful in return. She wished she could rise above her spite and show herself to be better. Except she would think about what it meant to want to be better. Didn't *that* sound spiteful, putting

yourself above somebody else? She wondered what right she had to put herself above 124. He had it hard. She would never want to be in his situation. But suppose she didn't try to be better than 124. Suppose that, instead, she simply let herself sink into her own spite. That wouldn't be good, either.

Upon reaching this point of finding her thoughts going in circles, Cora would tell herself to stop thinking. She would remind herself that 124 was a job, like the other fifteen. Her job was to put in her thirty minutes and then put 124 out her mind as far as possible as she moved on to her thirty minutes with 125. And if 124 was unpleasant, at least it came almost at the end of her shift, with only the simple respect of 125, 126, and 128 left to deal with. Plus 127, who had a tendency to become attached, but a pretty mild one.

Cora would tell herself, upon joining 124, to take a professional approach. She would enter. He would not acknowledge her. She would remove the standard-issue blue jumpsuit with the zipper down the front that made it easy to slip on and off. She would lie on her back, on top of the covers as he preferred. He would position his head to the right of hers, his face buried in the pillow. They never looked into one another's eyes. In less than a minute, they would be done.

She knew it took less than a minute because she would glance at her watch when she wasn't studying the ceiling. The exposed beams were the room's only interesting features. But they held limited interest because they had been painted white like everything else.

He would get off of her immediately. He would tell her she could leave, not looking at her face as he spoke. She would remind him, as she got out of bed to put her jumpsuit on, that it was her job to change the sheets. She would add that she wasn't free to leave. In fact, she had twenty-eight minutes and some seconds left.

She would drag out the changing of the sheets for as long as she could. But twenty-eight minutes would have been impossible. She found that by trying to make the bed as meticulously as she had read was required of some members of the military in some countries, she could take as long as five minutes. She always carried a coin with her for this purpose. She would finish making the bed, having pulled the covers as tight as her strength would permit. Then she would raise her arm above her head. She would drop the coin on the bed. It never bounced. But the labor had eaten up five minutes, so now she had twenty-three to go.

It was during those twenty-three minutes that her time with 124 became excruciating. He would turn away as if she had done nothing for him. This angered her because she knew that satisfying himself with her had to be better than satisfying himself alone. The proof was that he could have told her she wasn't needed. He could have told her to keep her jumpsuit on and to lie on the bed by herself for the thirty minutes. He never did that. Yet he would turn away from her to go back to doing what he had been doing when she entered. He would sit in the only chair in the room. He would face his desk and not speak.

She would prepare for those twenty-three minutes by bringing a book. She wanted to read everything Toni Morrison had written. Her books were increasingly hard to find, so Cora had made sure to buy every single one—used, when she could—before it became impossible. She had expected the guards to question her about her reading material, but they never said a word. They probably didn't know the name. But Cora had played it safe by tearing off any back cover or inside page that showed her picture.

If she loved the book she was reading at home, she would bring that one. If she didn't love it, she would look for one she had loved in the past and bring that. She would easily find her favorite passages because she had the habit of using a pen to make asterisks in the margins.

Yet no matter how much she loved the book, new or old, it didn't help. The magic she had found in the book at home, or in the bus on her way to work, would vanish when she was with 124. She would get through a couple of pages, barely noticing what she had read. Then she would close the book.

She would look at her watch. She would do that often. She wondered if looking at her watch made those twenty-three minutes pass even more slowly. Yet she couldn't help it since there was nothing else to do. In the beginning she would sometimes set the alarm on her watch and close her eyes and try to sleep. But it had never worked, so she had given up. She would stare at 124's back, marveling at his spitefulness and wondering how he could think she deserved it since she was practically in the same boat with him as a fellow sufferer.

Exactly a month into the job, Cora decided that she couldn't take it anymore. She didn't feel worse than she had any other day, but she thought that a month was enough. Maybe the job market was worse than ever, but even being out of work couldn't be as bad as doing this five times a week. She couldn't keep telling herself that enduring 124 wasn't so bad. Never mind that she had been lucky with the other fifteen and she was with him only two and a half hours out of the hundred and sixty-eight hours in a week. True, that made less than two percent. But that two percent was what she found herself thinking about most of the rest of the time.

She made a plan. She would finish her shift. She would march to her supervisor's office to say that she wouldn't be back the next day.

"What's your problem?" she said to 124 on that day that would be her last one on the job.

She had prepared herself for whatever ugly response he might give. The satisfaction of knowing that she would never see him again would get her through the ugliness.

"Is it because I'm black?" she said. "The ones who couldn't stand doing it with blacks were supposed to be filtered out for us. They were supposed to be set up with Hispanics or Asians. But I haven't done anything to you, so what else could it be?"

Cora thought about herself and her co-workers: blacks, Hispanics, Asians. No white people doing the job, of course. What other proof could you ask for that giving the detainees this service was not about treating them with some humanity? The point of the service had to be to humiliate blacks, Hispanics, and Asians by giving them the kind of work they were suited for.

She saw a flicker of movement in 124's shoulders. She thought he was going to turn around. But after the flicker there was nothing.

"Say something, dammit. Maybe I *have* done something to you. Did we know each other before? Did I do something to you that I don't remember? If I did, I'm sorry, but…. Look, I can't even give a real apology if I don't know what I did. Could you tell me?"

He didn't move.

"Maybe what I did was so bad you won't even accept an apology? Fine, I won't try to apologize. But just tell me what it was. No matter how bad it was, I deserve to know."

She got up. She walked toward him and stopped behind him. During the entire month, she had never been this close to him before except in bed. He didn't move. His chair had wheels. That was funny because she had never seen him use them. His upper body would move when he wrote or read, but the chair had always remained as still as if it were nailed to the floor.

Cora gripped the back of the chair. As she dragged it away from the desk, he looked up at her. As she made a wrenching motion with her arms to send the chair spinning across the room, he swore. He stamped his feet on the floor to stop the chair's movement. Then he jerked his head back as she came close to him, thrusting her face in his and forcing him to look straight into her eyes as he had always refused to do when he lay on top of her in bed.

"I've told you my name is Cora, but do you even remember? I think you believe that we're not individuals who deserve to have our own names."

She straightened up.

"Well, too bad. I'm telling you again that my name is Cora."

She crossed her arms.

"You have a name, too. What is it?"

He mumbled something.

"What?"

She was shocked. She had thought he would never speak.

"I'm sorry," she said quietly. "I didn't hear. Could you say it again?"

"124," he said, looking her in the eye. "The government says I'm 124."

"Fuck the government."

He shook his head.

"Very brave," he said. "That's 'Fuck the government' as in, 'They can't tell me what to do'? But I know you don't like doing this, so obviously they can. So, what's the point of your little show of defiance? The guards can see and hear everything we do, but you think they're impressed? They're laughing at you, Cora."

She hated hearing that the guards were laughing at her even though she knew it was true.

"That was 'Fuck the government' as in, 'I don't care what the government calls you.' And you think I don't understand that the government can tell me what to do? I wanted to go to college. But once the government started making it almost impossible to get financial aid—"

"Especially for people of your 'persuasion.'"

124 cleared his throat.

"You wanted to go to college?" he said. "To study what?"

"I love to read. You've seen me read. I wanted to be an English teacher."

"Good. There are never enough English teachers. But what about History?"

"History?" she said.

"If we had more History teachers, maybe this stuff would never have happened."

He spread his arms and looked around the room.

"I love architecture too," she said. "I thought a little about being an architect."

"Great," he said with more enthusiasm than she thought her foolish dreams deserved.

"Anyway, now I do this."

124 looked down.

"But I'm okay," she said. "And there's no justice in what they're doing to you, either."

She tried to look into his eyes again but he looked away.

"As bad as what they're doing to you is, at least you get this service. The gays get nothing."

She didn't feel right about saying that.

"You don't have to be grateful for any of this," she said.

She hesitated.

"How long have you been here?"

"A month," he said. "You're the first one they've sent to—"

"How much longer? 114's been here a month, and he gets out in a week."

"Five weeks total? Vacation, probably. It's not so bad for the ones who were on vacation."

He stood and walked the chair back to the desk.

"I didn't mean that five weeks here is okay."

"114 was in Italy," Cora said.

"Nice. But I have five more years. If I can take it."

Cora checked her watch. Her thirty minutes would be up soon.

"Cora?"

"Yes?"

"That jumpsuit's a nice color on you. A nice blue."

She looked down at the loose-fitting fabric.

"Royal blue," she said. "And I sure feel like royalty in it."

They laughed.

"You want to talk more tomorrow?" she said.

She had decided that if 124 had another five years in quarantine, she could last a little longer. She looked at the ceiling as if good ideas for conversations might be written there.

"You could tell me about living outside the country. I've never been anywhere else."

She looked at the ceiling again. Then she looked at 124.

"You could tell me about the places you lived."

"One of them was Italy. You love architecture? I could tell you about the old buildings."

"I'd like that," she said, turning toward the door and the guard's knock.

"Guards are punctual," she said. "They expect me to be punctual too."

124 smiled grimly.

"The idea that I could infect my countrymen with 'foreign ideas' because I lived abroad for five years is outrageous," he said.

#

The next morning a guard told Cora that 124 would be off of her schedule for a couple of days. The time would be needed to process a new occupant to replace the former one. During the night, the former occupant had hanged himself with a bedsheet.

The guard talked and talked. Cora didn't hear until he said something about architecture.

"A thing in architecture?" she said. "What's a thing in architecture?"

"Form follows function. That's a thing in architecture, right?"

He grinned.

"There's a reason the ceiling beams were left exposed."

LINDA HUGHES
THE SHAPE OF MY SKIN

I have things I don't want to let go.
Boxes of scribbles on scraps of paper
and filled note books.
Clothes I like, some I don't
but keep.
Dishes I don't use.
The mirror that held my mother's image,
my grandmother's, now mine.

A huge chifforobe follows me
into houses large and small.
Memories of pets and people,
experiences good and bad.
A bank account, my name.

(cont)

This menagerie of life's rituals
clings to me and I to them.
I have gathered these around.
They hold me in,
surround me like a skin.

Someday all will be tossed.
When I have nothing to say,
no need to cling.
Sold on eBay or in a yard sale.
This cup, these shoes,
that seashell.

The bird calling, doesn't know
it was mentioned
when we said its name.

Neither will I.

Hughes

CARMINE LOMBARDO
SOLILOQUY OF A LOW THIEF

18TH CENTURY

Jim Griggs' my name—
A low thief I am,
Who lives on the things I steal.
My parients—simple, ignorant folk—
Labored for ev'ry meal.
I growed in the streets
Quite loose and fast,
And made low crime my trade.
My parients, so poor,
Could never show
How fortunes could be made.
I shall always blame my parients for not edycating me. Had
I been liberally edycated...

(cont)

By God, it's my belief
With all the talent in my head,
I'd be a bigger thief.
I believe they call 'em defaulters.
I wouldn't swipe the petty loot
Like watches, rings and such,
Why I would have the princely sums
Right at my fingers' touch—
Thousands, hundreds of thousands!
The law would never reach me.
I'd be too shrewd to catch.
I'd get elected governor
And let 'em all go scratch.
Then you'd see.
I'd ride home in my carriage
To the house that suckers built.
I'd swill my gin and sugar
And revel in my guilt.
An investigation might be made, and some of the noosepapers
might come down heavy, but me, they would spare,
Cause I would have the money,
And the party boys would swear
That all was on the up and up.
The public? Would they care?
NO!
Money is the ruler
That buys you anything.
People beckon at your feet
And treat you like a king.
You get away with murder,
Fraud, embezzlement—
The power of those thousands
To my measly cent
But alas, unedycated
I'm only a wretched thief—
Taker of watches, rings and such
Headin' for prison's grief.
Oh, that I's been edycated
Liberally, liberally edycated!

(cont)

EPILOG—21st CENTURY

Three hundred years have passed
And like ol' Jim,
Things haven't changed.
It's still the same.
Money's still king,
And it rules the game.
Now they steal your identity
No matter how old—
Don't need to be edycated
To pocket your gold.
Treacherous it has become—
The times we live.
There are certain sins
Even God won't forgive.

Lombardo

ERIC SOMMER
LIFT TICKETS, PLEASE

On a day like today, Patterson Reece was kicking it hard into high gear.

Face it: life as bike messenger in Chicago wasn't worth a whole lot. The lawyers who wrote the stuff he carried were, as far as he was concerned, made as much sense as the Family Law Court judges who kept threatening him. Same ones hounding him for the child support he owed his ex. He was either a payment behind or one day away from a 30-day stretch in The Cook County Detention Facility on South State. Reese had never been ahead of the game.

He couldn't keep track of it all.

And he'd had a pounding headache for the past two weeks. She was calling the CPS every day looking for more money, and it was only a matter of time before he was back inside. He should never have been at that downhill skier's party five years ago in Aspen.

For Patterson it'd been one regret trip after another.

Now speeding down Diversey toward Halston, he had in his

courier bag his salvation: a $400 super rush express NOW NOW NOW delivery job that would bring his payments current, keep him free for another month and give him some beer money.

At Diversey he turned a sharp right onto Clark and let it all out. Superior Court was 3 miles dead ahead, it was 4:11 p.m. and he could make the filing just in time, with a little room to spare. Just enough for the $500 bonus which would make this day a score and bonus even the Chicago Black Hawks could appreciate.

He was flying along the center lane now, not too much traffic, ripping down the clean asphalt which was only going to last for another mile or so before it turned into a ripped-up construction job site for some sewer nonsense Cook County was always thinking up….

Patterson Reese let out a string of obscenities that singed his eyebrows: an Anheuser-Busch truck pulled in front of him out of nowhere, and now he was in the construction zone he dreaded. Traffic started to slow. He couldn't hit the sidewalks—too many police—his head was pounding with a vengeance and as he scanned the lanes and traffic…. He saw ahead of him, on the back of the Busch truck, a scene he knew so well in Aspen.

His eyes locked onto the huge poster now directly, and dangerously, in front of him. The snow, the skis, the impossible blue sky and white, white snow….

The sounds of the traffic, horns, wind and whistles faded into silence. He could only see the panorama ahead. The wind washed his face, the rush of the traffic, horns, tires braking, the smell of carbon monoxide, the swirling exhaust dissolved molecule by molecule into nothing....

He can't let go: the white slopes against a deep blue sky, a new snowfall trail. It is right in front of him. Untouched, waiting for the right moment to reveal its secrets to the lonely high mountain skier…the evergreens are heavy with fresh snow, and there is a wisp of snow trail, so fine, so delicate, so barely visible coming off the mountain wind-side. The panel is a photographic marvel, clear, shimmering in the gritty surroundings, a perfect escape hatch there on the back of a beer delivery truck in the middle of rush hour in Chicago. Patterson cannot take his eyes off it. He cannot escape.

The tires screech, the smashing sounds of metal on metal explode into a deafening roar. The truck has come to an abrupt stop but Patterson Reece, still in the picture, unable or unwilling to come back to the real world, plows into the back of the truck at around 60 miles an hour.

By the time the crowds are cleared, and the Chicago PD has

secured the area, all they find is a terribly mangled courier bike and an empty courier bag. The back of the truck shows no sign of the horrific impact: there is no blood, no body, no Patterson Reese. There isn't anything—not a dent, not a scratch—yet something *has* changed: the picture on the truck has changed.

Been altered.

It clearly shows the magnificent mountain panorama, the fresh snow on the evergreens…but now it includes the image of a lonely high mountain skier, shooting powder, far, far down the mountain.

ALAN MARSHALL CLARK
WAITING FOR THE GAS MAN

What worrisome things hang on when it's ice-
cold winter and the tank is dry and every
electric dollar spent only reconfirms that
the "pay no heed for tomorrow" folks are as
few as ever, and you're not one of them.

But then he arrives in his big fat truck and
Tyrone flies out his little cat door and now
the tank is thank god full again and all
the heaters cranking lovely, hellish heat,
and the sun is high noon high and the world
is white and grey-blue-yellow shadowed and
what's lingered of that young-old faith is back.

And now Ty is back in my lap as the day
picks back up almost where we'd left it,
before the visitation, re-begins with thanks,
and everything once again seems possible.

Clark

JENNIFER CAMPBELL
ABOUT THE TWO FELLED ADIRONDACK CHAIRS
FROZEN ON THE PATIO

I know what it looks like.
I'm sure the neighbors
think we've given up the act,
upper-middle order upended,
refused the fire pit and tucked away Tiki bar.

Not a failing, these light chairs
stay the course all winter,
whether frozen upside down
or blown across the yard,
reminders of endurance
and a touch of madness.

They are snow rulers
and weather barometers,
perches for the birds that decide
it is mild enough to stay.
Bark-brown, the plastic chairs have a place
against green or white.

And my husband and I watch them,
out the window, through
the sliding door, reporting
on their micro movements,
certain the toppled seats will remain
for the next time we desire to fill them.

Campbell

JIM BEANE
A PRICE FOR PICKLES

First thing I see when I walk into Gold's Deli on Saturday morning
is Officer Monahan manhandling a kid from the neighborhood. He's got

the kid pressed up against the lineup of shopping carts by the front door. Today, August 19, 1969, is my birthday. I am seventeen years old and working on my birthday to earn money so I won't have to work my senior year of high school. It is hellish hot in the city in August and everything simmers. Cops against the colored makes tempers flare, both sides. Monahan looks ready to erupt. Fat Sammy, my boss, stands in front of the deli counter, wringing his sausage fingers and smirking at the tussle. The bakery ladies act afraid but sneak peeks around the corner of their display. John the fish man, Izzy the butcher, Darrell and Freddie the stock boys don't come in until ten, and they never show up early. Alma, the morning cashier, leans into Mister Gold outside his office. No one is at her register. She is upset and Mister Gold is patting her back. No one sees me. No one knows it's my birthday.

Two older colored men follow me inside and huddle up in Aisle One. They lean on their canes and talk in whispers, sneaking glances at Monahan's handling of the kid. A woman, a regular customer I recognize, is frozen beside the fresh vegetables, staring. I see the kid's face more clearly. The other kids call him GT. His grandmother calls him George Thomas. Officer Monahan is overwhelming, and GT ends up face-smushed on the tops of the rack of carts.

"Don't rough that boy like that," one of the men from Aisle One chirps.

Monahan glances at the pair of old men and presses GT's cheek against the plastic cart handles. He uses the open palm of his meaty hand to lean on GT's head while he uses his other hand to hold GT's wrists behind the boy's back. GT is wearing jeans, black Chucks, and a baggy white T-shirt. He wears his Afro picked out. I wonder where his grandma is.

"Leave that boy alone," the other man says. He speaks louder than the first man. Both are twice Monahan's age.

"Police business," Monahan says. "This don't concern you." His free hand dismisses them, and I see how red his face and arms are from the heat. Sweat stains streak his shirt.

The woman by the vegetables leaves her cart and heads for the exit. But she knows me, so she stops next to me and moves close. I am a familiar face, a kid, someone who works behind the deli counter at Gold's Kosher Grocery. She looks up at me.

"It's all right," I say. I don't know what else to say.

To the old Jews, like this woman, I am a face without a name. I am a goy, so I am relegated to making sandwiches for the colored customers. Fat Sammy handles the kosher crew. It's cool. Mister Gold treats me fair, and I don't mind working. I drive my uncle's old '62 Ford Falcon as a result, and that car has set me free.

"No. No. It is not all right," the woman says. "Alma was robbed." She points her finger at GT. "Alma opens her register to give change, and that boy grabs the money from the tray and runs out the door. Who does such a thing?"

Not him, I think, but I don't bother to say it. I've seen GT's grandma keep him close, so it's weird seeing him without her. But it's not really my business. I know GT and his grandma from the store, that's all. I know lots of people in that same way.

"And *those* people," the woman says. She hits my arm to get my attention and points to the two colored men in Aisle One.

My mother uses *those people* when she wants to make sure Pop and I know who she's ranting about, and how *those people* have trashed her city. My old man joins right in, and pretty soon they are both blaming *those people* for everything happening to their world. I just go along. I mean, look at Mister Gold. He keeps Darrell and Freddie working in the basement of the store so his old loyal customers from the neighborhood will not have to deal with *those people.*

"Did you see GT take the money?" I ask.

"Well…no. But Alma screaming, Mister Gold running. My God, who does such a thing?"

I look at Mister Gold and Alma outside his office. Gold's a skinny guy with sloped shoulders and thinning hair he combs over a bald spot. He walks with a limp. I drift toward the shopping carts for a better look.

"Keep moving, son," Monahan says to me.

The city's swamp heat clings to me like second skin. Gold's air conditioning does nothing to cool things down. I move closer.

"Police business," Monahan says. He raises his voice. "Shove off." He jerks GT's wrist upward behind the kid's back and lifts.

"Stand up straight, boy," he barks. "Let's go." Monahan muscles GT toward Mister Gold and Alma. GT drags his feet and scuffs his Chucks on the worn linoleum.

"This him?" Monahan says to Alma.

Alma looks ready to faint. She comes from Russia and speaks little English. Leaning close to GT, she squints and studies the boy's face. Abruptly, she turns away from Monahan and faces Mister Gold.

"Not him," she says.

"What d'ya mean, not him?" Monahan says. "I seen him runnin' across the lot." Monahan's face is red and getting redder.

Alma takes a longer look at GT.

"Not him," she says again.

Monahan looks like a heart attack about to happen.

"You were runnin' after him," he says to Gold. "Down Longfellow. And he ends up caught, by me, tryin' to hide behind the Amoco. He's the one, right?" Monahan's gaze passes from Alma to Gold and back to Alma.

"Not him," she says.

Mister Gold raises his hands as if the matter is settled. Monahan is flabbergasted and can't talk. Finally, he collects himself and spits out, "But it could be him. Right?" He shoves GT a little closer to Alma and slaps the kid's arm to get him to look up.

Alma shakes her head slowly. Her fingers go to her mouth. Monahan shakes his head and speaks to Mister Gold.

"How 'bout you, Mister Gold?" he says. "Get a look at the guy?"

"No," Mister Gold says. "I heard Alma scream and came to the front, but by the time I was there, the thief was gone."

"Why'd you run?" Monahan jerks GT.

"Exercise," GT says. Monahan cuffs the kid on the ear with his open hand.

"You think this is funny, smart-ass?"

"No. I think you grabbed me 'cause I'm Black and I was running."

"All right," Monahan says. "That's enough outta you. Let's go. We'll see how smart you are at the station." Bit of a crowd has developed. Me, Mister Gold, Alma, GT, Monahan, the two old colored men, and Sammy. Monahan draws his nightstick, uses it to push me aside.

"Get outta my way," he says.

"Alma said it wasn't him," I say.

"Son, back away before you get in trouble."

"I'm not your son."

"Barry." I feel Mister Gold's presence behind me. "Let the police do their job."

"Alma says it's not GT."

Mister Gold touches my shoulder. "Go punch in, Barry," he says. "The police will take care of things."

Monahan unclips his walkie-talkie, brings it to his mouth, and starts talking. He ushers GT to the front doors and makes him sit on the floor with his back pressed against the carts. Monahan hovers over GT.

It's quiet as church for what seems forever until Darrell walks in.

Mirror shades cover his eyes and a leather strap corrals his afro. Thick mutton chop sideburns flare on his cheeks and a Fu Manchu droops from his upper lip to his chin. He's wearing his Army fatigue jacket. A peace sign is inked beside his name stenciled above the breast pocket. Darrell jerks the shades off.

"What you doing on the floor, son?" he asks GT.

Monahan looks out the plate-glass windows as if Darrell doesn't exist. Darrell reaches down, takes GT by the elbow, and helps the kid to his feet.

"Hey, what are you doing?" Monahan says. "Hands off. This suspect is waiting for transport."

"Suspect?" Darrell says. He dusts the boy off and gently pushes him toward the exit door.

Monahan is slow to realize what is happening; he is paying too much attention to Darrell, and GT takes off. Monahan makes a grab, but Darrell pretends to step in his way, and the interference lasts long enough for GT to scoot out the front doors.

"Stop," Monahan shouts.

But by then, GT is gone.

Darrell heads into the store, past Monahan, as if he were beginning any day. Monahan grabs his arm, and before Darrell can jerk free, Monahan clicks one cuff around Darrell's wrist and then the other.

"You are under arrest, smart guy," Monahan says.

"For what?"

"Obstructing justice. Resisting arrest. Name it. I'm fed up with you people. C'mon, I'm taking you in."

"*You people*?" Darrell huffs. "Who the hell is 'you people'?"

Monahan's mouth closes in a thin line. His hand rests on his nightstick.

"Enough," Mister Gold shouts. "This is over. Release my employee. No one is pressing charges against the boy or this man."

Monahan removes his cap and wipes his brow. As slow as possible and making sure he sends a pain message, Monahan uncuffs Darrell. He points his finger at Darrell and pulls the trigger. Darrell doesn't blink. Monahan slips out the front doors.

Mister Gold raises his hands and signals everyone back to their business. He touches my shoulder and directs me toward the deli counter. When he's sure I am on track, he signals Freddie from the top step of the cellar stairs to join Darrell and him by the office. Alma has disappeared. Mister Gold finishes talking with Darrell and Freddie and sends them on.

They walk away without talking and head for the stairs leading to the cellar.

Darrell stops on the top stair and scans the store. He does this a hundred times a day. But this time, Freddie appears from below and throws one arm over Darrell's shoulder to ease him down the stairs. I am glad they have each other.

On breaks, I always drift down to the cellar and hang out with them. They are not like anyone I know. They are men, Black men, and I like being with them. When I'm perched on a pickle barrel, listening to Freddie's transistor radio hanging from the floor joists blasting WOL soul music, I enter a different world than the one I live in. I bum Kools and smoke them to the filter, crush the butts on the bottom of my shoe, and flick them onto the damp floor like Darrell does. I try to be noticed by them, but mostly I feel invisible. Yet still, for reasons I don't quite understand, I like being with them.

But for now, I go to work behind the counter with Sammy. I catch Sammy smirking. I can tell he can't wait to spit something out at me.

"Sooner or later GT will get what he deserves," Sammy says. "They all do." He goes on to further his point for about the millionth time, that if Gold would move the registers away from the front doors, a kid like GT would never attempt a grab-and-run. Sammy rolls his fat head on his fat neck and blows out a breath of exasperation.

"What makes you so sure GT did it?" I ask.

Sammy looks incredulous, like how could I be so stupid.

"You're kidding, right? He looks guilty, Barry. They all look guilty. Can't you see that?"

"Did you see him take the money, Sammy?"

"Ahhh," Sammy says. "You and your *schvartzes*."

I pull the chain and a new number appears. I call it out.

A colored teenager steps to the counter. He leans on the glass and orders pastrami on white bread with mayo, lettuce, and hot peppers.

"Gimme two pickles," he says.

"Extra nickel," I say. The kid mumbles something. I add "+ 5 cents" to the price on the white paper wrap and hand him the sandwich with two pickles. He glares at Sammy before he spins away. Sammy gives pickles to his white customers all the time, but never to the colored, and he's not hiding it.

I pull the chain and call the next number. The overhead lights hum and buzz. A transistor radio echoes from one of the aisles.

A colored bus driver who comes in every day after his shift ends steps up to the counter and orders his usual carry-out corned beef sandwich. A transistor radio bulges his uniform shirt pocket. Soft soul music fills the space between us. He tosses his number on the counter.

Darrell appears at the top of the stairs and watches me.

"Hey, man, you all right?" the driver says.

"Sure," I say. But after today, I'm not so sure anymore.

Before I wrap the driver's sandwich, I shove two extra pickles in next to the sandwich. The driver watches me curiously, but says nothing. I wrap the white paper tight and write only the sandwich price on the white paper.

The driver grins. Marvin Gaye sings from the radio in his pocket.

"WOL?" I ask.

"Right on," he says. "Gimme that sweet soul music."

I hand him his sandwich.

"Thanks, man," he says. "You all right. I love them kosher dills."

As the driver walks away, I turn my head to see if Darrell has witnessed what I just did for the bus driver, but he is gone.

Sammy clears his throat and gets my attention. He points to the "five cents extra pickle" sign and taps the word "extra" with his fat index finger. But I don't care what Sammy thinks or does. Today is my seventeenth birthday, and I will drive away from here in my '62 Ford Falcon. I'll remember what happened today, but if I forget, I'll wind my windows down and listen to WOL.

STEPHANIE KAPLAN COHEN
GENEROSITY

We were generous
And gave them places
Of their very own.

Never mind, no water
Dry land, no crops
But somehow they made do
Until the conquerors
Needed that land.

(cont)

They gave them directions
For a long trail
Of starvation and death.

Little children
No more than bones,
Were buried on the way.

And so it has gone.

We, the Americans
Are the generous
Conquerors.

Cohen

KEN AUTREY
WOODEN BUDDHA

A carved Buddha, 5 inches tall,
sits on my dresser, dark polish gleaming.
I pause each morning to marvel
at the grace of his flowing robe,
the shaved head, the string of beads
hanging like seeds from his right hand.
I rub his belly for luck and imagine my father
doing the same aboard his ship at the end
of the war, cradling the squat figure bought
in some Asian port, then secreting it
in his sea trunk. The scent remains as it was
sixty years ago—mahogany, shellac,
cloves, incense. This brings my father back
to me more than the heft of his handsaw
or the cut of his double-breasted suit
hanging in my closet. The seated icon
is as patient as my father had to be
in those long months apart from me,
as patient as my memory of him,
gone now twenty years.

Autrey

DAPHNE VLACHOJANNIS
A CONGO STORY

Part 2 of a 3-part series

Summary of Part 1:
In Part 1, the author provides a bit of background leading up to her decision to move to Kinshasa. She tells us her first impressions upon arrival, and we get a taste of the dichotomies that exist in this vibrant city. We are introduced to the author's "Congo family," the group of friends she makes there, and are given a glimpse into the relationships and life she lived during this initial period. Part 1 ends with us wondering how life in Kinshasa will unfold for this most unlikely of inhabitants.

Risks

Something that really struck me when I moved to Kinshasa was the sudden loss of freedom of movement. I had never realised how unbelievably skipping-through-fields-of-flowers carefree I'd always been about *moving around.* I had taken for granted that I could move freely pretty much wherever and however I liked. Kinshasa, as I would come to learn, is referred to as a *"prison a ciel ouvert"* (open-air prison). As a large, white, almost reflective target, you end up going everywhere, including the grocery store, in an armoured vehicle. The biggest security risk, oddly enough, are boys as young as 5 and as old as 18, referred to as *"sheges"*— "street boys." These boys were either abandoned by their parents or grew up in shanty towns. They are dispersed in different areas of La Gombe, the expat neighbourhood, and as those who commit most of the robberies, have been categorised by the United Nations as the number one threat to expats. In a very typical scenario, you are in your car, stopped at a light or in traffic, and a group of *sheges* will try to open the doors of the car or break the windows. Interestingly however, in some neighbourhoods it is the *sheges* rather than the police who protect the residents. I have friends who relied on these boys to protect them from break-ins or from getting their cars vandalized. In fact, when my passport and documents were stolen from my car, it was our neighbourhood *shege* chief who made sure I got them back, and who chastised his fellow gang members for "messing with our friends." Thanks to my friend, I was able to purchase my passport back at a bargain price. Personally, I came to appreciate this backward sense of loyalty. People trust that the *sheges* are coordinated enough to prevent any criminal threats, unlike the police who are corrupt, dysfunctional and disorganised.

Aside from the *sheges*, who can be an actual threat, there are the constant perceived threats. Although far from a blanket truth, the general dynamic that has unfortunately developed between locals and expats is that expats have money, locals are poor, and expats should share their wealth. It is a very African mindset that if my neighbour has food and I don't, he should share his food with me. The difference between the western capitalistic, individualistic mentality, when confronted with this very communal way of thinking, adds anger and frustration to an already charged atmosphere.

This anger, combined with the risks, sets the stage for a deep divide that creates the proverbial Expat Bubble. Add the political unrest, and you have a general feeling that at any moment, things can explode. And in fact, they do—both literally and figuratively.

Living next door to the presidential palace in a post-conflict society where most people hated the president was, in hindsight, possibly not the wisest choice I've ever made. In my defence, it is very difficult to find a decent apartment in Kinshasa with both stable electricity and running water for less than 4,000 USD a month. I found a place on Rue la Vallée, a little street that wound and ran downhill in an almost charming fashion (my standards had dropped into the toilet by that time), just before hitting the first barrier of the presidential palace. I convinced myself that the presidential guards 10 meters from my door were a positive presence— they would no doubt protect me should things go sideways. And the security guard sent over by my work didn't seem concerned, so why should I be? Little did I know that several months later I would be hiding under my bed, listening to shots being fired outside my bedroom window and peeking my head out just long enough to catch a glimpse of a blood-covered soldier, his AK-47 dragging perilously behind him from a rope as he limped down our street. Ducking back under the bed, I once again shimmied out long enough to grab my phone and call Security. Our security officer informed me that he couldn't evacuate me because he couldn't reach my building. I was apparently "in the direct zone of danger." The roads leading to my house were all blocked. I was to remain calm and away from the windows. And—of course—to email HQ and inform them of the situation. Several moments later, a grenade exploded directly outside my bedroom window, and I started composing the email in my head: "Dear Colleagues, in case you haven't heard the news, there was an attempted coup d'état in Kinshasa today. Luckily, despite several close calls, the staff are all safe and well. We were, however, unable to carry out any of the programmed activities, and the daily report will therefore not be coming today. I apologise for any inconvenience this may cause. I typed this up and sent it the next day in what remains, to date, the most surreal work email I have ever written.

The Explosion

Several months after the failed coup d'état, I was woken up by my bed shaking and a crash outside the window as if something had exploded in the back yard. I went from horizontal to vertical with a velocity that made my head spin and tried to figure out if I had been dreaming. Then the second crash came. The windows shook, my bottle of hair spray fell off the desk, and people screamed outside. In a single move, I pulled on pants, grabbed my phone and passport, and darted out of my bedroom. My housemate was already on the phone with UN Security. "What's going on?" I whisper-shrieked. He held up his hand to shush me as if listening to a very important message. "Mm hm. Mm hm. I see. Ok, I see. Very good." Then he covered the receiver. "They have no clue what's going on."

I tiptoed to the front door and looked out the peek hole, half expecting to see the smushed face of a guerrilla warrior staring back at me. Nothing there. I opened the door and bolted across the hall to Tara and Paul's apartment. Paul opened the door holding five phones, Tara behind him looking shell-shocked. He yanked me inside and barked orders ("Get down and stay away from the windows you muppets!") as he tried to reach our security office on the satellite phone. The three of us crouched in the space between the bedrooms, the kitchen and the bathroom—the one part of the house without windows—and waited for the next crash. It came after about three minutes, shaking the walls and the ceiling. Tara looked at me imploringly. "We can't die, we're not even supposed to be here! We were supposed to have left by now!" The irony of the situation suddenly hilarious, I started laughing uncontrollably. "Imagine we die now? After three years here, and having already left? We weren't even supposed to come back!" Our laughter is hysterical. Misplaced. A mixture of disbelief, mania and dark acceptance: Served us right. Several months earlier, we had packed up our things and, without telling anyone (as if we knew it wouldn't last), had left with a plan of no return.

"Keep it together you fucking muppets!" We looked abashedly at Paul, the only one in control of the situation, and waited for him to tell us what to do other than pull at his alarmingly tattooed arms like two useless children. He put the phone on speaker, and we waited for UN Security to tell us what was going on. The mechanical, infuriatingly unclear voice came through the line. "We have received information that a plane that appears to be from Brazzaville is flying low over the Boulevard 30 Juin and is dropping bombs. A number of people have been killed." The boulevard in question was about 20 metres from our apartment. Panic set in as we realised a bomb could land on our building at any given moment. Just then my phone rang, and my ex, who worked in security at the French Embassy, was calling to check on us and let us know the crucial piece of information that the French Embassy had no idea what was going on. "*Je ne suis même pas là pour te protéger….*" (I'm not even there to protect you.) In disbelief, I sputtered "*Ce n'est vraiment pas le moment!*" (This is really not the time!) and hung up, followed by hysterical laughter from both Tara and Paul. "Seriously? Even now?" Paul's face conveyed his (understandable) disgust that only I could manage to interject a ridiculous broken-hearted ex into any given situation, no matter how absurdly out of place. After a few more crashes followed by a commensurate number of panic attacks, UN Security called back to inform us that they had been mistaken. There were no bombs dropping from a plane 20 metres away. In fact, there wasn't even a plane. To this day I do not understand how they got this so wrong, but what actually happened was that an old ammunitions depot, in which the weapons had been poorly stored, spontaneously combusted across the river in Brazzaville.

Dating in the Field

Considering the adrenaline-inducing, constantly charged atmosphere just described, now imagine what the dating scene was like. "Intense" doesn't quite convey the full picture.

There's a saying amongst the expats of Kinshasa that Kin time is double time. Two years in Kinshasa feels more like four years anywhere else. And one week in a new relationship somehow feels more like a year. Normally, boy meets girl, they develop an interest in each other, and things can move as fast or as slow as they choose. In the field, boy meets girl and whether he wants to or not, boy keeps meeting girl every day because everyone is at the same parties, the same bars, and the same supermarkets. Boy and girl therefore know what the other is doing every minute of every day.

But while the relationship is on turbo-charge, everything else is moving at a snail's pace. And when one's emotional world moves so much faster than the surroundings, it takes a much more prominent place in one's life.

Hence the ever-dramatic dating scene in our humid, emotionally charged metropolis.

I am slightly embarrassed to report that dance parties, house parties, and "clubbing" (yes, I said clubbing) are the scene of the crime. Certain song lyrics take on a whole new meaning in a lonely, desperate, anxiety-ridden expat community. Dancing, in turn, reaches a new level of inappropriate. White women who once bopped back and forth self-consciously are now backing that ass up for all to witness. Lyrics like "we found love in a hopeless place" and "gimme everything tonight, for all we know we might not have tomorrow" take on existentially profound meaning. We are convinced these singers feel our pain—know where we live—are in fact the ones who understand us best. As we bump and grind in dirty, smelly clubs, we unleash our desperate hopes of finding love in this hopeless place—of, against all odds, having the story go "and that's how I met your grandfather, in a charming out of the way place in the Congo." Never mind that the storyline is more likely to go "and that's how I got an STD from a Uruguayan peacekeeper and ended up sterile, and isn't that fortunate because that's when I decided to adopt your mother!"

Dating in the field generally involves four main types of actors, all male: MBAs (no ladies, not those highly educated in the field of finance, rather Married But Available)—those who have a wife and children back home of whom no word is ever spoken. In a phenomenon coined "bush marriage," a married man takes a "bush wife," i.e., a partner in the field. I am not referring here to formal polygamy; I am talking about an additional relationship that exists only in the field. It resembles a prototypical relationship in most ways—common friends, dinner parties, even co-habitation—except for one small detail: no one outside the field duty station knows it exists. There are lacunas in this relationship during which the man goes back on a visit to his "home" to see wife and children (swearing they sleep in separate beds and are only formally together for the sake of the children), and then nestles happily back into his bush life.

Ironically, these married men are often sought out by women in the field for their ability to provide stability. The rationale goes like this: They have so much to deal with back home that they don't have time to "polygamize" when they are in the bush and are happy to have a "monogamous" relationship.

The second type of man is the GS (geographically single). This guy has a girlfriend back home, but when he crosses the border into the field, becomes a full-on playboy. ("Sorry baby, I tried to reach you all night but you know how the phone network here is.")

Then there are the men who are actually single—notably those who never had much success back home with the ladies and are now overwhelmed by the countless options of vulnerable women. These men, who previously found themselves scrambling for crumbs, are faced with the prospect of fulfilling what was previously only a wet dream.

Finally, there are the non-committers—the men who fancy themselves Indiana Jones and are convinced they can stay forever young despite their deepening wrinkles and expanding waistlines. The field is the one place they can do this past age 40 without being labelled a-social.

Slim pickings is an understatement. The men who are both unmarried and emotionally available are referred to by the disgruntled women as tyrannosaurs. When one is found, he is not only admired but is studied for the rare species that he is.

The result, for better or for worse, is that in the field you tend to date people you normally wouldn't—*ever*—anywhere else. Whereas you may have heretofore had a weakness for bearded intellectuals, suddenly men who jump out of parachutes and crawl around in trenches seem normal—even appealing. You picture yourself walking arm in arm down the street with your beloved bespeckled intellectual, through swarms of militia and their AK-47s, and somehow having a partner who knows how to wield a rifle doesn't seem like such a bad idea.

And since these bush relationships are with people we would never have considered before, there follows an interesting bush exchange in which we learn new things. We fancy ourselves open-minded, having evolved so much that we have widened our comfort zone and can now mesh with people we would previously have discarded at first glance.

There is a grain of truth to this in that we stretch our systems of values and judge less than we would in other contexts. And while all well and good that we've stopped judging, the downside is that critical thinking has also taken a hiatus. While there are cases of bush relationships that prevail, for the rest of us the scenario goes something like this: One day, under the illusion that you have a legitimate relationship, you attempt to take it outside the field. You step off the plane, still fuzzy from the adrenaline that is constantly pumping through your veins, into the cold airport of, say, Vienna. Your first thought is that the warm sweater you threw into your bag is, in fact, not warm at all. The dress you're wearing, which is made of waxy *panya*, is quickly hardening like a cold pack in a freezer. You look over at the guy standing next to you, whose manly and protective embrace you've been nestled in, and notice as his hand grips yours that it's freakishly large and calloused. The cargo pants you found sexy suddenly look ridiculous and robo-cop-like in the sea of Brooks

Brothers cardigans and Armani suits. You experience your first (and not last) pang of embarrassment as he throws his He-Man-like weight behind you and lifts you off the ground in what is meant to be a show of affection, but now feels like a scene from an Alabama trailer park. The rest of the trip is a series of come-to-Jesus moments while you struggle with admitting to yourself what no one wants to admit—this relationship, along with much of your life, makes no sense outside of Kinshasa. Solution? Stay there forever, in a fuzzy cloud of denial, or make a break for it.

To be continued.

ELIZABETH WEIR
EMIGRATING FROM ENGLAND

"Please Mind the Gap,"
a warning on the London Underground

Always that gap
between
platform and train,
that potential trip
as you step
from where you are
to where your life
is taking you.

And when you arrive,
bereft of the comfort
of context, the gap gapes
an absence, a trap
over which you
must aim
to—
leap.

Weir

LEW FORESTER
LIFE BIRD

Earth tilts to October, the sun climbs
      a ladder of yellow leaves

in a season that lifts more than falls.
      Thrilled, stone still, our group

of seven bird watchers behold
      a Sage Thrasher. *Life bird for me*,

a woman whispers in birder lingo—
      after decades of looking through

field glasses, the first she's seen in the wild.
      A new entry for her *life list*, another

feather for memory's nest. We scribe
      entries in notebooks the way years

etch our faces, listen for bird calls
      over the distant drone of traffic,

the hum of our collective histories.
      Humans are steered by gravity—
birds navigate a different sky. We stand
      on a carpet of fallen leaves,

knowing wonder is presence on this earth,
      wings for a life too short.

Forester

GALINA CHERNAYA
THE COURT OF THE PEOPLE

Part 3 of a 3-part series

Summary of Part 1:
Winter 1986, USSR, the dawn of perestroika. Galina and her husband
Lonya have been living in Abramtsevo, an exclusive Stalin-built estate 40
miles north of Moscow where her father maintains the rights to a large
dacha as a member of the Soviet Academy of Sciences. Well-educated
professionals with budding scientific careers and two small children, the
couple is desperate to find housing in Moscow, a grueling five-hour daily
commute to work. This need becomes urgent as heavy snow descends on
the isolated, now-empty summer community, where they have no access
to car or phone, and the nearest train stop is a two-mile tromp down a half-
plowed country lane. When Galina's father refuses to pull strings at the
Academy of Sciences Housing Committee, which routinely obtains free
apartments for the children of its members in Moscow, the couple seizes
their last resort: two rooms in a three-room *kommunalka* in a remote
industrial district of chemical plants and factories plagued with the worst
air pollution in Moscow. Thus begins Galina's challenge to come to terms
with "the brilliance of the Soviet system that invented communal living"
where sharing daily life—one stove, a toilet, a bathtub, and even a single
phone line—with an utter stranger, also means an ear pressed up against
your bedroom door at night: "an observer watching your every step,
listening to every word, ready to report you for any reason or no reason at
all." Eyeing the dismal rows of identical gray buildings from her window,
Galina ironically recalls a Russian saying: "Love makes a castle." *Ha*, she
thinks. *We never should have left the dacha.*

Summary of Part 2:
A cast of colorful and often sympathetic characters parades through Galina
and Lonya's apartment, giving Galina a "real-life introduction" to the
industrial working class, whose ways and grammar were "akin to a foreign
tongue" in the circles where she'd grown up. While Lonya adjusts more
easily to communal living, Galina becomes possessed with the need for
privacy and a larger space than the 345-square-foot domain to which their
family of four has been consigned. When their co-tenant unexpectedly
moves out, Galina quickly realizes that the official housing code accords
their budding family priority over the empty room—making the entire

apartment "theirs" alone. When a local factory assigns the right of occupancy to one of their workers instead, Galina initiates legal action, unleashing a struggle with "justice, Soviet-style" that escalates upward from the Municipal Housing Office to City Court to letters addressed to the Supreme Soviet and even to Gorbachev himself. When the room remains empty despite her lost appeals, she wistfully wonders, *What if we get lucky? What if the factory has backed off, and the municipality lets us have the room?*

Dangerous Corner

> *Life's got too many dangerous corners*
> —*J. B. Priestley, "Dangerous Corner"*

Then came Tuesday, December 8. It was an ordinary winter day. Dirty snow was piled up around buildings, leaving messy slush in the metro and apartment hallways. At this point, Vera was watching the children in Abramtsevo, and we were staying in Pechatniki on Monday and Tuesday nights, thus cutting down on exhausting commutes.

I came home from work as usual around 7:00 p.m., and rode the elevator up to the eighth floor. The elevator slid open to reveal a fresh, unpainted wooden panel installed in our front door. Standing there, I already knew that my key would no longer fit—the lock to our apartment had been changed. Without informing us, a bailiff had executed the order of the municipal court and introduced the new tenant into the apartment. The authorities had broken in, installed a new lock, and given a set of keys to Viktor Stepachev. I rang the bell. No one was home.

Close to tears, I left the building and called the police from a pay phone. They confirmed what I already knew. No, they would not come and break the new lock, I had to wait for the new tenant to come home and let me in. All my hopes crashed down around me. They, the municipal court, the system, had exercised their power before our appeal had even been heard in city court. As I slowly returned to our building, I saw Lonya coming from the bus stop. I told him what had happened. He was not surprised. We rode the elevator back to the eighth floor, and sat, devastated, on the stairway beside the apartment door in silence.

People from neighboring apartments were going back and forth, some coming home from work, others going out on errands or to pick up kids from school. One glance at our door told them what had happened, but no one asked any questions. Around 8:00 p.m. the elevator opened, and a man we'd never seen before walked towards the apartment. It was Viktor. Without a word, he opened the door and let us in.

The first thing I saw were dirty footprints tracked all over the floor. Looking through the open door into Viktor's room, I saw only a bed, a chair, a television, and a suitcase. Our phone was sitting on the floor in the hallway. The door to our room was also open, although I clearly remembered closing it on my way out that morning. There too, the floor was covered with muddy footprints. I had a guess about what had happened that Viktor readily confirmed: since there was no phone in the hallway, he asked the bailiff to locate one. After all, according to regulation, the phone, like the toilet, was for everyone to share.

The bailiff, I later learned, was 23-year-old Marina Petrova, who had entered the apartment with two of our neighbors, recruited on the spot to serve as the witnesses required by law. Looking for the phone, she opened our bedroom door, discovered it on the table, yanked it from the outlet, and placed it on the hallway floor, indicating that it was for shared use. I told Viktor it was our personal phone and that he needed to get one for himself. He did not object, although he could have reported us for infringing the rules.

Numb, I washed the floors, then sat at the table in our room trying to think rationally about what had just happened, and how our life would change because of it. We'd obviously lost the battle for Antonina Dmitrievna's room. Now we were stuck with a new neighbor, a total stranger. Again, we had no hope for privacy. What should we do?

One thing was clear: I would not allow the authorities to roll over me. I refused to accept their actions. By entering OUR room without a warrant and removing OUR phone, *our personal property*, they had violated our privacy. I didn't yet have a plan of action, but I was determined. I was not about to let this go.

An Ordinary Guy

> I don't deserve your attention
> I'm hardly worthy of mention
> I've got a job and a pension
> Nothing remarkable
>
> —Michel Legrand and Didier Van Cauwelaert,
> *Amour*, Broadway musical

Meanwhile, we had to come to terms with living with a new

tenant. Viktor was in his mid-thirties, a guy you wouldn't notice in a crowd. Newly divorced and needing a place to live, he could have been lured away from his job by any other factory that offered him housing from its distribution list. To preempt the loss of a skilled employee, Viktor's current employer handily offered him Antonina Dmitrievna's vacant room. He happily accepted and remained in their employ.

Communal living with Viktor did not start out on good terms. It was hard for me not to see him as the cause of my crushed hopes. He felt my aggravation, and responded by declaring that he refused to do his part to clean the common areas. Cleaning duties in a *kommunalka* customarily rotated among households, but Viktor didn't care if common areas were clean or not. If I wanted them cleaned, it was my sole responsibility to clean them. I agreed to accept this duty in exchange for his promise not to bring any women into the house.

Viktor's daily routine was similar to Antonina Dmitrievna's: He left for work before 7:00 and came home at 5:00. He did not cook much. Every evening he made fried eggs and ate them in his room. We were fortunate that he was not a drinker. Although I occasionally saw a beer bottle in the kitchen, I never saw him drunk, not even once.

But Viktor had another addiction. Every night, the characteristic sounds of porn issued forth from behind his closed door as he watched his favorite tapes on his new VCR. Aroused, he'd periodically run out to the bathroom where he'd spill his bodily fluids all over the walls and floor, then rush back to his room to continue enjoying the show.

Our five-year-old daughter Katya was very curious concerning all the noises coming from Viktor's room. We sometimes brought the children to Moscow for doctors' visits, and on such occasions, it took all my creativity to keep inventing explanations about what was going on behind Viktor's door. Fortunately, Lonya was better at it than I was. One time when he was taking Katya for a bath, Viktor's door was ajar, and she managed to glimpse the television screen. "Papa," she asked, "How come all those people don't have any clothes on?" Lonya replied without skipping a beat. "Well, Katya, you know how we're going to take a bath now? Those people are getting ready for a bath too!"

Needless to say, it was also my duty to clean up Viktor's mess so we could use the toilet. He rarely spoke to us and paid little attention to the kids. It was as if they weren't even there. But all things considered, he was not a bad neighbor. A few weeks after he moved in, I asked him to spend a night somewhere else because I was having a party to celebrate receiving my PhD. He agreed and didn't even lock his room. The next morning, I was surprised to find two of my friends sleeping in his bed, totally wasted after the party. Viktor did not complain.

Galina Chernaya vs. The Court of the People

> *So you think you can stone me and spit in my eye?*
> *—Bohemian Rhapsody*

As life went on, I continued to burn with a slow, steady desire to strike back. I would not lie down and allow myself to be steamrollered: I would file a lawsuit against the system itself. An officer of the court had clearly violated our privacy, which was guaranteed by international laws to which the Soviet Union was a signatory. The first step was to get hold of the documents stating these laws. This would require jumping through some hoops.

I had to get my hands on The Helsinki Accords and the United Nations Universal Declaration of Human Rights. By signing the Helsinki Accords in 1975, the Soviet Union had adopted a number of principles, including the reunification of families, that allowed hundreds of thousands of Soviet Jews to emigrate in the 1970s and 1980s. From my dissident friends, I knew that the Accords also obligated participating states to act in conformity with the United Nations Universal Declaration of Human Rights. In the Soviet Union, the State controlled access to all information, let alone documents of such significance.

I now put my freshly minted PhD to use. The documents I needed were housed in the Lenin State Library, where membership was limited to those with graduate degrees. As a PhD, I could submit a request for any material, regardless of its source or content. One of my classmates had proudly told everyone how he'd cleverly put his education to good use by requesting recent issues of *Playboy*. His request was granted, and he just could not stop talking about those centerfolds.

Thus encouraged by the largesse of the Lenin Library, I put in my request to see the Helsinki Declaration and the Universal Declaration of Human Rights. A week later, I was thrilled to be notified that my request had been granted and I could come in to view the documents. On the assigned date, I went to the library, where I was instructed to leave my school bag in a locker and was then taken to a small room. I was allowed to bring along a piece of paper and a pencil. I was permitted one half-hour with the documents.

After a short wait, the door opened and a person walked in with what appeared to be a plain bound book with no title. The man looked totally generic, as if he'd spent a lifetime blending into the crowd. He instructed me that he would lay the book open in front of me, then stand behind me watching as I read. I was allowed to turn pages and make handwritten notes. He warned me that there might be redacted passages. On request, he placed the volume before me, open to the Universal Declaration of Human Rights.

My hands were shaking as I started to turn the pages. I was surprised it was so short. But how much was packed into those few pages! I quickly found the article I was looking for:

Article 12

No one shall be subjected to arbitrary interference with his privacy, family, home or correspondence, nor to attacks upon his honour and reputation. Everyone has the right to the protection of the law against such interference or attacks.

I copied Article 12 on my paper and asked for the Helsinki Accords. It was a long document. As much as I wanted to read it all, my time was limited. I had to hurry before it ran out. Fortunately, the section on human rights came early on, and I soon found the passage I needed:

In the field of human rights and fundamental freedoms, the participating States will act in conformity with the purposes and principles of the Charter of the United Nations and with the Universal Declaration of Human Rights.

I walked out of the library confident that I had a case. Now I needed to convince Viktor to be my witness in court. He readily agreed, assuring me that he would swear that the bailiff and witnesses had entered our bedroom without a warrant.

I drafted a letter of complaint requesting a reversion of the court's decision due to the unlawful action of a court official, and set up an appointment with our lawyer. When she heard my intent, she dismissed me as a client on the spot. Under no circumstances was she willing to risk her career by getting mixed up in a political case. She told me I was insane for even thinking about it, and advised me to drop all thought of legal action. I was not too surprised.

Fine, I thought, I'll do it myself. Lonya expressed support, but without much enthusiasm. We wisely agreed that I alone would be the plaintiff. That way, he would not be legally involved and could still take care of the children if something happened to me.

I submitted my complaint to the court the next day. A secretary assigned it a case number and filed it. The nerve-wrecking wait had begun. In a week or so, I got a phone call from the judge, the same Yuri Sergeevich from municipal court, asking me to come in for a meeting.

He sat me down in his office, sounding annoyed.

"Tell me, why are you doing this?" he demanded. "I promise you that the bailiff will be subjected to disciplinary action. Isn't that enough? What else do you expect?"

"I want the court to admit that they violated the United Nations Universal Declaration of Human Rights," I persisted.

"Never," he answered.

A Concurrence of Circumstances

> You've hit the dirt, do not cry tearfully.
> You are alone—no one is to blame.
> Even shooting stars fall to earth,
> And no one is there to pick them up.

> —Vadim Delaunay (1947-1983)
> Dissident poet and Abramtsevo neighbor

My hearing was scheduled for March 21, 1988. It was held in the same courtroom, with the same presiding judge, Comrade Luzhin, a secretary, and two different assessors. Present also were a very nervous Marina and her boss, a middle-aged woman in a suit, who kept whispering in each other's ear. Viktor showed up last, looking stressed.

The judge began the hearing by reading my complaint. The tension in the courtroom, already palpable, built further yet as he pronounced the words "in violation of the United Nations Universal Declaration of Human Rights." Next, Viktor was called to the bench to provide his testimony. After a series of routine questions, the judge asked him if he could verify that he'd seen Marina enter our room and pull our telephone out of the wall. Dead silence.

And then I heard Viktor say: "I didn't see anything. After entering the apartment, Comrade Petrova handed me the keys and I went to my room to unpack. I didn't see her leave."

I couldn't believe my ears. Even the judge looked surprised. I'm sure that he and Marina's boss had already agreed on a strategy for defense, but now it wouldn't be needed.

The judge turned to me. "Do you have any additional proof to support your accusation?" he asked.

I couldn't say a word. I was in shock.

"Case dismissed due to lack of evidence," he declared, and dismissed everyone but me from the courtroom. He then requested that I accompany him to his office.

"Didn't I tell you to drop it?" he exclaimed. "Now what? Do you know that Marina can sue you for slander? She has a solid case. You'll get imprisonment for up to a year. Do you know what will happen to you in prison?"

Of course, I knew what would happen to me in prison. I most likely would not survive a year. But I couldn't think. My mind went completely blank. The judge finished up his diatribe by informing me that he himself would initiate no action against me. But if Marina decided to go forward with a case, he would be unable to prevent it.

I don't even remember how I got home. Viktor was already there. He rushed over as soon as I walked in, begging for forgiveness. "I'm so sorry, Galina. I got so scared I couldn't make myself say it!" I myself was so frightened by the prospect of being sued and imprisoned that I wasn't even angry with him. All I could think of was our dissident young Abramtsevo neighbor, Vadim Delaunay, who'd returned from prison missing almost all his teeth, utterly destroyed in body and spirit.

> Just gotta get out, gotta get right outta here!
> —*Bohemian Rhapsody*

For the next several months, I opened the mailbox with shaking hands, fearful of finding a summons. Throughout this time, a passage from *War and Peace* kept running through my mind. It comes near the end, when Tolstoy takes us into the single, obsessive thought in Pierre Bezukhov's mind as he faces a potential death sentence:

> [W]ho was it that had really sentenced him to death? Not
> the men on the commission that had first examined
> him—not one of them wished to or, evidently, could
> have done it. It was not Davout, who had looked at him
> in so human a way. […] The adjutant, also, had
> evidently had no evil intent. […] Then who was

executing him, killing him, depriving him of life—him, Pierre, with all his memories, aspirations, hopes, and thoughts? Who was doing this? And Pierre felt that it was no one. It was a system—a concurrence of circumstances.

If worst comes to worst, I kept wondering, just who exactly will have sentenced me to prison for slander? It won't be the judge. Yuri Sergeevich is a good person who actually sympathizes with my hopeless efforts. It won't be Marina. She is young and blundering and has nothing against me personally. She is just confused and frightened. Is Viktor to blame? No, he sincerely feels guilty for being too scared to testify in my favor. No one is doing this—it is the SYSTEM. The SYSTEM is trying to kill me, to deprive me of my life, deprive my children of their mother.

Very fortunately, Marina took no legal action against me. I think back to that time with horror even today, and wonder why I was not pursued in the name of "justice." Perhaps my luck was also born of "a concurrence of circumstances"—in this case, the times themselves: In 1988, the Soviet system was rapidly falling apart and officials were far more worried about securing their personal futures than enforcing the rules of a dying system.

◊◊◊

Unlike my dissident friends, I can't say I grew up hating the Soviet system. After all, that very system provided all the privileges my father and our family enjoyed. I knew that you had to be cautious, that if you got in its way you could be ground down like Vadim. But I never would have thought that I myself would push so far that I'd overstep the bounds if personally confronted by the system's inherent injustice. I was not so naïve as to believe that the system would lose. But whatever the cost, I just couldn't give up the fight.

Nor did the reaction of our families and most of our friends surprise me. They were totally satisfied. It met their expectations. Once again, the system had exerted its power, justifying everyone's apathy and lack of courage to stand up against it.

My experience of these painful legal battles and the self-satisfied reaction of my family and friends profoundly impacted me. In just a few months, I lost my idealism; my entire vision of life was destroyed. Before, I believed that persistence paid off, that justice won over unfairness, that my family and friends would always support me. After, I knew that none of this was true.

One conviction crystallized in my mind: I knew with utter certainty that I would never be able to live within the rules of the Soviet system. Life was unfair, and it was just a matter of time before my rebellious character landed me in serious trouble. I did not want to be stuck continually risking my life fighting a system I had no hope of beating.

My fight with my country's system did leave me with another hope, though. Maybe I would be a better fit for a different society—one with more personal freedom and respect for human rights. *Just let me and my family out of here!* That one thought hammered in my brain. *But how? How could I make this actually happen?* We had no Jewish roots or relatives abroad. There was no legitimate way for my family to leave the country. The next three years were spent achieving the unachievable: beating the SYSTEM by leaving the Soviet Union.

CONTRIBUTORS

W ROYCE ADAMS, emeritus professor, Santa Barbara City College, has published over a dozen college textbooks, several academic journal articles, four juvenile novels, and a collection of short stories entitled *Against the Current*. He won the *Haunted Waters Literary Magazine*'s 2016 Grand Prize Short Story Contest, honorable mentions from *Glimmer Train* and *Winning Writer*, and received "Notable Essay" from *Best American Essays, 2017*. His works have appeared in *The Rockford Review, Black Fox Literary Magazine, Catamaran, In the Depths, Coe Review, Chaffey Review, Adelaide, bosque*, and others. He lives in Santa Barbara, CA.

MEGHAN ADLER honed her craft at The Writers Studio in NYC. Her poetry has appeared in *Alimentum, California Quarterly, Gastronomica, The Intima: A Journal of Narrative Medicine*, and *The North American Review*. Her first book of poetry, *Pomegranate*, was recently published with Main Street Rag Press. When not writing or teaching poetry, Meghan creates literacy strategies for educators and collaborates with neuropsychologists to develop learning plans for students with learning differences.

SAM AMBLER's writing has been published in *Apricity Magazine, Christopher Street, City Lights Review Number 2, Euphony Journal, Evening Street Review, Glint Literary Journal, Headway Quarterly, Hearth & Coffin, The James White Review, Nixes Mate Review, The Phoenix, Plainsongs, Poetry Magazine, Red Wheelbarrow*, and *Visitant*, among others. Most recently, he was featured in the anthology *Voices of the Grieving Heart*. He has a BA in English, specializing in creative writing of poetry, from Stanford University.

TRISH ANNESE (she/her/hers) is a writer and teacher from Rochester, NY, whose stories and poems have been published in *Hawaii Pacific Review, Five on the Fifth, Caliban, Santa Fe Writers Quarterly, Apricity*, and *Penmen Review*, among others. She is currently at work on a collection of short fiction.

KEN AUTREY is professor emeritus of English at Francis Marion University and now lives in Auburn, AL. His work has appeared in *Atlanta Review, Cimarron Review, Poetry Northwest, Southern Poetry Review, Texas Review*, and elsewhere. He has published three chapbooks: *Pilgrim* (Main Street Rag), *Rope Lesson* (Longleaf Press), and *The Wake of the Year* (Solomon and George). He is a coordinator of the Third Thursday Poetry Reading Series at Auburn University. He also won the 2021 Helen Kay Chapbook Prize (Evening Street Press) for his chapbook, *Penelope in Repose*.

JIM BEANE's writing has appeared in numerous print and online literary journals. His story collection, *By the Sea, by the Sea...*was published by the Wordrunner's eChapbook series in 2019. He is a mentor for the Veterans Writing Project and sometimes fiction workshop leader. He lives west of Baltimore with his wife of forty-two years and their dog Lily.

EDWARD BELFAR is the author of a collection of short stories called *Wanderers*, which was published by Stephen F. Austin State University Press in 2012. His fiction has also appeared in numerous literary journals, including *Evening Street Review Issue 4*, *Shenandoah*, *The Baltimore Review*, *Potpourri*, *Confrontation*, *Natural Bridge*, and *Tampa Review*. He lives in Maryland with his wife and works as a writer and editor.

BRUCE L BENNETT, at age 23 (in 1993), was arrested, sentenced to 33 years for murder and robbery. In solitary confinement, after an escape attempt, he discovered a love for reading and writing. In 2022, upon release, he hopes to publish his literary novel, *Regarding the Daughters of Joey Bright*. In prison, he earned an AA Degree and currently works as a state certified Wastewater Treatment Plant Operator.

RACHEL SQUIRES BLOOM's poems appear in journals including *Hawaii Review, Poet Lore, Main Street Rag, Poetry East and California Quarterly.* She published two local histories. She wrote her first poem at age six on a paper plate, and flowers still occasionally appear in her work, along with soup kitchens, pillbugs, passports, crickets, and the bones of Capuchin monks. Her inspiration is the heart and bustle of cities and the intense pleasure of solitude, usually simultaneously.

JENNIFER CAMPBELL is an English professor in Buffalo, NY, and a co-editor of *Earth's Daughters*. She has two full-length poetry collections, *Supposed to Love* and *Driving Straight Through,* and a chapbook of reconstituted fairytale poems, *What Came First*. Her poems have recently appeared in *The Healing Muse*, *Heirlock*, *deluge*, *The Sixty-Four Best Poets of 2019*, *Paterson Review, Little Patuxent Review,* and *Bond Street Review*.

GALINA CHERNAYA, the daughter of an eminent scientist, was raised in the upper echelons of the Soviet intellectual elite during the Brezhnev era. She received a PhD from Moscow State University and was engaged in a promising research career when she fell afoul of the Soviet authorities. Threatened with imprisonment, she emigrated with her husband and two young children to the U.S., where they were admitted as refugees in 1991, settling in Princeton, NJ. She now lives in Vermont with her husband and boxer, Ziggy.

ALAN MARSHALL CLARK (he, him) is a poet and artist living in Maine and when possible, Mexico. He's the author of two books: *Guerrero* and *Heart's Blood*, a play for voices and a story set in pre-Conquest Mexico, and *Where They Know*, poems. His work has appeared in *The Caribbean Writer*, *Little Star Journal*, *Adirondack Review*, *Numbat* (Australia), *East Coast Ink*, *Zocalo Poets*, *About Place Journal*, *Evening Street Review*, *Ekphrastic Review*, *Dime Show* and others.

TIM COE is a 61-year-old man who grew up in the Michigan, Indiana, Ohio region before a 4-year stint in the Navy. He attended West Chester University for 2 years before dropping out of college to raise 3 kids. He has been writing off and on for 30 years, taking online courses, and continuing to try to improve his writing skills. He is submitting a lot of poems hoping someone will read and enjoy them.

STEPHANIE KAPLAN COHEN's poetry has appeared repeatedly in *The New York Times* and elsewhere. Her work has also appeared in the anthologies *Lessons in Love: Gifts from Our Grandmothers* (Crown, 2000) and *Split Verse: Poems to Heal The Heart* (Midmarch, 2000). Her memoir is *In My Mother's House* (Woodley Books). Her poetry books are *Additions and Subtractions* and *Body Work* (Plain View Press). She has been nominated for the Pushcart prize twice. She wrote a column "Ask Stephanie" for the *Alzheimer's Association Quarterly* in Westchester and Putnam, NY. She is an editor of *The Westchester Review*.

RICHARD COMPEAN studied English at the University of California at Davis and now teaches English at City College of San Francisco. His short stories have been published in *Good Works Review, The MacGuffin, Menda City Review, The Penmen Review, Pour Vida,* and *Forge.* In his spare time, he enjoys hanging out on the corner of pop culture and spirituality, admiring the work of Bruce Springsteen, Bob Dylan, and John Lennon as much as John Donne, William Shakespeare, and Andrew Marvell.

FRANK H COONS is a poet and veterinarian. His first book, *Finding Cassiopeia,* published in 2014 (Lithic Press), was a finalist for the Colorado Book Awards. His second book, *Counting in Dog Years* (Lithic Press) was published in 2016. A third book, *A Flash of Yellow Wing*, is currently in press through Orchard Street Press. His work has appeared in *Caesura, Evening Street Review*, *Plainsongs, Pensive Journal, Santa Fe Literary Review, Pacific Review, Pudding*, and elsewhere. He was nominated for a Pushcart prize in 2019.

CRAIG COTTER was born in 1960 in New York and has lived in California since 1986. His poems have appeared in *Caliban Online, California Quarterly, Chiron Review, Columbia Poetry Review, Court Green, Gay & Lesbian Review, Great Lakes Review, Hawai'i Review, Ottawa Arts Review, Poetry New Zealand & Tampa Review*. His fourth book of poems, *After Lunch with Frank O'Hara*, is currently available on Amazon. His manuscript *After Lunch* was a finalist for the National Poetry Series. *ALEX*, was a finalist for the Tampa Review Prize. www.craigcotter.com

HOLLY DAY's newest poetry collections are *In This Place, She Is Her Own* (Vegetarian Alcoholic Press), *A Wall to Protect Your Eyes* (Pski's Porch Publishing), *I'm in a Place Where Reason Went Missing* (Main Street Rag Publishing Co.), *Folios of Dried Flowers and Pressed Birds* (Cyberwit.net), *Where We Went Wrong* (Clare Songbirds Publishing), *Into the Cracks* (Golden Antelope), and *Cross-Referencing a Book of Summer* (Silver Bow Publishing).

DEBORAH H DOOLITTLE has lived in lots of different places but now calls North Carolina home. A Pushcart nominee, she is the author of *No Crazy Notions, That Echo, Floribunda,* and *Bogbound.* Some of her work has appeared or will soon appear in *Albatross, Creosote, Plainsongs, Riversongs,* and *Thema.* She shares a home with her husband, four housecats and a backyard full of birds. "Advice from a Tyrannosaurus Rex" was inspired by a trip to the NC Aquarium's special exhibit on dinosaurs.

MIRIAM EDELSON is a neurodivergent social activist, settler, writer and mother living in Toronto, Canada. Her literary non-fiction, personal essays and commentaries have appeared in *The Globe and Mail, Toronto Star,* various U.S. and Canadian literary journals and on CBC Radio. Her first book, *My Journey with Jake: A Memoir of Parenting and Disability* was published in April 2000. *Battle Cries: Justice for Kids with Special Needs* appeared in late 2005. Her doctorate from the University of Toronto focused upon mental health in the workplace.

TINA EGNOSKI is the author, most recently, of the novel *Burn Down This World* and the fiction collection *You Can Tell Me Anything.* Her work, both fiction and poetry, has been published in a number of literary journals, including *The Carolina Quarterly, The Master Review,* and *Saw Palm Journal.* She leads community-based workshops in Rhode Island and online through Livewire Writing Workshops. Along with writing, she's a bookbinder and papermaker.

THOMAS ELSON's stories have been published in numerous venues, including *Ellipsis, Better Than Starbucks, The Cabinet of Heed, Flash Frontier, Short Édition,* Journal *of Expressive Writing, Dead Mule Scho*ol, *The Selkie, The New Ulster, The Lampeter*, and *Adelaide.* He divides his time between Northern California and Western Kansas.

MICHAEL ESTABROOK has been publishing his poetry in the small press since the 1980s. He has published over 20 collections, a recent one being *The Poet's Curse, A Miscellany* (The Poetry Box, 2019).

ROD FARMER has over a thousand poems, articles, and reviews published in journals, and 3 chapbooks. He is professor emeritus at the University of Maine at Farmington. His last chapbook is: *Fingers Pointing at the Moon* from Finishing Line Press.

MATTHEW FEENEY (www.matthewfeeney.com) is currently incarcerated in Minnesota. Matthew received 2nd place in the 2017 PEN America Prison Writing Contest for Fiction and more recently won the 1st Place/Grandview Award in the 2018 League of Minnesota Poets 34th annual poetry contest. His work has appeared in numerous publications including *The Analog Sea Review*, *Spotlight on Recover*, and *Pinyon Review*. He is a member of his prison's Restorative Justice Council and a trained conflict resolution mentor.

JONATHAN B FERRINI is a published author who resides in San Diego. He received his MFA in motion picture and television production from UCLA.

AARON FISCHER worked for 30+ years as a print and online editor in technology and public policy. His poems have appeared in *Briar Cliff Review, Crosswinds Poetry Journal, Five Points, Hudson Review,* and elsewhere. He is the author of *Black Stars of Blood: The Weegee Poems* and won the 2020 *Prime Number Magazine*'s poetry contest.

TIM FITTS is a short story writer and photographer. His works have appeared in journals such as *Granta, New England Review, The Gettysburg Review, Xavier Review, Boulevard, The Baltimore Review*, among many others.

LEW FORESTER is the author of the full-length collection *Dialogues with Light* (Orchard Street Press, 2019). His poems have appeared or are forthcoming in *Atlanta Review, Main Street Rag, Blue Mountain Review, Plainsongs, POEM, Slipstream*, and other journals, magazines and anthologies. A social worker and mMultiple myeloma survivor, he lives with his wife in Arvada, CO. http://www.lewforester.com

JAMES FOWLER teaches literature at the University of Central Arkansas. He is author of the poetry collection *The Pain Trader* (Golden Antelope Press, 2020). His poems have recently appeared in *FuturesTrading Magazine*, *Cave Region Review*, *Elder Mountain*, *The Poetry of Capital*, *Aji Magazine*, *Evening Street Review*, *Westview*, *Grand Little Things*, *Cantos*, *U.S. 1 Worksheets*, *Transference*, and *Dash*.

JULIE GARRISON has been writing for the past 20 years. Her work has appeared in literary magazines *Flash Fiction*, *Lily*, *Pow Wow Paper*, *Long Story Short*, *Evening Street Review*, *Aim Magazine*, and *Helium Holidays*, and in two books, *Apologetics Without Apology* and *One Woman's Anthology of Short Stories, Essays and Flash Fiction*. She was a regular columnist for the legal website of Cordell & Cordell. She lives in Southern California.

GRAHAM C GOFF is a college student in rural central Texas (two hundred miles from Nowhere). He collects and repairs typewriters, avidly consumes Russian literature, and plays tennis. He anticipates a future career in writing, law, professorship, or diplomacy—depending on who's asking. He is an editor at *Kitchen Sink Magazine*.

JOHN GREY is an Australian poet, US resident, and was recently published in *Orbis*, *Dalhousie Review*, and the *Round Table*. His latest books, *Leaves On Pages* and *Memory Outside The Head*, are available through Amazon. Work upcoming in *Lana Turner* and *Hollins Critic*.

LEE GROSSMAN's writing has appeared in *Moonshine Review*, *Freshwater*, *Stanchion*, and *Adelaide* magazines. His photographs have been featured in *Black & White*, CameraArts.com, and *Color* magazines. He and his wife, Jan Baeuerlen, are retired psychoanalysts living in Oakland, CA, where they are owned by two English bulldogs.

RED HAWK is an Earth name, received during a 4-day water fast at the Buffalo River in the dead of winter during the worst ice storm Arkansas had seen in many years. It was given by our Mother Earth, bought as answered prayer, paid for by enduring suffering. It is not an Indian name.

RUBY BONNELL HAWKINS is a retired lady who passionately loves reading and writing poetry. She writes from her own experiences of life, love, family, heartache, nature, fun and happiness. She enjoys reading, painting, quilting, walks in the park and spending time with her family. To her good fortune many of her poems have been accepted by poetry magazines. She lives in Marietta GA.

WILL HEMMER: "I am a retired college math teacher and after retirement, a play producer in Los Angeles. I produced seven plays and two concerts (I'm also a pretty good singer), then the money ran out. I was born on April 26 in Zanesville, OH. My mother told me she could hear the Angelus ringing as I was born. I don't know what to make of this."

CY HILL is an eleven-year Navy veteran. He also spent fifteen years in manholes and climbing telephone poles. He is currently majoring in biology.

SHIRLEY HILTON (she/her) is a personal coach, writer and visual artist. Her writing has appeared in *Rattle*, *The Edison Literary Review*, *Delmarva Review*, *Nixes Mate Review*, *Backchannels*, and more. Her poems "Dance" and "Marina Arena" have been set to music by award-winning jazz musician Ryan Middagh. She is currently completing edits on her first novel. www.shirleyhilton.com

PAUL HOSTOVSKY (he, him, his) is the author of numerous books of poetry, most recently *Deaf & Blind* (Main Street Rag, 2020). He has won a Pushcart Prize, two Best of the Net Awards, the FutureCycle Poetry Book Prize, and has been featured on *Poetry Daily*, *Verse Daily*, and *The Writer's Almanac*. Paul makes his living in Boston as a sign language interpreter. Website: paulhostovsky.com

LINDA HUGHES, a retired massage therapist, has a BA in advertising/ journalism. Her poetry has been published in *Abstract Contemporary Expressions*, *OVS*, *The Critical Pass Review*, *Mangrove Review*, *Art Alliance Broadsides*, *Drunk Monkeys*, *Blacktop Passages* and *American Journal of Nursing*'s *Art of Nursing*. She grew up in Oklahoma and now lives in Florida with her husband, three cats and various animals that wander from the jungle. She enjoys writing, painting, running and meditating.

LOWELL JAEGER (Montana Poet Laureate 2017-2019) is founding editor of Many Voices Press, Grolier Poetry Peace Prize winner, and recipient of fellowships from the National Endowment for the Arts and the Montana Arts Council. He was awarded the Montana Governor's Humanities Award for his work in promoting civil civic discourse.

JACQUELINE JULES (she/her) is the author of *Manna in the Morning* (Kelsay Books, 2021) and *Itzhak Perlman's Broken String*, winner of the 2016 Helen Kay Chapbook Prize from Evening Street Press. Her work has appeared in over 100 publications and she is the author of 50 books for young readers, including *Tag Your Dreams: Poems of Play and Persistence* (Albert Whitman, 2020). Visit her online at https://metaphoricaltruths.blogspot.com or www.jacquelinejules.com

MARC KAMINSKY is the author of eight books of poems, including *The Stones of Lifta* (Dos Madres Press), *The Road from Hiroshima* (Simon & Schuster), and *Daily Bread* (University of Illinois Press). His poems, fiction and essays have appeared in many magazines and anthologies, including The *Manhattan Review, The American Scholar, The Oxford Book of Aging*, and *Voices within the Ark: The Modern Jewish Poets*.

STEPHEN J KUDLESS is a poet and playwright whose work has appeared in journals, anthologies, periodicals in the US and abroad: *The Country and Abroad, Light*: *The Journal of Light Verse, Inverso* (Italy), *Freefall* (Canada), *The New York Times*. And on stages: *Beds and How Fish Breathe, All Souls Player*s, NYC *and Killing Time: What We Do, Gallery Players, Black Box Festival, NYC, 2020*. His poem "The Color Hazel" was awarded first prize in The International Lawrence Durrell Society's poetry competition in 2015. He retired from the English Department of Touro College in 2012. He lives in New York City, maintaining residences in Staten Island and Manhattan.

KATE LaDEW is a graduate from the University of North Carolina at Greensboro with a BA in Studio Art. She resides in Graham, NC, with her cats, Charlie Chaplin and Janis Joplin.

LESLEY L LAMBRIGHT is a professor emeritus of psychology at a large community college in Michigan. Having published scholarly articles, she is now focused on the challenge of poetry. Travel, culture, and politics inform her work. She is happy to share that their daughters recovered from Covid-19 but Michigan in March 2021 is deluged by the virulent British variant. "We've had our shots and wear masks everywhere."

AYMON E LANGLOIS (he/him/his) is a disabled award-winning writer and scholar-activist. From Belfast, ME, Langlois currently attends Skidmore College in Saratoga Springs, NY, where, as a member of the Periclean Honors Forum, he is pursuing a BA in English. Scholarship has appeared in the journal *Wordgathering* while fiction has appeared in *Canvas* and *Adelaide* literary Magazines. You can find out more by visiting his website (aymonelanglois.com) or following him on Instagram (@aytypical) or Twitter (@ay_typical_).

EDWARD LEE's poetry, short stories, non-fiction and photography have been published in magazines in Ireland, England and America, including *The Stinging Fly*, *Skylight 47*, *Acumen*, *The Blue Nib*, and *Poetry Wales*. His play *Wall* was part of Druid Theatre's Druid Debuts 2020. His debut poetry collection *Playing Poohsticks On Ha'Penny Bridge* was published in 2010. He is currently working towards a second collection.

CARMINE LOMBARDO began his writing career at age 16 and to date has written 12 children's books; many poems which have been published in magazines, newspapers and anthologies; 12 musicals; memoirs; short stories; and over 300 songs. In 2009, the 17th Annual Senior Poets Laureate Award, sponsored by Amy Kitchener's Angels Without Wings Foundation, honored him as Poet Laureate of Florida. Blessed with a wonderful family, he now lives in Cape Coral with his wife, Dorayne.

DS MAOLALAI has been nominated eight times for Best of the Net and five times for the Pushcart Prize. His poetry has been released in two collections, *Love is Breaking Plates in the Garden* (Encircle Press, 2016) and *Sad Havoc Among the Birds* (Turas Press, 2019.

ROD MARTINEZ was attracted to words at an early age. His first book was created in grade school; his teacher used it to encourage creativity in her students. His high school English teacher told him to try short story writing. He listened, and the rest, as they say, is history.

JUSTINE MCCABE has published op-eds in several Connecticut newspapers including The *Hartford Courant*, and essays in *Green Horizon Magazine*. She also has several academic publication credits. She is a cultural anthropologist who received her doctorate from Duke University, as well as a practicing clinical psychologist. Among her interests are doing play therapy with children, and writing letters to editors, many of which have been published, including by the *New York Times*.

IVANA MESTROVIC holds a bachelor's degree in philosophy from Yale University. She has worked in arts management for sculptor Mark di Suvero for over thirty years and runs his Spacetime Studio. She has studied poetry with Marie Howe and Ellen Bass. Her work has been accepted for publication by *Brief Wilderness, Cider Press Review, Doubly Mad, Oxidant Engine, Plainsongs, Slant,* and *Visitant Lit.*

ANTHONY J MOHR is a five-time Pushcart Prize nominee and a 2021 fellow at Harvard University's Advanced Leadership Initiative. His work has appeared in, among other places, *Brevity's blog, California Prose Directory, The Christian Science Monitor, Commonweal, DIAGRAM, Eclectica, Hippocampus Magazine, North Dakota Quarterly, Superstition Review, War, Literature & the Arts*, and *ZYZZYVA*. He enjoys hiking, travel, and improv theater.

ROSEMARIE MOORE MORELL is a writer, keyboard musician, and retired preschool teacher. She has been published in *Bandshell, Connections in Black, Legacy, The Entertainer, Christian Times, Daily Challenge, Message,* and *Shooting Star Review.* She has also written the music and lyrics for two gospel songs.

CECIL MORRIS, after 37 years of teaching English at Roseville High School, has turned his attention to writing what he once taught students to understand and (maybe) enjoy. He has poems appearing in *2River View, Cobalt Review, Evening Street Review, Midwest Quarterly, Poem, Talking River Review,* and other literary magazines. He enjoys the work of Sharon Olds, Billy Collins, Tony Hoagland, Carrie Fountain, and Morgan Parker. He prefers ice cream to cruciferous vegetables.

GWENN A NUSBAUM, psychoanalyst, teacher, and creative coach, received a Pushcart nomination, honorary mention, and Gradiva nomination for her poems which have appeared in several print and on-line journals including *Edison Literary Review, Diverse Voices Quarterly, Louisville Review, Plainsongs, Rattle, Salamander, Schuylkill Valley Journal, The Phoenix, Verse-Virtual,* and *Voices de la Luna.* She is engaged in charitable giving to organizations that support poetry, human, and environmental causes. www.gwennnusbaum.com.

BRUCE OVERBY lives and writes in California's Santa Clara Valley. He holds an MFA in writing from Queens University of Charlotte and is a former winner of the Lorian Hemingway Short Story Competition. His stories about family, love, loss, and addiction have appeared in *Storyglossia, Green Mountains Review,* and the anthology *Home of the Brave: Stories in Uniform.* He is also a contributing writer for a number of publications on Medium.

M A PHILLIPS grew up on a family farm in Pennsylvania. After graduate school, he explored America for some few years in a VW van, eventually settling in Southern California, where he is now managing a self-storage facility, and putting the finishing touches on a novel. Two of his stories have been published in *Red Rock Review.*

DONNA PUCCIANI, a Chicago-based writer, has published poetry worldwide in *Shi Chao Poetry, Poetry Salzburg, Acumen, Mediterranean Poetry, Gradiva, ParisLitUp,* and other journals. Her seventh and most recent book of poetry is *Edges.* (She/her/hers)

SARA QUAYLE is a native Vermonter. Her love of nature and experiences as a mother, daughter, wife and pediatrician inspire much of her poetry. She is afflicted with multiple sclerosis, which became disabling in 2014. Some of her writing is about her illness, its impact and the ensuing loss and self-reinvention. She's is currently collaborating with her daughter on a collection of their original poems. She now lives with gratitude at The Boston Home, a home for people with severe neurological disorders. She enjoys the outdoors, theater, reading extensively and watercolor painting.

PAUL RABINOWITZ is an author, photographer and founder of ARTS By The People, a non-profit arts organization. His works have appeared in many magazines and journals including *New World Writing, Burningword, Evening Street Review, Adirondack Review, The Montreal Review, Grey Sparrow Journal, The Oddville Press*, and others. He was a featured artist in *Nailed Magazine* in 2020 and nominated for Best of the Net in 2021. He is the author of *Limited Light*, and *The Clay Urn*. His short stories are the inspiration for 4 short films. https://www.paulrabinowitz.com

CHARLES RAMMELKAMP is prose editor for BrickHouse Books in Baltimore. Two full-length collections were published in 2020, *Catastroika,* from Apprentice House, and *Ugler Lee* from Kelsay Books. A poetry chapbook, *Mortal Coil*, was published in 2020 by Clare Songbirds Publishing.

BRIAN RIHLMANN lives and writes in Reno, NV. His work has appeared in many magazines, including *The Rye Whiskey Review, Fearless, Heroin Love Songs, Chiron Review* and *The Main Street Rag*. His latest poetry collection, *Night At My Throat* (2020), was published by Pony One Dog Press.

JUDITH R ROBINSON* is an editor, teacher, fiction writer, poet and visual artist. A 1980 summa cum laude graduate of the University of Pittsburgh, she is listed in the *Directory of American Poets and Writers.* Teacher: Osher at Carnegie Mellon University and the University of Pittsburgh. *publication info and credits, art exhibitions, awards, including Pushcart nomination, on request or at: www.judithrrobinson.com

ZACK ROGOW is the author, editor, or translator of more than twenty books or plays. His ninth book of poems, *Irreverent Litanies*, was issued by Regal House Publishing. His most recent play, *Colette Uncensored*, had its first staged reading at the Kennedy Center and ran in London, San Francisco, and Portland. His blog, Advice for Writers, has more than 200 posts. He serves as a contributing editor of *Catamaran Literary Reader*. www.zackrogow.com

R CRAIG SAUTTER (Sawt-ter) is author, co-author, editor of 11 books, two of poems, *The Sound of One Hand Typing* (Anaphora Literary Press) and *Expresslanes Through The Inevitable City* (December Press) and three on presidential conventions and elections (www.presidentialconventions.com.) His short stories also appeared in the *Chicago Quarterly Review*. He was 47th president of The Society of Midland Authors and served two terms on the Abraham Lincoln Presidential Library Advisory Board. He teaches at DePaul University.

YVETTE A SCHNOEKER-SHORB's poetry has appeared in *The Midwest Quarterly*, *About Place Journal*, *High Desert Journal*, *Weber: The Contemporary West*, *AJN: The American Journal of Nursing*, *Terrain.org*, *Medical Literary Messenger*, and elsewhere. She holds an interdisciplinary MA from Prescott College and has been an educator, a researcher, and an editor. She is co-founder of a 501(c)(3) nonprofit natural-history press. Her chapbook is *Shapes That Stay* (Kelsay Books, 2021).

ANN SILVERTHORN is a storyteller from northwest Pennsylvania who explores a variety of writing genres. She shares reflections and observations of past and present social conditions and experiences. Her poetry has appeared in anthologies such as *Picture This* and *Poetry Leaves*. Her creative non-fiction has appeared in the *Medical Literary Messenger*. Please visit www.annsilverthorn.com.

DIANNE SILVESTRI is a poet and retired physician. *Naugatuck River Review*, *Poetry South*, *The Main Street Rag, Barrow Street*, *The Journal of the American Medical Association*, and *Pulse* are among her publishing credits, as are anthologies including *The Practicing Poet: Writing Beyond the Basics*. A past Pushcart nominee, she is author of the chapbook *Necessary Sentiments*.

ROGER SINGER is the poet laureate of Old Lyme, Connecticut. He has had over 1,200 poems published on the internet, magazines and in books, and is a 2017 Pushcart Prize Award nominee. He is also the president of the Shoreline Chapter of the Connecticut Poetry Society.

ERIC SOMMER is a writer, musician and photographer who grew up in Southeast Asia, Northern India, and Boston, MA. He toured with Little Feat, Leon Redbone, Gang of Four, Mission of Burma, and Dead Kennedys. Eric holds an MFA from George Washington University. Through the years he's never stopped writing: songs, journals, prose, poetry, and letters.

JEANINE STEVENS is the author of *Inheritor* and *Limberlost (*Future Cycle Press), and *Sailing on Milkweed* (Cherry Grove Collections). She is winner of the MacGuffin Poet Hunt and The Ekphrasis Prize. *Gertrude Sitting: Portraits of Women,* won the 2020 Chapbook Prize from Heartland Review Press. She recently received her seventh Pushcart nomination. She studied poetry at U.C. Davis and Community of Writers, Olympic Valley, and is faculty emerita at American River College.

DON STOLL is a Pushcart-nominated writer living in Southern California, near Palm Springs. His fiction has appeared recently in *The Honest Ulsterman* (tinyurl.com/4d65pz6h), *The Galway Review* (tinyurl.com/y6nxt9nv and tinyurl.com/y4vdsqhe), and elsewhere. In 2008, he and his wife founded their nonprofit (karimufoundation.org), which continues to bring new schools, clean water, and medical clinics to a cluster of remote Tanzanian villages.

SARAMANDA SWIGART has a BA in postcolonial literature and an MFA in writing and literary translation from Columbia University. Her short work, essays, and poetry have appeared in *Oxford Magazine*, *Superstition Review*, *The Alembic*, *Fogged Clarity, Ghost Town, The Saranac Review*, and *Euphony*, to name a few. She has been teaching literature, creative writing, and argumentative writing and critical thinking at City College of San Francisco since 2014.

J TARWOOD has been a dishwasher, a community organizer, a medical archivist, a documentary film producer, an oral historian, and a teacher. After a life spent in East Africa, Latin America, and the Middle East, he currently lives in China, and has published five books: *The Cats in Zanzibar, Grand Detour, And For The Mouth A Flower, What The Waking See*, and *The Sublime Way*. He has always been an unlikely man in unlikely places.

VINCENT J TOMEO is a poet, archivist, historian and community activist. He was twice nominated for the Pushcart Prize and has been published in *The New York Times, Evening Street Review, Comstock Review, Mid-America Poetry Review, EDGZ, Spires, Tiger's Eye, Byline, Mudfish,* and others. He has 999 published poems/essays; won 106 awards; and presented 141 public readings. His book, *Cemetery Friends*, is a garden of encounters at Mount Saint Mary in Queens, NY. Blog: vincentjtomeo.com

VINCENT VECCHIO is an on-and-off-again writer from Vancleave, MS. He's had poetry published in the online literary magazine *The Write Launch*, as well as *The Dead Mule School of Southern Literature*.

CHRIS VINER is a writer based in New York City. He is the author of *Brief Tenancies* (J. New Books, 2021) and *Lemniscate* (Unsolicited Press, 2017). Both of his books were nominated for a Pushcart Prize. His work appears in *Colorado Review, Critical Read, Culture Trip, The Festival Review, The London Magazine,* and *Woven Tale Press,* among others. He holds degrees from Goldsmiths, University of London and St Anne's College, University of Oxford, where he was a recipient of the F. H. Pasby Prize for his writing. He is poetry editor of *The Twin Bill.*

DAPHNE VLACHOJANNIS is a New York-qualified international human rights lawyer who has worked in London, Florence, Sarajevo, Brussels and Kinshasa. In 2013 she settled in The Hague where she lives with her husband and three children. She is passionate about languages and creative writing

SUSANNE VON RENNENKAMPFF immigrated from Germany in her early twenties. She writes from her home on a grain farm in north central Alberta, Canada. Her poems have appeared or are upcoming in a number of literary magazines in the US and Canada, among them *Room, The Antigonish Review, Prairie Fire* and *Grain.* A chapbook of her poetry, *In the Shelter of the Poplar Grove,* was published by The Alfred Gustav Press in 2014.

MARGARET H WAGNER is a writer, dancer and artist based in the Bay Area of California and has published poems in various literary journals, written articles for *World Screen,* and won three *Travelers' Tales* Solas Awards for Best Travel Writing. A certified Open Floor and 5Rhythms® dance teacher, Margaret is the founder of WRITE IN THE BEAT, workshops that pair mindful movement with written poetry and visual art. Visit her at https://margaretwagner.com/.

J ELIZA WALL (Joy Elisabeth Waldinger) is an artist, writer, filmmaker, and educator from Philadelphia. Her work explores family dynamics, the human condition, nostalgia, and connection to nature, in an attempt to restore connections in a fractured world. She recently published *Like The Sun Holds The Moon: A Children's Book.* Lately, she has turned her poems into short films, which have been featured in a variety of national and international film festivals.

PAUL WATSKY, a Jungian analyst practicing in San Francisco and Inverness, CA, and former poetry editor of *Jung Journal: Culture and Psyche*, has had poems in *Smartish Pace, The Carolina Quarterly, Interim, The Puritan*, and elsewhere. Kirkus says in a recommended review of his second book, *Walk-Up Music* (2015), that he "does the work of 10 poets."

JANET AMALIA WEINBERG is a former clinical psychologist, a founding member of one of the first feminist therapy collectives and the editor of an anthology which was an Independent Publisher Award finalist (*Still Going strong; Memoirs, Stories, and Poems about Great Older Women*). Her stories and articles have appeared in *Room, Mused, Wild Violet, Crack the Spine, ChangingAging, The Medical Literary Messenger* and elsewhere.

ELIZABETH WEIR grew up in England and lives in Minnesota, USA. Her book of poetry, *High on Table Mountain*, was published by North Star Press and was nominated for the Midwest Poetry Book Award. Recent work has appeared in *Evening Street Review, North Meridian Review, Comstock Review, Gyroscope, The Kerf*, and *Turtle Island Quarterly*.

MARTIN WILLITTS JR is a retired librarian. He has 25 chapbooks including the *Turtle Island Quarterly* Editor's Choice Award, *The Wire Fence Holding Back the World* (Flowstone Press, 2017), plus 21 full-length collections including the Blue Light Award 2019, *The Temporary World*. His new full-length book is *Harvest Time* (Deerbrook Press, 2021). He is the judge for the New York State Fair Poetry Contest. He is an editor for *The Comstock Review*.

PAULA YUP returned to Spokane, WA, after a dozen years in the Marshal Islands where her husband taught. She published four hundred poems in *Exit 13, Evening Street Review, J Journal, Conestoga Zen Anthology* and other places. Her book of poetry is *Making a Clean Space in the Sky* (Evening Street Press).

R G ZIEMER (he/him) was born and raised on the south side of Chicago, where he learned the value of a good story. He has worked in construction, practiced genealogy, and taught writing in junior high school and college. He enjoys sharing poetry and fiction with writing groups and at reading venues around the Chicago area. His novel, *The Ghost of Jamie McVay*, was published in 2019.